Art Is a Spiritual Path

PAT B. ALLEN

SHAMBHALA
Boston & London
2005

SHAMBHALA PUBLICATIONS, INC.
Horticultural Hall
300 Massachusetts Avenue
Boston, Massachusetts 02115
www.shambhala.com

To find out more about the artists whose stories appear in this book,
to contact the author, or to learn about opportunities to experience
the studio process firsthand, please visit www.patballen.com. The
site also contains an archive of the images in this book in full color.

9 8 7 6 5 4 3 2 1

First Edition
Printed in the United States of America

Designed by Jeff Baker

∞ *This edition is printed on acid-free paper that meets the*
American National Standards Institute Z39.48 Standard.
Distributed in the United States by Random House, Inc.,
and in Canada by Random House of Canada Ltd

Library of Congress Cataloging-in-Publication Data
Allen, Pat B.
Art is a spiritual path / Pat B. Allen.—1st ed.
p. cm.
Includes bibliographical references.
ISBN 1-59030-210-9 (pbk.: alk. paper)
1. Spiritual life. 2. Art and religion. I. Title.

BL624.A54 2005
203'.7—dc22

2004025879

Contents

List of Illustrations

Acknowledgments

When I finished my first book, *Art Is a Way of Knowing*, I had the shocking realization of how isolated I was as a person and how artmaking had kept me alive. My experience this time around is vastly different. For the past ten years, working in and teaching the studio process described in this book has served to connect me to a vast number of people in profoundly important ways.

The Creative Source has been exceedingly generous in sending me companions along the way. I am deeply grateful for Dayna Block and Deborah Gadiel, my partners in the original Open Studio Project, and Kim Conner, whose loyalty, support, and loving witness made both the existence and the demise of Studio Pardes a central blessing in my life. I thank the artists whose stories appear here: Annette Hulefeld, Dave King, Lisa Sorce Schmitz, Sallie Wolf, Barbara Fish, Kim Conner, and Dayna Block. I thank my daughter, Adina, whose images weave their way through my life like golden threads.

As I began to think about whom I might mention in these acknowledgments, I became overwhelmed remembering all the fellow artists, many dear friends, children, and teenagers, some of whom only came once to a studio session, others who have made intention, art, and witness a central part of their lives. I despaired of coming close to naming all the people whose images and witness writings have instructed me in the studio process, all the colleagues who have engaged in formative discussions of these ideas, and all the students and workshop members who have welcomed, embraced, and enlarged my work. You have all made real for me the beautiful image of life as a net of interconnected threads, each of you a pearl at a crossing of lives.

I am honored by the work of Kendra Crossen Burroughs, who is exceedingly knowledgeable about all spiritual traditions as well as all things editorial, and that of her colleague Jacob Morris, who sharpened and helped to shape this book into its present form. I am also honored to be published once again by Shambhala Publications.

Finally, I thank the Creative Source for my husband, John, who has provided unwavering support of my work since the moment we met and has been an active participant in the studio process as it has unfolded in our lives.

Preface

This work grows directly out of my first book; *Art Is a Way of Knowing* (Boston: Shambhala Publications, 1995). There, I recounted my own journey through art, and the nascent concepts of intention and witness in relation to artmaking were first explored. Just as that book was published, the Open Studio Project in Chicago came into being. For six years, Dayna Block, Deborah Gadiel, and I experimented with how to make art and be of service. Along with many others who came to our workshops and joined us in this journey, we were graced with direct transmissions from the Creative Source. In that way, we received the studio process described in this book. Open Studio Project was the crucible in which the process of intention and witness was refined. For four more years at Studio Pardes, in my hometown of Oak Park, Illinois, I was privileged to develop my thinking, share the process further, and write the present work. Open Studio Project, now located in Evanston, Illinois, continues to provide the studio process to the public as a vital arts and social service agency; Deborah Gadiel continues to evolve the process in a mental health setting. Studio Pardes has evolved into a virtual studio online at www.studiopardes.org that encourages the participation of everyone who chooses to travel the path of art. The Creative Source continues to guide all these manifestations of Its unfolding as well as new ones that appear every day. My piece is to articulate the studio process as a spiritual path, which I believe is its fundamental purpose. From that place we can enrich and enliven any work in the world we are called to perform.

ART IS A SPIRITUAL PATH

Introduction

Artmaking is a spiritual path through which we are most able to explore Divinity by participating in the act of creating images. In the broadest sense I have discovered three aspects of artmaking that we are invited to explore, which seem to grow out of the very delight of the Creative Source with Itself:

Inquiry: Art is a place to raise any question about any subject.

Engagement: Art is a means to enter, to play with, to dance with, to wrestle with anything that intrigues, delights, disturbs, or terrifies us.

Celebration: Art is a path to meaning, which includes all forms of honoring, sharing, memorializing, and giving thanks.

This book will describe how inquiry, engagement, and celebration through acts of art and writing constitute a spiritual path.

There is an intelligence, the Soul of the World, calling forth new ideas at all times. The call is urgent in this time of great change throughout human cultures and the earth itself. I have seen these ideas arrive in my images and the images of many others. All of us are being called to midwife a great transition of consciousness, and artmaking is one of the best ways to receive new understanding in this process. We are living in a time when old ideas are wearing out and new ones are needed. Institutional forms of all kinds are crumbling and we have the opportunity to envision new ways to make meaning in how we live, treat one another, express reverence and awe, solve conflicts, and steward the planetary resources with which we have been entrusted. Artmaking, especially in small groups, can serve as sanctuary, asylum, ashram, therapy group, think tank, and village square. Art is a vehicle that allows us to transcend linear time, to travel backward and forward into personal and transpersonal history, into possibilities that weren't realized and those that might be.

When we take a concern or a problem into the "place of all possibility" through image making, we reduce the tendency to act reflexively, doing what we have always done. We can fully experience all the paradoxical aspects inherent in every knotty problem but, owing to the unique qualities of artmaking, we are able to refrain from simply acting to reduce the tension we feel in paradox. Instead, the action of making art reduces the tension sufficiently that we can allow new information to arise.

When we work in the discipline of artmaking, we gradually become vessels for new wisdom. Slowly our long-held beliefs are loosened and our minds and spirits and even our bodies become more flexible. We develop a tolerance for ambiguity and a resilience that comes from reclaiming play as the primary means to learn. O. Fred Donaldson, in *Playing by Heart*, says that "it is play's underlying emptiness or absence of cultural categories and boundaries that enables it to encompass the fullness of life" (1993, 14). We can work at whatever pace suits us and we will be gently urged toward more. We learn in depth what our cherished beliefs really are and we practice letting them go and trying on new ones.

I have struggled for many years to find my way to a spiritual home through many paths: first Catholicism, into which I was born; sporadically in Eastern religions and yoga; later on in Goddess worship and the women's spirituality movement; and especially and most satisfyingly, in the Torah, among my adoptive tribe, the Jews. I love parts and places of all these worlds and traditions and have been formed and nourished by each. Finally, however, I realize that art is my spiritual path. I am a trans-denominational soul and art is my prayer, my ritual, my remembrance of the Divine. Art is the way I knit together the beliefs and practices that guide my life. Art is not a religion but a practice and a path. As a practice it has its own demands and discipline. As a path it can take us more deeply into whatever place it is that our soul calls home whether that place is a church, a *shul* (synagogue), a mosque, a dance studio, a soup kitchen, or a deep forest. Through receiving and giving form to new images, we breathe life into ancient scriptures and eternal teachings. Art also leads us to new places in ourselves, our work, our relationships, and our communities.

For the last thirty years I have been experimenting, studying, and sharing with others means of using art and writing to tap into the creative energy that is the essence of what we share with the Divine and is our core as human beings. It might be more true to say I have felt the presence of the Divine in my life as a force that guides, challenges, and pulls me along a path to question how I see the world and think about it. A series of practices have developed that prove to be a reliable guide for walking the spiritual path of art. These practices are simple and humble; they do not demand special skills in art or writing, special places or materials. They are accessible to anyone from any walk of life or age or background.

My journey on this path using these practices has led me into imagery and insights about the feminine and about Judaism, to a deeper understanding of my family and friends, my place in the order of nature, and my purpose on earth. I have come to know that each person I encounter is my teacher, none more so than those with whom I make art. I have seen art lead each seeker to his or her own personal wisdom teachings. These personal teachings strengthen and elaborate that which we know most deeply and will lead us to new understandings of teachings we may have grown up with that no longer seem to fit. Our images lead us to and support us in the work we are meant to initiate or complete in this lifetime. What we receive depends upon our diligent use of two simple but central methods that bracket the artmaking experience: our *intention*, in which we state our inquiry as an active desire to receive something, which then guides our artmaking; and our *witness*, a writing practice through which we engage with and integrate what has appeared in our artwork.

In this book I will share how a personal practice of artmaking has developed into a spiritual path and is being shared with others. Through my story and theirs, our images and writings, it is my fervent hope that you, too, will take up paintbrush and crayon, revision scraps of daily life into the poetry of everydayness, retell the old stories so that we can call upon the Divine in new ways of joy and peace and help create new maps for where we might as people go. The next step, already being taken by many, including some who are featured in this book, is addressing the question of how to take right action. Any valid spiritual path must lead both inward to the personal and outward to the Anima Mundi, the Soul of the

World. How do we take action in the world with clarity and discernment, with compassion and justice? We do so by facing our personal challenges, listening to our unique sensitivities, and letting them lead us to the knowledge locked within their challenges. Everyone has pieces to offer to clarify and rewrite old stories, reclaim pages of lost stories, and celebrate new ones. Through art may you find your piece and your peace.

Elements of Studio Practice

Introduction to Part One

Intention, our direct statement of what it is we hope to receive through our images, is the first step of art as a spiritual path. We can make art to find our way into and through personal issues, if that is our intention. Our images help us untie knots in the threads of our consciousness that come to us through our family lineage, our individual karma, or present life events. Depending on what we ask for, images come to us that reveal our fears, clarify decisions we must make, provide hope and direction, help us articulate a vision for our individual future, and allow us to see obstacles we are ignoring. Threaded through our seemingly personal dilemmas are also gifts of wisdom that nourish those around us indirectly when we choose this work.

As Kim (whose story appears in chapter 5) creates her mandala paintings and collages at home, her young sons learn that the dining room table is a place to feed the soul, an act as important as feeding the body and therefore conducted at a central location in the home. Kim's stated intention may be to calm and center herself by working on the mandala. An implicit aspect of her intention is also to unite and weave together her roles as artist and mother. In doing so she presents the possibility of integration to her sons, a subtle but crucial lesson in our culture, which still separates work from life to a great degree.

weave together artist + priest roles.

I believe that our imagery comes not only to nourish our own understanding and to influence those around us in a subtle way; it also comes to speak to our communities and the world. It isn't merely content that wants to be conveyed; it is also new ways of thinking, of absorbing experience and information, of participating in life, of being, and of being together. The path of art is a tutorial in the process of intuition. As we grow in our artmaking our intentions become clearer, and we can ask for what we need. We can also make it our intention to serve the needs of others and of the world, and to gain guidance about sustainable ways to be of service.

thesis

Having stated our intention, we prepare to *make art*. The first step of artmaking is playful. Artmaking can be simple or complex, can occur alone or with others, can involve simple materials or complex multistep processes. Each person finds their own way to the right art experience by following the energy, flow, and pleasure that comes with opening ourselves to the guidance of the Creative Source. In a studio, for example, participants may walk around and look at materials on the shelves until something catches their eye or may be drawn to a color of paint or the texture of working with fabrics. In the classes I facilitate, we often begin by simply making marks on paper while we play CDs of drumming music to help us let go of our thinking mind. There is no right or wrong way to begin. Artists also take inspiration from the images created by others in the studio, from nature, dreams, books, gallery visits, or ancient symbols. Artmaking as a practice stops time, opens us to rest our thinking mind, and nourishes our senses. After a sustained period of artmaking, enough to have an experience of merging with the Creative Source, we stop to step back and see what has arrived, an experience of separation. Each art experience moves through a cycle of inquiry, engagement, and celebration. We step in, become immersed, lose ourselves, and emerge enlarged. The cycle of the artmaking process reveals itself repeatedly over a lifetime of artmaking. It spirals through the raw material of our life and leads us into an ever-deepening relationship with the flow of Nature as She bestows our own truth and teachings. These ideas will be discussed more fully in the section on artmaking.

The next practice is that of _witness writing_ about the image. We first recognize the image as fully as we can by becoming still in its presence, becoming aware of our body and breathing. Sitting before the work in a chair and just looking and receiving its message can take several minutes at least. Next, we write in a journal or notebook kept especially for our witness writings in the form of descriptions, observations, intuitive responses, and, especially, dialogue with the image. Witness employs freewriting where spelling, grammar, and punctuation are not important. In fact, "slips of the pen" often yield additional levels of meaning that enrich what we "meant" to say. An essential part of art as a spiritual path is reading the witness writings to the artwork aloud in the presence of others, allowing the message from the image to attain its true power and significance by giving it the resonance of voice. The listener or listeners simply silently receive what is spoken, without verbal comment, although sighs, and sometimes tears or laughter, are not uncommon. When engaged in this act of deep listening, we function as embodiments of witness consciousness for one another. *Witness consciousness* is that attribute of the Divine that does not judge but simply holds, hears, and cherishes.

While there may be a facilitator of a particular art experience, each artist is in charge of their own experience. The ultimate goal of art as a spiritual practice is to actualize the artist archetype in each person. The artist archetype activates the ability to see things from an aesthetic perspective, discern harmonies and dissonances, and initiate new combinations or interpretations of life. Every artist develops and deepens their relationship with the Creative Source, the internal guide from which inner wisdom comes, and learns to express and share Its gifts. We learn to recognize and honor that wisdom in each other, learn from each other, and take our ability to see the Divine in every person into our daily life.

Part One distills the essence of studio practice: stating an intention, inquiry, engagement, and celebration through artmaking and witness writing. These elements constitute a form of "meditation in action" that will hold an infinitely varied content while providing a structure that ensures both safety and depth. Studio practice gives us the means to explore new ways of being together that allow both intimacy and privacy through the disciplined use of imaginative creation. Some of the rules that make studio practice effective, such as the practice of no–comment, are unfamiliar and only make sense through committed use over time. I am always happy to engage in dialogue with anyone who makes use of these methods. My Web site, www.patballen.com, provides a virtual studio, forum for questions, and an environment for the continued unfolding of art as a spiritual path.

1
The Practice of Intention
Divine Alignment

The first act of initiating an art experience, before making a single mark, is the creation of an intention to guide our work. We take a few moments to become quiet and go within to create a space that will ignite the spark of imagination. We must make room, clear out whatever distracts us to discover our intention. We may meditate, focus on our breathing, or free write until an intention takes shape. We may arrive knowing what we seek. More often we arrive with worries and tasks to do later clinging to our consciousness like so many Post-It notes.

Write the intention down in a journal or a notebook in the form of a present tense, straightforward statement, without using the verb *want*. To "want" is to remain forever lacking, preventing the Creative Source from catching up with what is underneath the lack. Make the intention as clear and concrete as possible, addressed to a force of great compassion that intends what is best for you, as if it were a prayer that has already been answered. When beginning this practice you are more likely to see the effect with a concrete intention that has some built-in limits. For example, you might ask for guidance about whether you should accept an invitation to some event or decline it and use the time for rest and quiet rather than just saying, "I am open to whatever comes." You are working toward the overriding intention of being in alignment with the divine intention; but to begin, keep it simple, recognizable.

Intention is always a co-creative process. It is not as if there is a Divine Puzzle Maker who "knows what is best for us" but withholds the information and makes us guess at it. Who co-creates? If we reflect even briefly, we recognize that every interaction we engage in has its own distinct energy. When two people are in a conversation, each of them contributes to its shape. I will discuss this further in chapter 3, which reflects on the edges of knowledge and the challenges inherent in art as a spiritual path.

Intentions that ask for change must be for oneself, not for another person; and they cannot violate any natural laws. It is fine to ask for guidance about how best to deal with a difficult person, but not correct to have an intention for that person to see that you are right about some disagreement. We turn over the outcome and the details of how it manifests to the Creative Source. As we gradually become conscious of the power of intention and the limits of our individual understanding, it becomes easier to let go of specific outcomes and open to a greater reality. Common beginning intentions in the studio include "to enjoy myself," "to let myself explore my creativity," "to receive guidance about a personal decision or health concern," "to make an image of my sorrow," and "to open to the creative source." As artists begin to create images, intentions also grow out of the relationship of the artist to the image as a teacher. The acceptance of the image as teacher often takes a long time. For many of us, especially those trained in art, the image is a thing we make; imagining it to have a life of its own or seeing it as an expression of a consciousness beyond our thinking mind can be a challenge. Shaun McNiff says, "If we imagine paintings as a host of guides, messengers, guardians, friends, helpers, protectors, familiars, shamans, intermediaries, visitors, agents, emanations, epiphanies, influences and other psychic functionaries, we have stepped outside of the frame of positive science and into the archetypal mainstream of poetic and visionary contemplation" (1992, 74).

The word *intend* derives from a Latin root, *tendere; in-tendere* means to stretch toward (Ayto 1990, 302). One way to think about intention is to ask yourself what you are willing to stretch toward. What are you yearning for? What is asking to be born through you? And can you imagine that a force of great compassion is also stretching toward you, with information that both you and the world need? What do you wish to be near—peace, wisdom, harmony, compassion, purpose, community, justice, truth? Although intention seems like a very simple idea, it is a practice; one must *use* it to reap its rewards. For example, in my first book I suggest some sample intentions (Allen 1995, 197) such as, "I want to know the meaning of this image." One day while reading a book whose title I forget, I came across the idea that to use the word *want* when forming an intention creates a state of lack. The words "I want" are a statement to the universe of an existential reality of lack or scarcity. What follows those words is re-

Elements of Studio Practice

ceived as so much static because wanting is a reality of not–having. I wish I could recall the book or even the subject in order to thank the author, whose words seared me and shifted my perception. I can only confirm over and over that these ideas belong to all of us and to no one in particular. They arise from a collective knowing that is the birthright of every person. How they are expressed will vary according to the circumstances, special gifts, and limitations of each person who chooses to express them.

After the insight about "want" I began to listen more closely as others read their intentions. I began to notice that many of us are in a state of chronic want that has to do with our forgetting. We forget what we asked for yesterday; we ask for something that contradicts that request; we forget to notice what we have; we forget to express gratitude. It comes as a surprise to many of us that the surest way out of want, which is a perception, is to make an inventory of what we have and then find something to give thanks for or, even more powerful, to give something away. Often there are things filling our lives and the spaces of our minds that prevent what we "want" from arriving. Sometimes the best intention is simply to make space to notice what *is* before trying for something new. In that space, our attention catches on something and the imagination is sparked. The spark is our intention, ignited by the attention we give it through making art. Our intention can be to see what we are holding on to that is filling our space. A refrigerator with old, spoiling food that doesn't nourish can't be replenished until it is emptied of moldy items crowding the shelves. New relationships, work, or life purpose will not manifest with clarity if we do not make space by acknowledging and letting go of some of our busyness and doing of what is no longer working. The architects of the Truth and Reconciliation Commission in South Africa at the end of apartheid in 1994 had a clear intention to let go of fixed ideas when they stated in the Promotion of National Unity and Reconciliation Act of 1995 the need for "understanding, not vengeance, reparation, not retaliation, *ubuntu* (humanness), not victimization" (TRC 1995). The TRC created the space necessary for new ideas to arise in the face of historical atrocity.

I believe that the Creative Source intends for each of us to manifest fully and joyfully. I also believe in the relational aspect of the Divine. I must ask in order to receive; I must come to the realization that my will is not the only factor in determining what will manifest but neither can it be completely superseded by divine intervention. It is part of the practice of intention to discern what we are really asking for and then to let go of worrying exactly what the result will look like. It is important to review our intentions on a regular basis to notice contradictions in our requests. Wording and language is important in crafting intention. Once, in the early days of Open Studio Project, discussing the notable absence of men signing up for workshops and our belief that men "needed" to be there, we decided to make a formal intention for more men to come to the studio. In the following weeks we were treated to random visits from several men. One offered to sell us art supplies that had "fallen off a truck." There was an earnest young artist who, unbidden, plopped himself down with slides of his art and recited his life story. And several city workers, taking a break from repairing the sewers, came in to ask if they could use our restrooms. The Divine has a great sense of humor but didn't fail to manifest our vaguely worded intention. The statement of intention crafted by the TRC allowed for a new cultural form to emerge that has been adopted in many other countries. While not perfect, it has opened the way for us to see that violence need not beget violence, if that is truly not our intention.

As with any practice that seems simple, it is easy not to give intention its due. Today I was running late and feeling impatient to get to the studio and write. I hurried through the rituals I have created over the years to foster mindfulness—including writing an intention. I had written something down, slapdash, but couldn't even remember the words. "Hmm," I thought, "I better go back and see what I wrote." My journal reveals the result of my hurry: "I do some writing, I do some art." After this terse summary, I had tacked on a reminder of what I needed to bring home at the end of the day. "Some writing" can be a grocery list or phone messages. If I am serious about working on this book, I will revise that intention. I write: "I align myself with the Creative Source as I receive refinements of the book I am writing." Better, but the new intention makes me stop and wonder, "What is necessary for that alignment to take place? Is it just an act of my will?" Well, if I'm really distracted by those tasks, I better figure that out. I get up and collect the items I need and put them in my bag to bring home later. Now am I aligned? I sit in my chair and notice my feet on the floor, grounding me. My body must be aligned. I offer a silent prayer to plug into earth energy and invite it to come up through my feet so that what I write is practical and useful to others. I feel the energy begin to surge upward, and I become aware of my heart: "May my words be openhearted so that they convey the joy that I feel when I am in alignment with the Creative Source, and may I be given the words to extend that joy to others. The heart of the world desires to touch your heart." Suddenly my mind says: "Whoa! How could you have forgotten to remind everyone that checking in with body, heart, and mind is part of the practice of intention?" May these words be simple enough, the thoughts clear enough, so that it makes sense to other people to take the time to line up body, heart, and mind, which is how we make way for spirit.

Body, heart, and mind are like a series of doors that the soul knocks on in different ways. If I get too caught up in thinking, I might trip or bump into something or develop a sore throat; so I can't broadcast my overheated ideas without being reminded that the body has some wisdom to contribute to ground the flight of my ideas. When I write when I am really tired and should be sleeping, a crabby self-righteousness can creep into my words. When I become enamored of a metaphor or story and try to force it into the text, the writing gets like over-yeasted bread, too full of hot air to nourish. When I haven't resolved a dispute with a friend, I find myself writing to instruct her, rather than listening to the flow. All of these things are my lessons. I take them into my art. I ask for guidance about working when I am tired, and sometimes I get the message that I need to take a nap. Sometimes I learn that I can work very small and accomplish what is needed. I make an image to learn the way to resolve my dispute with my friend. All of these subtle alignments are aligning me with the Source, which is in and of me, in and of my friend, in and of us all.

My daily intention is to be open to my learning about how to serve the Soul of the World with joy and to be an instrument of peace. Even so, I forget this intention at least a hundred times a day. Rereading my notebooks, I am constantly amazed at how fleeting mindfulness is. Taking an action to remind us of intention can really help. My friend Jackie gave me a bottle of essential oil called Joy once after she heard me read my intention to serve with joy. It is in a tiny brown bottle with a pink label. I place a drop behind my ears and on my wrist, when I remember to, and the scent helps me. Wearing a certain piece of jewelry or color of clothing can be an act of remembrance supporting our intention. Often when writing I wear a cloisonné amulet, a gift from my friend and colleague Janis Timm–Bottos, with an image of a woman writing on each side. It stays empty to signify my intention to have the words I write supplied by the Creative Source. When I especially intend to keep my daughter in my heart and mind, I wear a silver ring inscribed with the Hebrew name, Adina, that she and I share. We all have many, many "good intentions" that never manifest because we do not pay attention to them. Yet we can cultivate a space for intention to blossom by paying attention with mindful gestures that support our connection with the Creative Source. Mindfulness requires space. We must come to a stopping place to notice exactly what will support our intention. When our gestures of homage become rote, they begin to lose efficacy. There is no power in a charm or an idol; the power arises only from our directed attention, of which the charm is a sign to remind us. Without careful cultivation of attention, the Source cannot send us what we need.

Important insights can occur anywhere and anytime. Ideally, intention should permeate our lives. Each morning, before getting out of bed, I try to remember to recite the Modeh Ani, a Hebrew blessing in which I thank the Divine for the return of my soul, which has been journeying on my behalf in the dreamtime while I slept. Otherwise, I just say thank you for whatever I see or feel first—usually the simple fact of being in a body. My intention is gratitude. One morning, I become aware that I have taken on too many responsibilities for others. I have not set the limits and boundaries I need to accomplish my own creative work.

I am walking the dog in the early morning darkness. She sniffs an object; I bend down and pick it up. It is a battered little plaster burro from a Christmas nativity scene. I laugh at the beleaguered little work animal and my mind takes off to the manger scene under the Christmas trees of childhood (figure 1). Would the Divine Child have survived if the donkey and ox hadn't been breathing their warm breath over him instead of out plowing a field or hauling wood? I take the figure to the studio as a reminder to stay focused on my work even when others want to drag me off to plow their field. I acknowledge how much easier it is sometimes for me to respond to a request from someone else than to face the rigor of my own creative work. When I am away from my art and writing, a sort of

Figure 1. Plaster burro. Found object.

callus grows over my heart. At these times, my life becomes a sort of dutiful martyrdom that leaves me feeling resentful toward others for keeping me from my work. I often imagine that I must get all chores and
obligations out of the way before I sit down to make art. When I remember to make an intention to connect with the Creative Source and also ful-
fill my obligations, time expands. I engage in artmaking from a place of
dedication to the Creative Source, and duty becomes joyfully rendered.
The paradox of how that happens is the work of the Creative Source, not
my rational planning. The Creative Source doesn't issue ultimatums for us
to neglect whatever is true service in our lives, but does challenge us to
get all our parts into perspective.

When I am the facilitator of the studio, I make an intention to do no
harm, to receive no harm, and to be a worthy conduit for what needs to
come into the group. If I am rushing in without a moment to spare because I decided to do three errands on the way to the studio, it takes
longer for me to re-center and become present. Yet that is not my only
task. In every studio experience, I also make a personal intention based

on my life at the moment. I am not present solely for others, but also for myself. So, as I create an art piece for my daughter, I may have an intention to be present to my feelings about her going off to college. At the same time, I trust that my intention to be present to the group will also manifest. After years of teaching this process to my students at the School of the Art Institute of Chicago, I found myself becoming bored. The image came to me that I had lost traction; I was spinning my wheels in the same ruts but not moving forward. Students continued to tell me how much they got from the class, but it was becoming a chore to me. It isn't enough to have the intention to share the process with my students; I also have to have a personal stake in being there if the Creative Source is going to keep showing up for me.

Sharing examples from the past is useless unless I learn something new. I made the intention to discover what more, if anything, was there for me in teaching this method, or whether it was time to stop teaching the class and move on. I realized how many projects I had begun in my studio work and had not shared with the students. I had grown to rely on presentations of my past work that I had already put together and had resisted creating new ones. Then I realized that until I fully shared the new work, it was in fact not complete. I required other voices to respond, to witness what I had done, before I could truly know it (Watkins 1999). I gained awareness of how many unfinished projects I had in my life and in the studio, promising efforts that I had allowed to wither and die because of lack of time or the intrusion of other obligations. Each of these projects holds a certain amount of energy, a lingering charge. Our creative field can become like a computer with too many programs running in the background and not enough "memory" to accomplish any new work at hand. I made it my intention to inventory and clear out projects and let them go if they had no life. I prepared new presentations based on the responses I received in sharing the work. This helped me celebrate and come to closure with major projects. New energy flooded back for me when I shared work around a ritual I designed for my fiftieth birthday. I remembered the excitement of sharing work that is on my edge. I felt confirmed in my efforts when one student asked for some readings about women's rituals to share with her mother, who was facing a major birthday in the coming year.

18

Intention is how we join with the Divine and how we access our internal wisdom. It is how we ground and center ourselves and prepare ourselves to receive the image, which is the medium through which the Divine communicates with us. It is how we remind ourselves that "I" am not doing anything; I am serving a higher force. Intention is an exchange of energy. We put our physical, mental, and emotional energy at the disposal of the Universe. We open ourselves to the energy of the Universe but in a focused way. Once the intention is written down, it is best to forget all about it during the artmaking process. There is no need to try to hold the intention in mind while creating artwork; in fact it can interfere by preventing you from following the image. You will check in again with the intention when you write your witness.

At the last session of a six-week basic practice group at Open Studio some years ago, I forgot to write an intention down before I began. The final session is always used for review. Instead, after rereading the work of the previous weeks, I began with a quote from a past witness writing. Immediately, a small sculpture of an old wise woman guide called *Maud* (figure 2), one of the images I had been working on in that session, began to speak, and I got some very intense information. She began: *People can feel violated by insights if they are unready to receive them. . . .*

Maud went on to tell a long story of Saul of Tarsus and his conversion experience and all the contradictions in it:

MAUD: *Saul was knocked from his horse by a flash of light, he experienced a conversion. From being a persecutor of the clandestine followers of Jesus he switched and founded institutional creativity* [I meant to write "Christianity"], *as we know it. He represents the externalizing of insight; we "honor" him and don't question his finding an external solution to what originated as an internal challenge. But that manner of response is no longer applicable, sustainable. As a Jew, Saul must have known, felt, some of the institutional atrophy of Judaism within the Temple system of the day. What if he had taken the path inward to find his own atrophy and renewal? Would Christianity have spawned pogroms, the inquisition, the crusades, the witch burnings in the name of Jesus who spoke of—Get this, LOVE YOUR NEIGHBOR AS YOURSELF and LOVE GOD, which I understand to mean Love Godness, wholeness, God includes all, there is nothing that is not God. There is no division, no separation, yet all uniqueness*

Figure 2. *Maud*, by Pat B. Allen. Plaster gauze, mixed media.

is honored. Old age and youth are not valued differently, male and female, rich and poor, allness. Justice is love and the opposite of love, as it has been said, isn't hate, it is indifference. But indifference leads to, breeds hate, revenge, attack. If contact is denied overtly, it will happen in indirect ways. Union will happen. How ironic that in the war between Serbians and Croatians that rape is so often a weapon of war. The enemies believe that they are destroying the ethnic purity of their enemies by forcibly implanting their seed in the women and girls. What better image of self-hate? I put myself in you, against your will, as if I, myself, am poison. But also, what more awful, poignant fact—I must connect, even in this degraded, brutal way.

ME: *I feel a chill, it seems you are saying that the universe will accomplish the union of opposites at any cost, it seems heartless and cruel.*

MAUD: *Mother Kali has but one oneness, the continual manifestation of truth. The truth can be brutal and here it has hidden sweetness. Those who become mothers through rape are asked to do a vicious service, but they will*

also love the infants who issue blamelessly from such infernal unions, some
of them will love these babies who are the manifestation of truth. The free
will of humans does not allow you to violate truth, only to make it a
painful struggle, and endless suffering.

ME: *So back to Saul/Paul?*

MAUD: *It's evolutionary but clearly humans will not survive without reac-*
quainting themselves with truth and giving up their silly notions of exclu-
sivity. Kali doesn't negotiate; honor Her and the unfolding is wondrous
because you can perceive truth without fear.

ME: *Why is all this coming to me today?*

MAUD: *You didn't begin with an intention and so I took my opening to de-*
fine the territory according to what I need to say.

ME: *I can limit you with my intention?*

MAUD: *Of course, but be aware that alignment with the intention of the uni-*
verse will occur, with or without your cooperation. It's like this—your free
will doesn't cover certain things, like if you jump off a building, which you
are free to do, you cannot will yourself to fly. Once you exercise the will to
jump, the laws of truth apply and you go splat!

As always, the job is to practice discernment or, as the Buddhists say, "discrim-
inating awareness." Consider that the building you jump off is internal and
not the World Trade Center.

ME: *Look, I miss making art.*

MAUD: *Next time include that in your intention, you can stop me at any*
time.

This witness writing occurred about five years before the events of
September 11, 2001. The witness speaks clearly about distinguishing what
is actual from what is symbolic. What if the intention of the Soul of the
World is to manifest Its oneness now, after many centuries of manifesting
differentiation and the separations that requires? And what if we, individually and collectively, are Its means to realize this intention? And what if
we are not in alignment, are not cultivating the intention to manifest the
highest good for all humankind? What if those of us with the clearest intention, paying the most attention, can only see as far as maximizing corporate profit? What if another group can only see as far as making the
world into the image of their religious beliefs and sees their proselytizing

as a gift, not an intrusion on freedom of belief? Our intention guides how we manifest our thoughts, beliefs, and desires. I often wonder how mindful we are as Americans of exporting our culture and ideas around the world. The destruction of the World Trade Center towers made us aware that there are cultures in the world that do not share our beliefs. What if we make the intention to turn inward to create oneness, each of us, one unique being at a time, instead of creating a global monoculture? Is it possible that the manifestation of McDonald's restaurants everywhere is a misguided kind of temporal oneness? In other words, there are forms, ideas, truths that *will manifest*, no matter what. Our work is to cultivate sufficient imagination that what manifests will be artful and not horrendous. This is a particular strength of art as a spiritual path: it gives us a means to cultivate imagination as a tool of discernment in the process of reality manifesting.

Although <u>intention is a tool I usually think</u> of as focusing awareness, <u>it also has the function of creating boundaries</u>, something I had neglected to do in the session described above. In its boundary–creating capacity, intention limits and helps give shape to what we receive. Once in an ongoing class where many artists frequently engaged in dialogue with their images, there was one woman who was an accomplished watercolorist. After the first few weeks, she began to bring her own materials rather than use the more humble tempera paints and tape and foil the rest of us were using. She came with her Arches watercolor paper stretched on a board and her own brushes and paints. She worked in the style that had earned her prizes in local watercolor exhibits. She often lamented in her witness writing that her paintings never spoke to her the way others spoke to their artists. Yet she never asked her work to speak and never made an intention to speak to her image. The Creative Source respects our limitations. Had this artist continued in the process, she might have become aware that she "had no intention" of changing her methods or her relationship to creating, no intention to speak to or listen to her images. Students have often asked me why I didn't point out to her that she hadn't invited her work to speak. I only know I asked that question internally and heard guidance to not meddle in her process. It is not our job to foist our insights on others, but rather to be fully ourselves in each moment.

Each of us is a conduit for truth; but how much we receive, and whether or not we can put the truth we know to use, depends partly on how well we modulate what we receive. The Surrealist artists of the early twentieth century made a game of tapping into the universal stream of information through automatic writing and spontaneous drawing techniques like the "exquisite corpse" (Martin 1999). This practice began as a game where a phrase was written on a piece of paper that was then folded over to conceal the writing. Next it was passed to another person who wrote another phrase, folded the paper, and so on. The final amalgam was read as a "poetic fragment" of the group mind. The name comes from an early attempt at this exercise: *Le cadaver exquis boira le vin nouveau*" or "The exquisite corpse will drink the young wine." The game was later adapted for drawing as well. Overwhelmed by the powerful images and energy brought forth by these games, a number of people experimenting with them became disoriented and emotionally destabilized. In the studio, being in the presence of others engaged in similar work provides a form of grounding that makes each of us more capable of receiving and expressing images that might overwhelm us individually.

When working together with others, the intention to do no harm is crucial. It prevents us from making thoughtless remarks and helps to raise difficult feelings like envy or competition to the surface. What would the world look like if corporate CEOs shifted their intention from maximizing profits to doing the greatest good for all while doing no harm? I suspect we would have fewer costly and unhappy ecological disasters—not as a magical outcome, but because consciousness expands with clear intention into how to make that a reality. Without clear intention our insights are like brief wildfires extinguished by flash floods; they appear then vanish without lasting effect. The place from which the information comes contains all things; many of us receive information that needs to come into the world but do not necessarily have the grounding to bring the information in safely. The community of the studio, where there is no risk of judgment, is an ideal place to receive the wisdom that awaits us and to gain support for manifesting that wisdom in form. The "forgetting" that I often observe in rereading old witnesses may have the function of protecting us from knowing too much at once.

Sometime the image takes the lead and challenges me about my overall intention. This was the witness to the *Narrow Drawing*:

IMAGE: *How much life force energy are you willing to have pass through you?*

ME: *I "want" to say "a lot." I say a lot—I let a lot of life force energy pass through me. I will be a pathway for life force energy. As I say that to myself I feel my face change to an eagle, then a fox, then a jaguar, then talons spring from out of my fingers I have a sharp, curved beak . . . then I am covered in sleek black fur, stalking my prey I am a panther I feel a growl in my throat. Then I stop my kaleidoscope vision. I feel a trap door close at the level of my heart.*

I say "a little," I'll take a little energy and I feel my throat constrict my breathing feels labored. A trickle of energy is flowing through me I feel smaller, my shoulders stoop and round, gravity pulls the flesh of my face downward, I feel my bones drying and shrinking no words come from my throat, I'm dying.

What does this mean?

IMAGE: *You asked whether or not to get involved. Life is involvement, death is disengagement. Work to open more to life until you are one with whatever you do as you do it, like when you are drawing.*

ME: *You seem narrow to me now, at different times you felt more open. I chose a narrow piece of paper to feel boundaries.*

IMAGE: *You are always held by invisible bounds unless you work to destroy them, you are always utterly safe in the life force; widen the path as you feel comfortable.*

ME: *What about fear?*

IMAGE: *Fear is a speed bump stay with it and honor it and it will dissolve.*

There is a sense of power and sacredness in allowing our inner voices to speak aloud and receive witness. The language of parable, story, and metaphor, which for most people arrives only in dreams if at all, begins to feel more natural in our waking state. It is important to use intention as a means to ground ourselves in our daily life. I believe this practice allows us to listen to what is below the words spoken in ordinary discourse for the soul and heart meaning. There is a multiplicity of voices within each of us. Mary Watkins (1999, 2), referencing a phrase coined by Sampson,

Elements of Studio Practice

calls this the "'ensembled self,' aware of multiplicity on all levels." Over time we become less judgmental of others and otherness in ourselves, and are able to hear the image on a soul level when it speaks, which allows us to respond with compassion and gratitude. Artmaking is the vehicle by which we enter the place of all possibility. Intention determines what we manifest when we return from that place.

I often wonder how our foreign policy would change if the tool of intention were used in policy planning sessions. How about urban development or the affordable housing crisis? What if we made the intention to house every citizen in a way that would most support both body and soul unfolding? I spent time in Cuba recently and saw the effect of intentionality on urban planning in Havana. To determine the effect of a new building on the environment, surrounding buildings, and population, a *maqueta*, or scale model of the city, is carefully consulted before any new construction is begun. Cuba began to enter world markets following the collapse of the Soviet Union in 1991. Losing its only trading partner opened the way for both chaos and opportunity in Cuba. By mindfully entering into joint ventures with foreign investors, the Cuban government is struggling to deal with the paradox of legalizing the dollar and trying to maintain the values of socialism for its citizens. There is a clearly stated intention to preserve the dignity and rights of workers as a cornerstone of the ongoing Cuban revolution. What if Cuban and American artists were invited to envision together an even larger shift, one in which the greater good of all concerned was the guiding intention? What new forms of commerce might emerge that could aid developing nations and even our own sagging model of capitalism? Cuba, like South Africa, has resisted the demands of globalization in planning a smaller, sustainable, and just economy.

Imagine mindfulness guiding our interventions in nature. Imagine if our elected officials saw themselves as serving the Creative Source, whose compassion knows no bounds and observes no national boundaries. What if the imagination was considered our primary resource and was nurtured as such? What if artists were engaged through intention to serve as advisors to those in positions of power? Oracles had their place in the ancient world in just such a function. What would the world look like if power were exercised by those with alignment of body, mind, and heart? What is our intention, as individuals, as citizens, as creatures of the world? To go beyond our superficial answers and our despair, to touch our inner truth, we engage in artmaking, which takes us to the realm of all possibilities and revives in us the ability to imagine.

2
The Practice of Making Art
The Eros of All Possibility

Making art thrills and terrifies me. Here's how it begins: I am attracted to something, say the way green and orange look together. I begin to notice those two colors and see them everywhere, orange and green peppers piled next to each other in the grocery store, orange zinnias and green foliage spilling out of a flower box at the front of a house when I am taking a walk. I compliment women wearing these colors; they look ravishing to me. I wear those colors myself and feel more alive. I stare at a scarf a friend is wearing when we meet for tea. It is a shade of yellow orange gold, with purple and metallic threads, and I don't hear what she is saying—she might be reading the phone book—but she is gorgeous, and I love looking at her. I come into the studio and mix paints, multiple shades of orange and green next to each other, all around, shapes light, bright, muted, mixing, flowing into each other overtaking each other's essence and creating an all-new, never-been-seen color. I feel my body; it's like I am eating these colors and I can't get enough. They nourish a hunger I didn't know I had. Then purple gets into the act. Oh yes. "Oh yes" is what art gets us to do. Oh yes, I am alive, oh yes, color is food for my soul, oh yes, I am hungry, oh yes, you are an exquisite magnificent being, oh yes, I am in love with life. Mission accomplished.

Emerging from this encounter with orange and purple and green and gold, I am happy, refreshed, open, full. My judgments have receded. Time has elongated and widened. My shoulders have dropped, my gait is easy, and my hips are open. I am open. Washing my paintbrushes regrounds me into everyday life. Where have I been? I have been to Eros, the place of all possibilities, where I have let pleasure guide me to fulfillment.

✓ This place scares the bejesus out of me. I am scared by this place partly because of all the teaching I have received about love and lust and proper use of time and energy and all sorts of half-baked, overcooked substitutions for real soul food, heavy on the artificial ingredients and sanctimonious platitudes that have passed for spiritual sustenance. The fact is I am far more likely to do good in the world in the post–artmaking state than in any other. If I walk out of the studio and see a threadbare person who asks me for a dollar, there is no doubt I will give him that and perhaps even more because I am flush, I am rich, and I don't need a dollar to remind me of that.

In short, when I am in the moment, I am not afraid, and I desire to ignite delight in others the way I have been delighted. Here, now, I want to share my wealth, to see it reflected back in the eyes of another. In these moments I know that even money is Eros, another guise of the energy flow from the Creative Source. *Webster's* says that Eros is "the sum of life–preserving instincts that are manifested as impulses to gratify basic needs, impulses to protect and preserve body and mind" (1993, 394). We have narrowed our understanding of Eros to sexual expression, which is one but hardly the only way to preserve and protect body and mind. We can place so much weight upon our sexuality, in the form of expectations and simultaneous taboos, that it may be worn out as a reliable path to Eros. Artmaking reminds me that I know where the switch is and how to throw it to the on position. Art is a little subversive, very subversive; it gets underneath the surface and reveals what is there; it is a Geiger counter for truth.

What is there, under the surface of our fixed ideas, is everything, all possibilities. Once I am momentarily, fearlessly, in flow, once I have loosened my headlock on myself and released my clutching desperation to figure things out, to make a plan, to get it right, answers to previously unsolvable dilemmas float up into awareness. The Creative Source never says, "Well, that's just the way it is, you better get used to it." Always, new visions of what might be arise.

Why on earth would I resist this? Why resist pleasure, that sense of energy flowing through me, that quality of seeing everything through a lens of love, the edges of particularity etched so clear? Because it ends. Because there is death: "to know what Paradise means presupposes knowledge of its opposite, and the burdens and sufferings of earthly existence. The very idea of Paradise contains simultaneous grief over its loss" (Jacoby 1985, 26). The practice of staying fully alive takes courage. Art is a path of being exceptionally alive and dying small deaths over

Elements of Studio Practice

and over and over. It is a practice of learning the rhythm of living and dying. I know this in my bones and still I resist. My friend Don Seiden has been my greatest teacher of the art of dying in the practice of art-making. Over the more than twenty-five years that I have known Don, he has consistently made his art. I always try to see him when a new body of work is finished. Every time, he says, "I wonder if this is it." When he is in that spot right before the show is installed and friends come to congratulate him and admire his work, he sits, just him, soul and bones, wondering, "Is this it?" Whether or not Don makes another body of large work like his herd of antelope, I know he will continue to practice living and dying through his art and inspiring all of us who know him. For most of us, the pain of something coming to an end prevents us from ever fully engaging, as if that holding back would preclude the pain. Other times, we can trick ourselves into thinking, "Well, if death is inevitable, then don't even bother starting something."

When my imagination is really juiced and I am relaxed and not contracting in fear, I can even imagine death itself as a creative act complete with the whispers and seduction of art. The shadow of annihilation stands near every flirtation with creativity because, in some way, we do die; whoever we are before a creative act, we are not the same afterward. We know something new. The price of that renewal is a small death. The French speak the same way about orgasm, le petit mort, a price for the blissful union. Every entry into art is a time to renew our membership in life. There is no hard evidence to support what many adolescents and the truly sad hope for, that physical death is the answer to make pain stop. It is more likely that when we face and engage our pain, it begins to soften and open and change into something else. Many traditions tell us that death is the moment that all the demons we didn't face in life show up and confront us one after another. How we respond determines the set of challenges we return to in the next life. I suspect we get a little down time and then boom, back in another body to try again. Life loves itself and isn't trying to pull the plug. I believe the Creative Source is trying to get each of us to paint our way clear, to learn how to have an aesthetic response to life's challenges, to learn to see everything as a puzzle to be solved, an opportunity to high-five life over and over, to stay fearlessly in Its flow, like a surfer on a wave.

So why, being able one day to write these words, an anthem for aliveness, am I today, as I reread them, crying and feeling they apply to anyone but me? There is probably a connection between how each of us relates to the Creative Source and how we learned or were taught about sex, pleasure, love, and death. Everything we were cautioned about ties a knot in our energy flow. No matter what you learned, it wasn't the whole picture. It's like we were each given part of a torn letter; and then to claim our soul, we must find the other pieces and read the full text. Even a crumb of truth is freeing but maddening. The whole thing is like a scavenger hunt: we get the pieces we need from being with others, making our images, and seeing theirs. There are no wallflowers at a shindig thrown by the Creative Source. Nobody goes home alone.

No wonder con men succeed with the pitch "You are already a winner, just send money." We respond to such scams because on a certain level they represent the truth of our relationship to the Creative Source: we have images to express; we must simply send energy. We constantly exchange energy with others in the hope of gaining a bit of what we are here to learn. The perverse, false specialness of "Maybe I'm the exception, the only one whose Christmas stocking is empty" is a game played by our wish to feel safe. Today I am in that place because I am afraid of what I will find out next.

I have a pretty nice life, lots of people respect my work, and I am a pillar of my community, for goodness' sake. So isn't that enough? Shouldn't I just sit back and enjoy what I have? Isn't it greedy to think there's more? Or is it blindness not to see there's more to do? The fear of what's next means the fear of giving up the picture postcard of the present, which may be beautiful or could be painted in shades of gray respectability—but it is known. The fear is of what will happen if I really engage again in this creative process, and then I find out about how my life is connected to those who are not so fortunate or so safe. If I really engage, maybe the lens will begin to open wider. There is always the fear of being called to sacrifice what we love. I suspect that I can readily trace that fear to the story of Jesus that I grew up with. God supposedly loving his son so much that he okayed the crucifixion. Yet when I am willing to sit with my fear, I often find that synchronicity follows. New experiences arise to engage our enlarged capacity for understanding.

Elements of Studio Practice

As I am mulling over the idea of how the greater awareness of others beyond my personal sphere might occur, I find myself today in the Betty Rymer Gallery at the School of the Art Institute of Chicago, face to face with memory cloths sewn by South African women. I am in the presence of art that is about women reclaiming the images of their lives under apartheid. For a historical archive, women in the rural townships are sewing pictures about the violence they have endured. Art is returning their dignity to them and giving their stories to all of us.

In an essay that accompanies the exhibit of the work, Carol Becker writes: "The New South Africa will never know from whence it evolved if these stories are not told. Were they to remain buried, they would only return to haunt society, slowly, or not so slowly, eroding its underpinnings. The women of Amazwi Abesifazane (Voices of Women) understand that the transformation of society begins with creativity" (2004, 12). Am I ready to engage with how the strawberries I put on my cereal got to my table or how the country I am a citizen of conducts business on my behalf around the world? Creating images makes it possible to face personal fears; I know this for a fact. But can it also allow us to face the world? The women of Amazwi Abesifazane, who stand at a crossroads where the personal and political are so closely overlaid as to be indistinguishable, have much to teach those of us who believe we have a choice about facing the world or dealing with just ourselves.

Actually, I believe that the Creative Source is encoded in our DNA such that if we resist too long, our body makes images out of its cellular raw material by creating tumors, rashes, pain, and quantities of gelatinous body fat. A male yoga instructor once remarked to me that when he sees men in his classes with protruding bellies that don't shape up no matter what they do, he suggests that they take an art class. He thinks that they have something within waiting to be born, that they are pregnant with a neglected creative urge. Creation will always create. Yet when we glimpse that particular crumb of truth, our minds want to print bumper stickers that say "Make art, not tumors" and plan a seminar to serve that crumb to others. Instead of seeing that crumb as but one on a trail of crumbs leading us somewhere as yet unseen, we want to reify and market our small morsel of wisdom. "Oh! Bad metaphor," you say. "The trail of breadcrumbs was eaten by the birds, and Hansel and Gretel never got back to where they started." True, but we have to be willing to risk that.

Where we end up will not look like where we began or like the pictures in a travel brochure. We do not get the itinerary ahead of time. Sometimes following the trail will take us to the witch's house. Sometimes you have stay there and live with the witch for a while and get to know her. Sometimes the witch eats us alive or pushes us into the fire. That is exactly right. Sometimes what grabs me and activates the creative process isn't gorgeous sensuous colors but a paralyzing deadly gray sensation like being encased in cement. Sometimes it's "No!" with a capital N, and I feel myself apart and drowning and useless and hopeless. Somehow I have learned that if I can notice the cement, become aware of it—the particular nature of this shade of gray—if I can feel its coolness and solidity, then it begins to soften and it, too, opens a doorway into the place of all possibility, where nothing is as it seems at first glance.

And by the way, it's February in Chicago and that gray stuckness is the truth of Nature—why shouldn't I feel it? The February weather in Chicago tacitly begs the question, "Do you or don't you want to live?" I read somewhere that severely ill people die at higher rates during February and March than at any other time of year, and that makes sense. But yesterday being outside in the February absolute gray I knew the still point that I come to in the point of merger with artmaking simply by being with the trees. Suddenly the winds of March made a whole different kind of sense. True movement must arise out of true stillness. True stillness feels like death and, yes, it is a door to Eros.

I am always grateful for the Jewish holiday, a minor and lesser-known one, of Tu b'Shevat, the New Year for Trees, which occurs in the month of Shevat on the Jewish calendar, usually in February, though January this year. Among its many meanings, it is said to mark the moment that the seeds deep underground begin to move, sprouting and breaking through their casing and reaching out into the still-frozen soil. Everything that lives begins in secret darkness that just the moment before was utterly dormant, its spark coiled deep and hidden (figure 3). Regardless of whether the first stirring toward creation is pleasure or pain, the path leads to the same place—the place of awe and wonder and aliveness, the eternal now, the place of all possibility, Eros. Engaging with the obstacles

Elements of Studio Practice

Figure 3. *Seed*, by Pat B. Allen. Tape and foil.

is part of the artmaking process; unpacking what seems to get in our way is part of recognizing our particular images, our raw materials.

The first stage of artmaking as a spiritual path is *inquiry*. This stage is play with materials and ideas; it is about not having a plan. In the best of all worlds, we each played a lot if not enough as children, in a safe-enough place, unencumbered by too many lessons too soon, with enough stuff but not too much, with unscheduled time when we were accountable to nothing but our own imagination. We had challenges but not soul-stopping traumas. Of course, that's not how it always or even usually unfolds. Some of us were called out of the playground by family problems, and some of us were expected to turn play into achievement way too soon.

I told a mother who came into my studio asking about classes for her six-year-old daughter, who loves to draw, to set up a corner at home where the child can play with art materials, alone or with mom or friends. There she can inquire about what intrigues and interests her. In contrast, a class is likely to instruct her, to guide her toward a finished product, reassuring mom that her money was well spent. I saw the woman's eyes get a little teary as I spoke about just safeguarding a space for her daughter's imagination. I could tell this mom got the message, because she asked if she and her daughter could come back and just walk through the studio to get ideas of how to set up their own. The most important thing she could do for her daughter was to say Yes! to support what was already growing without turning it into an obligation and another stop on the carpool. In the best of all worlds, a parent is a

Figure 4. *Death Pulls Up a Chair*, by Pat B. Allen. Tempera.

child's first agent of the Creative Source. All of us need someone in our life who sees us clearly and says Yes!

If you get into play late in life, in adulthood, it is about flirting and playing the field and allowing yourself to be seduced. It is about letting yourself be recruited by life, for life. But maybe attraction and relationship are skewed too, because of abuse or loss or a rotten adolescence. It is never too late. Salvador Dalí described his work as an "erotic triumph over death." In a film on his life, he relates that his elder brother died at the age of seven, three years before Dalí's birth. His birth was seen by his parents as a replacement for his brother, and Dalí was even given the same name. Dalí says his parents never recovered, and "their anxiety never left me." He experienced the persistence of his brother's presence "as a trauma and a sense of being outdone." Because death is experienced as being so close, Dalí says, "everything is such a great pleasure." Everything is experienced as erotic, hence the celebration of life in his art (Low, 1988). Unlike Dalí, many people don't encounter death until later in life when aging casts light on the fact that death has pulled up a chair to our table (figure 4).

Elements of Studio Practice

Whenever it emerges, an awareness of death, if not suppressed, can make the Creative Source accessible. Death is a scary but reliable door.

Many people have practiced a form of inquiry about such things through journaling techniques in which they arrive at insights through writing about their thoughts and memories. A lot of therapy takes this approach and has its value. James Pennebaker, a psychologist at Southern Methodist University in Dallas, has done research showing that writing about traumatic events causes immediate changes in autonomic nervous system activity (1993, 539). Inquiry through art has some very different properties. Artmaking gives us the tools to remake and enlarge our story when it starts to chafe and bind and simply not fit anymore, once we have unearthed it and told and retold it a while. Images take us to a state where our perceptions and sensations are not yet mediated by words—a state of magic realism, where everything is real and everything is magic. We learn what pleases us and how to explore without conscious goals and without judgments. We learn again to play. Play is restorative in that it allows us to drop our edges and boundaries and attain the primordial sense of oneness. What art alone can do is allow us to become one with an infinite range of possibilities. We can imagine and therefore create what never was. I imagine that when the women of Amazwi Abesifazane sit together and tell their stories and stitch by stitch commit them to cloth that they release the stories from themselves but also experience the pleasure of creative focus and the support of each other.

The attitude we bring to the state of inquiry is important. We must cultivate the mind that resists quick conclusions and labeling. We show up with the intention of openness, emptiness. This is especially necessary if we have lost or never had a connection to the Creative Source through art. It helps if we can practice not wanting a result right away. We cultivate a mind of rising and falling. Now what I am painting seems like a tree, now a giraffe; now the giraffe is disappearing into green. Even realistic artmaking at its best works this way. A portrait painter does not exactly sit down to make a picture of his sitter, but rather to render the subtleties of the shade of violet that is next to the shade of pale orange that to the onlooker is named as the shadow under a cheekbone but to a painter is an abstraction of exquisite tone, color, and energy. This journey into Eros, into the pleasure of seeing without naming, works best at first with a time limit so that you can let go of fears of falling into something and not getting out. This is also why working together with others in a loosely structured way is helpful. The support of others breathing nearby and knowing everyone will stop at the same time is helpful in beginning to develop self–regulation. This is also a practice of nonattachment, a goalless foray into *being with*, rather than the production of a prescribed outcome. A challenge to many of us when beginning to connect with the Creative Source is to stay too long and then fear returning. At this stage, every possibility, any possibility, is great. The inquiry stage of artmaking as a spiritual practice occurs each time we begin on a small scale; on a larger scale it heralds each new body of work as well.

It is exciting to see an accomplished artist find their way back to the rudiments of inquiry, to come into the studio needing to return to the sandbox stage and let all their skills melt down to mud. Eileen was a successful decorative painter and interior designer when she arrived at my class burned out and questioning whether she had come to the end of art for herself and needed a new career. After several months of working with tape and foil and tempera paint and laying down the mantle of profes–sional artist for a while, she was delighted and surprised to find herself re–filled with energy for her decorative work. During her studio sojourn she also took the time to explore and work through family issues that had been draining her energy and joy for life. She untied the knots, let in the surge of energy that had been blocked by fears about admitting her daughter's eating disorder, and resumed her art career. Taking the time to reconnect with her internal wisdom through art as inquiry and find her way to what was blocking her energy, Eileen dissolved her relatively minor obstacles.

It is often at the borders of our experience that we encounter fertile opportunity for inquiry through art. If we focus on bodily sensation, we may feel a sense of fatigue or futility. An unseen barrier is preventing ac–cess to our usual reservoir of energy. We may resist or fear going places or doing things off our beaten path. We all live with multiple, highly elabo–rated systems of order: maps, addresses, bus routes, phone numbers, deeds, surveys, computer passwords, clocks. All contribute to our belief that things are either "this" or "that," "here" or "there." Phone lines were once party lines, which served several families who shared the same number and could enter one another's conversation by accident merely by picking up the receiver. We extend our belief in boundaries into many areas where blending, overlapping edges are a closer approximation of the truth.

I once was on a plane sitting near a young woman who had never flown before. Looking out the window, she expressed genuine surprise that the earth did not indicate where one state began and another left off with the sure lines of a map. Cities melt off eventually into plains and mountains; there is no "city limit" etched into the earth to be seen from above. Janis Timm–Bottos likes to compare the place of creativity to a swamp. Neither terra firma nor exactly a body of water, swamps never-theless teem with life. Many swamp inhabitants are beautifully adapted for life in multiple worlds, spending time both in watery abodes and on dry land. Through artmaking we begin to play with adapting ourselves to multiple landscapes, we loosen our fixed ideas by traveling to boundary-less places within ourselves. We resist monoculture and monotony.

To summarize inquiry, it is how we locate ourselves and find out what our work of the moment is. We do this by excavating our past, looking at old photographs, visiting the places our ancestors lived, reading about events that occurred during our parents' lives that shaped the zeitgeist into which we were born. This is as vital to an individual as it is to a cul-ture. We look around, notice what intrigues us, attracts us—what colors, what shapes, what kind of images in galleries and museums, what kinds of trash and pieces of junk on the street. What gives us cause for celebra-tion? We also notice what annoys us and what makes us cry, what ideas keep us up at night. What wounds me and makes me embarrassed to be a part of the human race? What piece of music stops us dead in our tracks? Anything can be a breadcrumb that begins to lead us back to the wellspring of our energy, to Eros, the Source. Who or what is laying claim to our energy through fears, secrets, or illness? We pay attention to our physical energy, to what gets our heart beating, what makes us laugh, what makes us jealous—especially what makes us jealous. Jealousy is shunned as a bad character trait, but actually it is a signal flag sent up by the Creative Source. You will notice, if you think about it, that there are countless extravagant or exquisite things that you do not yearn for. There are achievements and awards you do not covet or even think about. Yet there are some things that others have or do that arouse our envy. It is these things that instruct us in the unfulfilled potential of our deepest self.

How do we listen to hear what is aching to be made manifest through us? We experiment with materials, colors, and shapes. We envision the color and consistency of the mantle of doom weighing on our shoulders. What does it look like? Maybe we sew it and practice putting it on and taking it off. We collect found objects and label boxes to store them in. What images, when you see them, make you wish they were yours? Inquiry begins the art process, but inquiry never ends. Even when you are deeply engaged in a project, other little things will show up to tease you about what might come next. Put them in a box or folder, like a squirrel saving nuts for winter—for future inquiry. We inquire into the messy and dark feelings that we have instead of simply whitewashing them cheerfully and doing penance by being even nicer. ①

Challenges to inquiry abound. The first and worst is staying too busy to notice what attracts you. Fear may deafen us to the resonance that builds into a full-scale love affair. It is also possible to become drunk on the energy that builds in inquiry without clearly protecting the time needed to fully engage in the work that is calling. I am a sucker for this one. When inquiry really starts to bubble for me, my energy grows. At such moments, I am excited, happy, and at great risk for saying yes to things like being on committees, volunteering to read other people's projects, and deciding to redecorate. I see no end in sight to my energy. It's hard for me to turn down offers of work, invitations to speak somewhere, drumming in a peace parade, because the whole darn world just seems so fantastic and so connected to what ever it is I'm jazzed about. This is the delirium version of the interconnectedness of all beings. Of course, in a few days or weeks, when inquiry has morphed into engagement and the work requires me to settle down and pay attention for long periods of time, this is when all those obligations come due and suddenly my art and I are having a lovers' quarrel. Something like:

ART: *Didn't you beg and pray for me to show up? And now I'm here and you have a meeting about the appropriate height of hedges near the expressway?*

ARTIST: *Yes, but, really, it seemed connected at the time, and besides the meeting is over at eight and really, I'll meet you right after that, I promise. Except I'm fifty now, and I need to be in bed at ten o'clock.*

Elements of Studio Practice

Other challenges to inquiry are self-consciousness and self-criticism. It is crucial in the phase of inquiry to suspend judgments. One should simply ask oneself, "Does this please me?" If so, keeping it up is a good plan. If not, witness-write and find out what would be more pleasing. The process of judging art calls forth a very different kind of energy; it is the energy of pruning versus the energy of cultivation. In the stage of inquiry we must cultivate all leads. Related to our own judgments and equally dangerous is allowing others to name or direct our inquiry. It is important in the inquiry stage to avoid the comments of others, even positive comments. When we hear "Oh, I really like that!" an aura of preciousness can begin to form like a crust around an image, and it can be hard to allow it to continue to evolve. Finally, premature naming of our inquiry can lead to stunted growth. When the Creative Source is leading us along a path, we feel energy flowing through us, the physical sensation of being very alive. Sometimes, when we say, "Oh, I get it, this is about thus and such," the energy goes away because there is no point in continuing if we already think we know where we are going. We broadcast that we are content with the same story we have told before. There are certainly artists and people in all walks of life who simply do the same thing over and over. A consumer society demands that a product be consistent. The Creative Source pulls back and lets us proceed but without the fire and light we had before. We have stepped out of a gift economy and into a commodity economy. We have exchanged the passion of a love affair for a business relationship. Inquiry requires that we remain playful and open, noticing our energy and following it wherever it leads.

Engagement comes next. I really thought when my friends and I created the Open Studio Project, where we invented and refined the most simple ways of teaching others to gain access to artmaking, the basic form of art as inquiry, that I would make art only that way forever. I felt sure I would have no other needs. My work could be created and then hung on the refrigerator of the Creative Source forever and that was enough. Simply recording the rising and falling of an image, seeing it as ultimately just a piece of paper without any intrinsic value beyond the joy and message it brought to me, was fine. The image was the canoe, the snowshoes, the rappelling rope that took me down the path as the path appeared beneath my feet at any given moment—whether as a mountain to climb, a river to cross, or a trapdoor to fall through. Friends, especially other artists, and art therapists, would visit the studio and ask, "But where's your *real* work?" Writing, too, became the witness to the daily images.

I was always skeptical of Carl Jung, who spent a period of his life practicing art and writing in a similar way, making spontaneous paintings, which he did not call art, in contrast to his conventional landscape paintings. Jung transcribed dialogues with the images that appeared in his work, including Philemon, a wise old guru who showed up in Jung's now–famous Red Notebook. I thought Jung was shortchanging the process of active imagination, that instead of continuing to do art and active imagination he stopped and wrote about it and mined the few years of work for the rest of his life in all his academic books, for he spent the next thirty years writing his experience into theories (though I am deeply grateful that he did this). Time and again I watched artists, new and experienced alike, do the equivalent of lowering a bucket into the endless well of the Creative Source and pulling up gold. I couldn't imagine a need for more than that.

Then, gradually, imperceptibly, I began to feel a shift. I no longer felt the same sense of connection working alongside others in the simple and rudimentary ways of the basic inquiry of studio practice. Several hours of artmaking was no longer enough to feed my soul. The simple materials began to annoy me. I felt called to work with oil paints. I needed a space where I could leave my unfinished work out and not clean up with the group at the appointed time. I needed a messy adolescent's room, not the orderly space of the nursery. My faith in the process was complete. I knew if I showed up, the Creative Source would show up, too. But I began to feel It was goading me forward. *What about life outside the wonderful sandbox of your studio?* it seemed to say. *What about smelting some of that gold ore into bells and bracelets or wedding rings? What about moving up from the kindergarten team at least to Little League? What about if not a marriage, the possibility, at least, of engagement?*

But I've seen so many folks do that and fail. Their "real" art never achieves the sincerity of those early efforts; self–consciousness creeps in, or their technique isn't up to par. To go to the next level requires critique and commentary, which are anathema in the play stage. Many of us should have stayed longer in kindergarten, but the bell rang and what we had to bring to critique was still a mud pie and was not greeted with joyful acceptance. I myself barely made it out of art school, having just discovered the sandbox spirit that free expression evokes. I worried that I was being unfaithful to the process by wanting to paint again in oils, to make portraits, and to study skills. But the process called me there, and so I went.

How do we become intimate with what is ours, take the bait that the Creative Source is holding out for us, and become one with what is unfolding? How do we successfully move past the stage of inquiry into full engagement? As with any love affair, you have to have a place to meet. The first step is to create space and time to nurture, support, and revel in what has arrived. Let go of extraneous pursuits, cancel magazine subscriptions, disconnect the phone, or at least put a serious message on the answering machine. It was a breakthrough moment for me to put the message "I am writing today. Leave a message, and I'll call you back later" on my studio answering machine. Not only did that prevent interruptions, but when I did call back, I got lots of support from friends for setting that boundary around the creative process. Supporting engagement can also mean inviting in things that amplify whatever we are doing: narrowing down our search for images, collecting objects, gaining knowledge about a technique that would improve our skills, immersing ourselves in whatever the substance of our work seems to be. Instead of watching TV to relax, you might drop in on a figure–drawing class at the local art league or walk in the woods or lie on the grass and stare at the sky.

Engagement requires time for things to cook and simmer on the back and front burners. The mind can't be burdened with arguments and political discussions, unless that is what your work is about. Minimizing the errands, wearing the same clothes so you do the wash less often, negotiating with your family to cook a meal—all these can help make space. Most of all, engagement means showing up and working: in other words, discipline. Witness writing can be especially helpful in the engagement phase; for when we become deeply immersed in our work, the image becomes very eloquent about what it wants next. Rather than simply using our own visual sense, we must recognize that the image is a being in its own right that will direct its own unfolding if we choose to listen. Do we still say Yes! now that the place of all possibilities becomes the one and only possibility? That is the question the Creative Source poses to us. It says, "Here is something the world needs, are you up to it?"

Studio practice allows for simple engagement to occur in a single artmaking encounter. When an image begins to take shape from the marks made on paper, we decide whether or not we will engage. Gradually there is a growth in our capacity for engagement; and instead of ending the encounter at the end of a single studio session and starting something new next time, the artist takes out the piece in the next session and works her way back into it after asking what it is that the image requires. Facing the image a second time can feel like jumping back into the pool after your bathing suit is dry; we may have a little resistance, a fear of messing up whatever we accomplished before. To fully receive what we are being offered requires that we learn to sustain engagement beyond the first blush of energy. Tolerating the unfinished without abandoning it is a crucial skill gained in artmaking as a spiritual practice. In the seven-week series I have taught, artists were encouraged in the last week to revisit all their work and witness writings in order to see opportunities to deepen engagement. Forgoing the novelty of starting something new can be hard, but it is crucial in building the discipline of a spiritual practice.

This review also helps us to notice what is not our work, to recognize images that fulfilled their purpose in the moment and can be thanked and released. Once our receptivity to the Creative Source is activated, there is sometimes a struggle between the thinking mind and the deeper, intuitive faculty, which is what we are aiming to cultivate in art as a spiritual practice. Getting a clear-cut "idea" of what "we" want to express is often a signal that the thinking mind is trying to supersede the organic unfolding of the creative process. When we "know" what we are about to create, the trail is often about to go cold. The Creative Source wants to enlarge what we know by helping us to manifest new depths of truth or by discarding outworn perceptions. Engagement is a commitment. It is startling to realize what is being asked of us: a faithfulness to continue, a pledge to forsake other possibilities. We are asked to travel forward without knowledge of our destination. We are asked to trust that just about everything is a part of our path. We are asked to cultivate the sense of knowing in our body when we are on the right track, to recognize the signals of distraction such as aches, pains, sudden inspiration to start something else, and to gently turn away.

I learned some of the subtleties of engagement through my work with an image of the Akedah, the biblical story of the binding of Isaac (figure 5). I was called to this image in a workshop my colleagues and I facilitated at the Spertus Museum of Judaica in Chicago. After writing an intention, we were taken on a tour of the collections by the museum director. Each person was asked to choose or be chosen by an artifact and to write a witness to it in the gallery. We then returned to a classroom and created an art piece and witnessed a second time. I felt called by a silver platter depicting Abraham with his sword raised over Isaac, about to slay him—so he thought—at God's behest. Abraham "knew" where he was going and what he was going to do. This story is among the most challenging in the Torah and is often interpreted to mean that God was testing Abraham's faith and that when he proved faithful, God let him off the hook. My image tells a different story, one more closely aligned with a retelling by Rabbi Michael Lerner in his book *Jewish Renewal* (1994). Lerner says that Abraham is hearing the voice of the god of his childhood, the god he grew beyond, telling him to do to his child what was done to him. Abraham, born in the era of child sacrifice, had himself, legend tells, been passed through the flames. Abraham is stopped by the true voice of God, urging justice and compassion. As Lerner points out, "in this moment Abraham must confront the central problem facing every religion and every historical manifestation of God in the world: the difficulty separating the voice of God from the legacy of pain and cruelty that dominates the world and is embedded in our psyches" (p. 45). We are all at the mercy of the voices of the past, of our limitations, the known and the voice of the Creative Source, ever evolving and urging us to new possibilities, greater compassion and consciousness.

In my image the most prominent figure is the yellow angel, whose color and design resembles many other manifestations of life-force energy in my work. This is the voice that guides us toward true engagement, the voice of the Creative Source, of divine wisdom. Creating the image, I found that it wanted me to depict more than the four central players in the drama—Abraham, Isaac, the angel, and the ram for the sacrifice. In fact, three other figures showed up. One is Ishmael—the son whom Abraham cast out into the desert—pictured as a red, demon-like figure sitting on the ground next to the altar where Isaac is bound. One

Figure 5. *The Akedah (Binding of Isaac)*, by Pat B. Allen. Watercolor.

is a flying figure of Hagar, mother of Ishmael. She is pointing up to the sky with one hand and down to earth with the other. And entering the painting from the deep far–right corner is Jesus, carrying a lamb over his shoulder.

> HAGAR: *"This isn't the end of it, until my son, Ishmael, whom you demonize is also redeemed, the story is not complete. As above, so below, until you cease sacrifice of all the children, the sword will not rest."*
>
> JESUS: *"I am returning the lamb to its mother as well. This destruction, too, is unnecessary."*

In the background of the painting, two trees grow on the hillside, the originally united trees of life and knowledge. The angel is a definite male presence; he speaks with hands upraised.

> ANGEL: *"Offer your praises, not your sacrifices. Go back to the sacred groves and learn anew the sacred cycles, sing, dance, pray under the trees, remember nature and bury the sword."*

The red figure, who introduced himself after a long while as Ishmael,

Elements of Studio Practice

crouches under the sacrificial altar. He carries all the attributes of Satan: cloven hooves, red color, tail, and horns. He remains the scapegoat. No wonder he was the last figure to identify himself.

These figures emerged over many months to populate this small painting. I was quite stunned when Jesus appeared, even though I know that the place of all possibility exists in the art space. There is no reason why Jesus can't enter this story and add his two cents as an embodiment of compassion. I could not have planned this painting ahead of time. The insights are not my own, but messages from the place of all possibility that we enter when we engage in art as a spiritual practice. It is not some definitive truth, but one of infinite possibilities to try on, to consider, helping us to enlarge the stories we are used to; stories want to evolve. I was simply open to receiving them because the studio environment does not have a dogma that draws a line between religions or anything else. Each of us embodies a particular confluence of factors that allows us to be receptive to different facets of truth. The courage to engage comes with practice but also requires the presence of nonjudgmental witness in the form of fellow artists.

During the engagement phase of artmaking, one must be careful not to lose balance by forgetting to eat, sleep, exercise, or otherwise maintain a healthy routine. Jung wrote that when he was engaged with his images from his unconscious, he needed to maintain his practice of seeing his patients in analysis as well as being involved in his family life in order to stay grounded in everyday reality. The hoary myth of the starving, smoking, drinking artist reflects struggles with resistance and personal demons, not the consequences of receiving images from the Creative Source. Like the voices Abraham heard at first, they are of the past and will not bring us new learning. They can dull the truth of your work and even derail it altogether. Like Jung, we all must maintain attention on our families and our work in the world in order to reel ourselves back in to daily life. We must learn to both cherish and manage the gift of energy that flows through us when we are deeply engaged in creative work. Often, however, there is a greater risk of becoming scattered, of leaving our work for so long that the trail grows cold and the breadcrumbs have all been eaten by the time we try to reenter the work. This obstacle can be overcome by witness writing. Before attempting to pick up a paintbrush, sit before the

[handwritten marginalia: stay connected to family, work, routine]

[handwritten marginalia: show up.]

image and engage in conversation. Apologize for leaving it for so long; ask for guidance about how to begin.

Inner obstacles will arise during the engagement phase. We will lose heart and energy for our work. Although I felt deeply moved after viewing the work of the women of Amazwi Abesifazane, I also became momentarily despondent about my writing. I found myself judging it harshly as being horribly self-absorbed, self-indulgent, and irrelevant. This sort of response almost always indicates that there is a knot to be untied in our attitude or awareness that will lead to greater freedom if we go forward. The key is to continue to show up in our workspace, but also to honor the resistance we feel and not try to force the work. Soon it became clear that I was being challenged to stand in another border space between personal and political work and to notice what happens in the place where the two overlap. One of the main reasons I closed Studio Pardes was my growing feeling that the work being done by artists there was too self-absorbed, too unmindful of the world outside the studio. I felt that in providing sanctuary for a few hours a week, I was helping maintain the status quo rather than subvert it. So my work is to engage the question: how does art move one to action? I have no right to judge the motives or experiences of the other artists. I cannot demand that all the artists in the studio become activists. I do have the responsibility to sit with my discomfort and see where it leads me. I have the responsibility to remain engaged with the questions that arise. I was led to close the studio and open space in my life without knowing what would come next.

Sometimes we are told that sitting is exactly the right thing to do. These times of struggle allow us to develop compassion for ourselves as well as for the image that is struggling to be born. If we keep it up, we begin to notice that our compassion flows to all beings we encounter. Sometimes just being in the space and sweeping the floor is a good idea. This is an act of service to the work. We notice the energy we feel and where it seems to be leading us. Sometimes the image needs something we do not yet have, and the direction to go and find a certain color paint or cloth or an image of a crow will come to us just as we finish sweeping. The important thing is not to break the engagement by abandoning the work. Another challenge in the engagement phase of art is isolation. In truth, a considerable amount of solitude is necessary to perform creative

Elements of Studio Practice

work. Yet it is also very helpful to make contact with others who are also engaged with similar concerns. Bubbling under the surface, sheltered from the light of too much scrutiny, our images can work in us while we engage in such contact.

When we are receiving information or moving through images to new understanding, it can begin to feel unreal or too intense to carry on the work alone. The engagement phase is a time when witness from others is valuable. Invite one or more trusted friends to witness your work. This is not a social event. Do not ask for witness from those so close to you that they cannot have any discernment. If you've served them hot dogs three nights in a row, don't ask your family. Do not invite a friend who is miserably stuck in his own work. Do cultivate witness pals whose opinion you value and trust. Remember this is an important and honored role for someone to take. Be grateful. Describe what your hopes and fears are concerning the work, and ask the witness to remain silent until you are finished. Then ask for a witness. A good question to ask of a witness is: "What in this work has energy for you?" When we witness this way for others, we always write an intention first, which includes the statement to do no harm and then can be elaborated in terms such as, "I respond with honesty and clarity to Jane's work in a way that will help her continue." The ideal state for a witness is that of compassionate disinterest. Responding to the creative work of others is an extraordinarily difficult task that few writers have explored. I hear horror stories frequently from art students whose professors say shockingly insensitive things that often seem to arise directly from their own fear or discomfort with the student's image. Art, music, and dance teachers should have to take a Hippocratic oath to do no harm. Themes of engagement often come into and out of prominence in our work. Most of us have several strands of work, either different images or preferences for materials that we revisit over a lifetime of practice. The collage paintings incorporating family photos that I began more than twenty years ago have become cloth hangings, the photos affixed to the cloth with computer technology and transfer techniques. My love of words and writing has joined my visual pieces through the use of rubber stamps, stencils, and witness writing directly onto art pieces. I have recently returned to drawing and painting portraits from life, the first art practice I began in college.

Inflation is a danger of the engagement phase of work. When we become inflated with our imagery, we have forgotten that we are engaged in service to the Divine. We may think our images and our process are the most important things in the world. We neglect the feelings of those around us, our obligations to family and friends. We may entertain fantasies of our own greatness. Adolf Hitler, once an art student who was denied entry to the Academy of Arts in Vienna as a young man, became dangerously inflated with his images of a new story for Germany's past and future. He created elaborate pageants and museums that depicted a heroic past that never was (Barron 1991, 34). His undeniably creative use of imagery to transform his own woundedness intersected with the collective wounded pride of the German people to horrible effect. Hitler reminds us that the Creative Source will manifest through us and is guided by our intention and level of discernment. Hitler was operating from his own mind's ability to split good and evil and to project evil entirely onto designated scapegoats. He is perhaps the most potent example of the dangers of creative inflation in history. While few of us will ever be at the crossroads of history that allows our personal blindness to have such a devastating effect, we must acknowledge that the same principles apply to us. Our engagement in creative work will manifest according to our strengths and limitations. It is our responsibility to work with our intention toward right action and discernment and to notice and resist any grandiosity. We must constantly question and ask for guidance in our intention and witness process.

A lack of balance will harm the work as well as our relationships to others and the world. At such times art can become an addiction rather than a spiritual practice. The rush of energy that comes from deeply engaging in creative work must also be allowed to ebb away until we come to the still point that begins the cycle anew. Witnessing our life and noticing what needs pruning is a good way to begin. Acknowledging our finite self and rededicating our self to our work while simplifying our life will lessen inflation. The Creative Source never asks us to act in ways that harm others; neither will it prevent us from doing so. To discern right action requires time, mindfulness, and discipline about seeing what is truly important. Stepping outside ourselves to perform mundane acts of service such as writing a condolence note or visiting a shut-in friend is an antidote to inflation. The final challenge is to resist coming to premature closure or forcing work to be finished that simply isn't. Some work needs a very long time, years even, to be complete. If possible, keep the image visible in your space or at least in your mind's eye. If some part of you remains engaged, the image will unfold itself in its own time.

Engagement can expand from brief encounters to the long embrace of a life's work. If we are true to the process on a regular basis, the bigger picture will come into focus by itself. As our stamina for engagement with the Divine grows, we may become more conscious of which people and activities nurture our process and which hinder it. Changes in our habits occur more or less spontaneously as we come into greater balance with the Creative Source. We become aware of foods, activities, or relationships that we have used to distance ourselves from our inner wisdom, and we begin to change those. In particular, as we make images of truth, our tolerance for consumption of the imagery of cultural products is likely to change. In his essay "Diet for a Mindful Society" (in Badiner 2002), Thich Nhat Hanh says:

> When we ingest toxic substances into our body, we get sick. When we ingest toxic "cultural products" into our consciousness, we also get sick. Our society has so many kinds of spiritual and cultural foods that are toxic. Television is poisoning us and our children, as are many magazines, news images, and so on. We practice watering the seeds of anger, fear, and violence every day. We have to learn to live our daily lives in a way that can help us refrain from taking in more poisons. When these poisons enter our store consciousness, they weaken our power of mindfulness. Without some kind of diet for our consciousness, it is very difficult to practice mindfulness. (p. 239)

The practice of artmaking gently substitutes forms of pleasure and gratification that make typical TV fare fade in appeal. One of the challenges in changing our visual and spiritual diet can be fear of alienating those around us. For decades the television has served as an electronic hearth around which people have gathered. If this is true in your experience, try occasionally to offer a joint artmaking time to family and friends instead. Collage is a good transitional activity. Engaging with the very images that bombard us and remaking the messages can be very liberating. The Creative Source welcomes the engagement of everyone, not merely some privileged class of artists. It is the mother and and father, nurturer and supporter of all beings, and welcomes all of us to wake up to life's abundance. Our engagement with art leads us to engagement with our bodies, spirits, and with each other.

(Celebration) is the stage of closure in the artmaking process. It is a time to be with and appreciate what has come to us, whether at the end of an individual session of artmaking or at the culmination of a body of work. We honor both what the Creative Source has offered and what we have done with what we have been given. Honor is connected to honesty, which means we must tell the truth. We review and assess and take measure of what we have done. We notice our emotions of joy, disappointment, and contentment. We account for any inflation: Did we imagine that this painting, this image, this idea would somehow elevate us over others? Do we remember that all the images belong to us but also to everyone? We begin the ending process by noticing what we have gained, or let go of, how we have been enlarged by the image or images that have come to us in this round of the creative process, whether it is one day or the culmination of months of work. As an artwork nears completion, we are called to a state of gratitude. It is time to thank those who have touched and inspired us in any way, as well as those who have challenged us. At the end of every workshop session we come together as a group; and each artist who wishes to, reads aloud their intention and witness. Afterward, expressions of gratitude are common. Gratitude at this stage helps to empty us out and brings in the support we need to tolerate the space of ending before the cycle can begin again; it ensures that the flow will return. By expressing our gratitude, we humble ourselves. We acknowledge that we have received what we have expressed, that we are vessels and serve the Creative Source, bringing into being the images needed to sustain the Anima Mundi, the Soul of the World. In the Bible the Hebrew word for "create" is used only in reference to God. God creates; humans make.

This aspect of the celebration phase of artmaking is my closest understanding of the Buddhist notion of no-self. Paradoxically, the making of

Elements of Studio Practice

images, the presence of these actual objects, relieves me of the burden of self. I experience a profoundly charged emptiness that comes from giving my all, my energy, in service to truth. I can also experience the subtle difference when I have served the images less well, when I have written the witness off the top of my head or for the benefit of others in the room rather than receiving it as welling up from the soul, from the image itself for me. Instead of a fertile emptiness, I feel a cluttered, mildewed sense alerting me that I have more work to do to prepare for the moment of celebration. Witness writing to that feeling is a crucial step in the process. Sometimes there is an image left unfinished or a request made by an image that I have not honored. The inner teacher will wait patiently for me to find the loose thread and finish the seam.

At the end of a seven-week course, artists put up all their work and reread all their witness writings, a deeper version of what is done weekly. At times we have put together a show of artists' work with witness writings displayed alongside images and sometimes read out loud or performed before an audience. Heather's celebration took the form of reading her witness to a painting, *Monsoon*, aloud, while standing on a chair. Drummers accompanied her dramatic reading, in homage to the Creative Source welling up in her like a great storm, punctuating the primal energy with sound. *Fred* (figure 6) is a guide-dog image that came to Kim, reminding her to lighten up, that help and support are nearby always like a faithful dog. His tag reads: "Kim's Guide God." She gave her witness writings about Fred to Warren, an artist who especially resonated with the dog. An actor as well as an artist, Warren created a reworking of Kim's witnesses expressively in Fred's voice, complete with barks, howls, and panting. Witnessing Fred come alive through Warren's rendition gave Kim, and all of us, the true joy of celebration. Hearing our words spoken aloud by another is a profound gift. To be publicly witnessed in this way allows us to integrate our unclaimed vitality, to celebrate and be celebrated.

I always imagine during these events that we are tapping into something ancient and deep. Our ancestors who returned from vision quests and initiations to a feast prepared by their village shared their stories and enacted them, to the awe and delight of their community. These events allow us to share our practice with the larger community as well as to

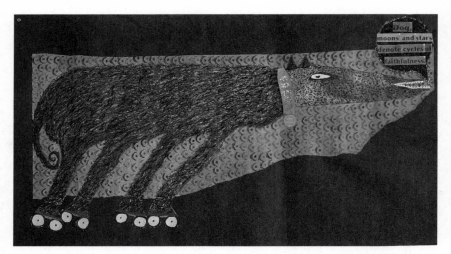

Figure 6. *Fred*, by Kim Conner. Oil pastels.

honor the work itself and the Creative Source. While some images require traditional methods of presentation, such as framing, we encourage artists to listen to each image regarding what it needs to be completed. Celebration can include performing rituals that grow out of images, creating memorials through art, or joyfully giving images away.

I made *Ovoid* (figure 7), a sculpture that embodied the hungry-ghost energy of my unfed soul in the early days of Open Studio Project. As hideous as she seemed to me, I knew she carried potent teachings. So, although she didn't seemed finished, I never discarded her. Periodically she would nudge me to take her out and work on her some more. I always thought I was finishing but somehow never did. Awhile ago she asked to be placed on the altar in the studio and simply honored. As my fiftieth birthday approached, I found her speaking loudly, saying that at long last she was to be burned in an act of transformation. With the help of Annette, an artist and healer, I planned a ritual burning. She asked to be burned to release all the tension, fear, struggle, and want held in her form. Eight women joined me in the ritual, which took place in my home.

In addition to burning the sculpture in the fireplace, we spoke an invocation. Then each woman was invited to speak something she wished to release and to symbolically burn a piece of paper with the words stating her intention. We read a witness dialogue that I had had with *Ovoid*.

Elements of Studio Practice

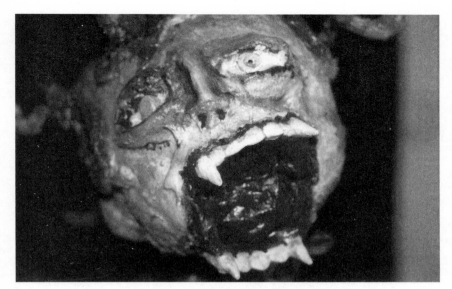

Figure 7. *Ovoid*, by Pat B. Allen. Plaster, sticks, acrylic paint.

Each woman read a part of the ritual, and my friend Dorie sang a song she had written. Annette offered a keening, wordless vocalization and shook a ceremonial rattle as *Ovoid* burned. As she finished her sounding, the head of the sculpture burned through and fell to the floor of the fireplace. Afterward, we gathered some of the ashes and buried them at the base of a tree we planted to honor the new name, Asherah, that I took to mark this life passage. Annette had prepared a reading of the principles, gleaned from a system of astrology she is studying, that guide my particular life transit.

In addition to the ashes, there were several pieces of the sculpture that did not burn completely. A few days after the ritual, I gathered and witnessed these remnants. I learned that they, too, needed to be honored and so I created a reliquary to house them (figure 8).

The witness to that piece reads:

*When you do not have a mother there are certain things you do not know.
Like what is enough? Or when to rest; when to be quiet. Then again, there are
other things that come to you as gifts through that space, that emptiness left
by her absence. You will always carry the imprint of her fears, her unrealized*

Figure 8. *Ovoid Reliquary*, by Pat B. Allen.
Wood, photo transfer, acrylic plastic, ashes.

dreams the unfinished and half begun possibilities. Remember that her spirit
is always near with wise guidance ask! Ask! Then be very still out of the void
will come what seem to be demons stay, STILL allow your eyes to soften to
soften, soften see that they are angels and that everything is revealed!!!

I learned that those tendencies that I intend to relinquish remain in
potential form and are never entirely extinguished. In addition, they de-
serve respect and honor; for they mark my best understanding of how to
live at a certain challenging period of my life. As time unfolds, I learn
more and more how this intention to change will manifest as I slowly let

Elements of Studio Practice

go of intense striving and settle more into breathing into each moment. A friend offered the wisdom "'Live every day as if it were your last" when I complained about change being hard. I realized that those were exactly the words I had lived by, but my interpretation had always been to pack as much as possible in, to do as much, to take on as much as possible because I felt I never knew when death would, as Dalí said, catch me. The ritual teaches me that there is another way to interpret those words— namely, to slow down and savor those things that have heart and meaning, while letting go of concerns about achievement.

ritual

There are many wonderful books containing suggestions for planning rituals and life–transition events (Broner 1999, Gottlieb 1995). Mindful witnessing of the images as well as consultation with close friends also yield directions for specific personal rituals. I have no doubt that these types of activities are important to our well–being. For myself, involving an elder friend as well as my daughter and a friend of hers in this ritual made it a form of repairing the links between generations. My daughter and her friend are able to see women engaging with the process of aging and change in a meaningful way that revises goals and claims power. Rather than simply chasing after physical youth, we celebrate the wisdom that comes with growing older.

The challenges in the celebration stage of artmaking include avoiding the culmination of the work by stopping short of finishing. An occasional artist is just too "busy" to come to the last session of a class and simply leaves her work behind to languish in a drawer rather than retrace her steps and see where she has been and where she may be called to next. Sometimes artists become too caught up in the celebration phase by framing and pricing work to sell without ever listening to the Creative Source about what the work needs in order to be honored. Work that is prematurely pushed out into the world creates an expectation in the artist of working to sell, which can interfere with art being a true spiritual practice, instead making it a kind of indentured servitude. In such cases images often dry up or become repetitive until the artist deflates the ego a bit and listens again to inner wisdom about what the art requires. Other artists err in the opposite direction by grasping on to work that would be embraced by others if it were put up on the wall for sale or demeaning their work by disbelieving that someone else could

Blessing Cup?

appreciate its value. Some images require going out into the world for their completion.

Although this process cannot be encompassed by any rules or prescriptions, there is a reliable way of determining how best to honor and celebrate the image one has received: listen carefully to the image. Celebration is a time when the comments and involvement of others are crucial. Shows and rituals are not solitary events. They are performed to serve both the individual and the community and therefore require collaboration. We support one another and the images when we work to best display them. Hanging a show is a powerful experience. In turn, each artist comes to be regarded by the group as special and helped to best present their work. Some artists will feel concerns about others' work eclipsing their own; sharing and working through these issues helps to move the overall process forward.

An intention for a public show is very important: Is the work simply to share? Is it for sale? Are artist and image ready to part? I have had the honor of being invited for a number of years to exhibit work in *Art of Remembrance*, a show at our local art league that takes place in late October and early November to coincide with Día de los Muertos, the Day of the Dead. I placed a recently completed wall hanging from the series that uses photographs of my mother as each piece's central image. I did not bother to price the piece, assuming it was too personal for someone else to want. When I received a phone call that a buyer was interested, I was surprised to find that the image clearly informed me to let it go. The letting go made space for more images to arise, exploring the themes of faith, loss, and attitudes about death. The image has its own work to do, in the world as well as in our lives, and we are to serve its purpose as much as we can.

Making art as a spiritual practice challenges us to engage with the public aspects of showing and selling art with the same discernment that we cultivate in making and witnessing the art. Crafting an intention for the public life of the art helps us consider right livelihood: that is, a livelihood that serves the image as well as our material needs.

As inquiry gives way to engagement, one image often will lead to the next to create a series. Sometimes it is the image of one artist that leads another onto the same path. This step of the spiritual path involves making a commitment to a relationship with the divine wisdom within, along

Elements of Studio Practice

with a willingness to see all others who are in our life as spiritual teachers or what I call "near occasions of inspiration." Sometimes there are images "in the air" asking to be explored and expressed. My friend Annette, who is studying new forms of dream work, says the same is true with dream images. She participates in several dream groups and an online dream exchange in which the similarity of dreams shared by people from different backgrounds and regions is often striking. The dreamers believe that we are doing work in the dreamtime that will make changes in the world. I believe the same about the studio. Our work with images brings new consciousness into being.

Engagement happens when we get "hooked" by an image, when mystery shows up and we find ourselves wanting to know or experience more. This is an energetic phenomenon; we feel more alive in the presence of, or when seeing and working with, certain images. We sense something is especially nourishing in using a particular shade of red or drawing a certain elliptical form. Engagement occurs when we respond to an energy coming toward us by answering back with energy of our own. I became intrigued with a photograph of my mother displayed in my sister's home. In it she was young and smiling, before marriage and kids, before illness claimed her. I created a series of fabric panels using a transfer of the photo in the center. I became engaged with the idea of my mother as a person, a woman, someone who once was not my mother. I began to separate the person from the archetype, so that it seemed I could engage in dialogue with my actual mother's spirit as we both shared our experience of the energetic force that is the Mother (figure 9). The witness was created on the piece, a new development in my art practice. This piece led to a series of cloth hangings that are more fully described in chapter 7.

We may be engaged by an image of another artist, one whose we see in a book, gallery, or museum. If we are fortunate to have a group of others to work with, we are often engaged by an image that arrives in the art of another. We also can take images from the culture and media— whether they attract or repel us—into our practice and work with them. Another artist, Lisa, who hadn't viewed my fabric hangings about my mother, came in one day with a beautiful collage book she was working on about her mother (see Lisa's story in chapter 7). After seeing Lisa's work, I shared my pieces with her. Kim was so moved by Lisa's work that

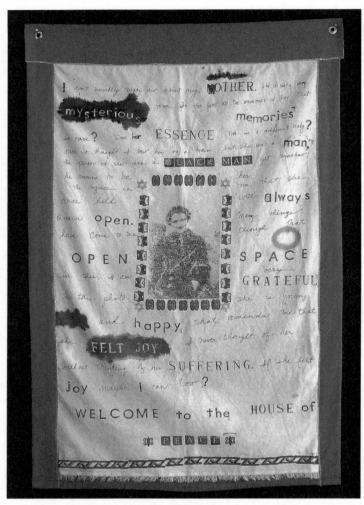

Figure 9. *Mother*, by Pat B. Allen. Cloth hanging, photo transfer, stamps.

she went home and pulled out photos of her mother and grandmother. She began a triptych exploring her life with her mother and her grand-mother, who had been a surrogate mother to her when she was young. She learned the following week that her mother had just been diagnosed with cancer. The work allows her to focus her energy on her mother and perhaps contain some of the anguish of waiting to learn what will un-fold. Illness and other major life events are opportunities to connect more deeply with the people in our lives; artmaking creates a medium in which to dissolve old hurts and remedy the effect of distance. The Mother archetype seemed to be speaking loudly in the studio.

After several of us listened to Lisa read aloud the witnesses to her book of her mother's story, an idea for a show arose, inspired by Lisa's mother's remark, "Make it up." We honor her by calling the show *Mother: Real and Imagined* to acknowledge the idea that our actual experience and our created experience overlap but are not the same. In the place of making art, the place of all possibility, new ideas of what Mother or mother means are excavated and shared. In this way we extend our work into the community, invite others to reflect on how it is we come to know or neglect the stories of our lives, and make a space both for personal mothers and for the idea of mother to be explored and witnessed.

My work has often taken place in a studio dedicated to art as a spiritual practice, where the methods described here are practiced day in and day out by groups of artists. But individuals can, without setting aside a space exclusively for this work, deepen their connection to their art into spiritual practice simply by adopting the practice of intention and witness writing. Planned or impromptu witness writing and reading circles can be convened in living rooms, classrooms, or outdoors under a tree. Celebrations of artwork involving exhibits witnessed by whole communities can be staged in libraries and other public forums. Groups of artists might decide to get together to make art and witness around a particular community issue or opportunity to become clear together about right action. Celebrations can be created and performed using genuine images in lieu of mass-produced card-store items to honor rites of passage, times of loss and joy, and other personal and community milestones.

The goal of art as a spiritual path is to live a meaningful life, full of active participation with our own hands, minds, and hearts, and appreciation of the joy and pleasure and depth of soul that is possible. It is to take the time to focus our attention on our hopes and dreams and nurture them to fruition. Over time we become able to listen closely and hear: what is it that wants to be born? We take charge of shaping such a life for our families and communities, and in doing so we awaken from the haze of consumer culture and the hunger it creates. We can then consider making alternatives. We have the means to reconnect with the flow of life-force energy that animates us, to guide it toward peace and reconciliation, allowing us to enjoy living while still facing and engaging with the problems life presents in an active, creative, and even joyful way.

A number of years ago I stopped watching television news. The incessant predictions of disaster made me feel anxious and depressed, and yet the disasters themselves never seemed to materialize. I was in a chronic state of low-level depression from consuming images designed to create fear and to give the impression that only professional newscasters could warn me of the dangers lurking around the next corner. And to what end? Apparently so that I would keep tuning in and watching all those commercials for products designed to allay my fears. When prescription drugs for anxiety and depression began to be advertised along with deodorant and shampoo, I guess that was too much for me; I swore off TV almost entirely—and not just news. I realized that watching cop shows and violent dramas before bed probably gave my spirit too much work to do. How can new images of hope and peace arrive if my mind is busy processing toxic images I willingly ingest? We need not allow our precious lives to be dominated by false needs created by images of the prevailing culture. We have a human, inalienable right to decide which images we will consume, to create those images from real experience, and to connect with others rather than let ourselves be divided by fear. If we begin to withdraw our energy from these toxic images, the images will disappear or at least be deprived of their power. Censorship and suppression are not as effective as disengagement.

Art as a spiritual path is one simple means to a life of joy and connection, truth and authenticity; and if enough of us take part, perhaps we can effect a renaissance of community culture—small scale, local, and loving. As the women of South Africa teach us, we do not need to shy away from tragedy; rather, we can engage its energy directly through art. We must be authentic both in our celebration and in our grieving.

Elements of Studio Practice

3

The Practice of Witness
Breathing In, Breathing Out

The practice of witness is the state of being present to our images and to each other in compassion, without voicing judgment. Not *voicing* judgment is different from not *having* judgments. Judgments are inevitable and contain important information; but our judgments are information for ourselves, not for the person whose work has elicited our judging response. My judgment is a mirror of my values, my fixed ideas. When the image of another calls forth my judgment, I have a chance to become curious. Where does the judgment come from? Can I trace its origin? Is it a valid bit of discernment, or is it due for some revisiting? When we act as witness to another person, we are acting as an embodiment of the witness consciousness that is the Creative Source. Our goal is to personify compassionate disinterest.

Like intention, witness requires stillness. For intention, our stillness calls forth our inner truth: Who are we in this moment? What are our questions, our needs, our fears? In witness, our stillness makes space for answers to arise. Intention is our human call; witness brings the divine response. The medium of exchange is the image. Sit in front of your own image, the image that has chosen to appear before you today. Allow yourself to settle into awareness of your body, your sense of fatigue or alertness. Feel your feet on the floor; notice your back against the chair. Breathe in; breathe out. Relax into what is.

Witness begins with a conscious return from the place of all possibility that is artmaking to the present moment, to this one particular image that has arrived in answer to your call. It is a return from the merger of engaged artmaking to the sense of self-awareness of you—living in this body, sitting in this chair—with this image before you. We return from that merger gently. In the studio, I usually give a warning that the artmaking time is coming to an end and gradually lower the volume of the music playing in the studio as a subtle signal. Some artists choose to clean up

Figure 10. Goddess triptych, by Adina B. Allen. Cloth, feathers, paint.

during the transitional time, feeling their way into witness through a grounding activity like washing paintbrushes or their hands.

In its focus on the connection between artist and image, witness shares aspects of the artmaking time of merger. As the music stops, it is as if we now meet our dancing partner and introduce ourselves and begin to learn more about the dance we and the art have just performed together. At the same time we begin to shift into our sense of separateness by stepping back, regarding this "other" that has arrived, and paying attention to what comes up as we do so. Like artmaking, witness is a practice with a number of steps. The first step is to turn our attention to the *physical* reality of the image. We return to our bodies with awareness by attending for several minutes to our breathing. We become able to concentrate on the image and notice simply what it looks like. We use writing both to extend the creative act as well as to record our experience of the image by focusing our attention. Moving my hand to write brings me into my body. Begin with a description of the image. To describe is to honor and to really look, really notice. Normally, our brain allows us to notice only to the point that we receive enough information to name what is before us. In our witness writing, we resist the urge to name. Even if I think the image I have painted is "me," I describe what I see at first, not

Elements of Studio Practice

what I think I know. In my witness I write, "I see an image of a woman," not "I see me." Naming is a judgment that stops the transmission of information. We resist this for a while.

I see three images affixed to a gold sparkly cloth. There are eight feathers on the edge of the cloth: white, red, brown, green, beige, orange, yellow, red. Beginning on the left is an image of a tree in full leaf, bigger than the page. It has a thick, strong trunk and light behind it. The second image is a landscape, green mountains in front, brown hill behind, a sun behind the hills. The final image is a dark crescent shape against a background of yellow, purple, brown, blue and green. The words "goddess cycle" are stamped under the central landscape. The words "Virgin," "Mother," and "Crone" adorn each image in succession. A mixture of typefaces from rubber stamps are used in creating the words. Glitter and stars adorn the words [figure 10].

The image I am witnessing was created by my daughter, Adina, as a gift for my birthday. This fact affects the second stage of witnessing, which ② is to notice my _emotional_ response to the image. As I take time to really *emotional* look, the piece begins to unfold for me. The use of multiple rubber-stamped type styles references some work that I have done. Referencing is the act of incorporating elements of another artist's work, like a quotation in a written work. I smile at this. The subject matter, images about the feminine, is a familiar one to Adina, who grew up around my artwork. We are joined together in a common discourse. My work called out to Adina, and she responded. Referencing is the joyful secret language of artists, and I am pleased that she has used it.

The tree in the first image is full, so full it extends off the page. I realize that Adina is in the fullness of her Virgin state. Beyond the details of age or experience of sex, the Virgin state describes a woman who still belongs most fully to herself. This is a tree of Summer; she is well past the Spring state with its tender buds and tentative leaves. She is a college student, growing and learning in leaps and bounds. I feel love, pride and a trace of sadness. This image seems to clearly represent the stage of the Goddess cycle she is living. Since the tree is too big for its space I can't help but also see that the inevitable transition to the next phase of Mother is beginning already in this image. Adina may be years away from physical motherhood but a sense of her own fecundity permeates her creative life as she absorbs information and experiences, writes papers, makes art.

What will the mother phase be like for her? Will she become a mother of actual children? Will she extend her nurturing to the world through her work in social activism and environmental studies? It is too soon to tell what the contours of the landscape of her mother image will be like. I feel the strength of life force in her images and feel happy for her, yet also apprehensive. Will she resolve the dilemma of work and family in a way that sustains her? I respond to this image from the place of mother as well as the recipient of the image as gift. I respond also as an artist receiving homage from another artist through her referencing of my work; I feel nourished by her bright exuberance. The crone image intrigues me most. The crescent shape is narrow and dark. It shows the shadow of the waxing moon without a sense that the rest of the moon's sphere still exists. The background is more abstract and mysterious. Shapes angle upward, lifted by the lightest shape, the yellow on the bottom. I feel a sense of tension but also magic as I look at the image. This image reflects my life stage and is far in the future for Adina. At first I smile, realizing that young women at Adina's age often see only the constrictions and limitations of aging and not its fullness.

It happens I am traveling to visit her tomorrow, and this witness feels like a preparation. I am reminded that I contain all the phases of the cycle; that is the gift of age. In the presence of Adina and her friends, I access my own possibilities, reconnect with some of the threads dropped during my Virgin days. I bask in the sense of offering them the possibility of Mother and Crone: someone still growing, learning, and creatively alive. I record this in my witness writings, but still I remain on the surface. I am telling my story about what feelings and thoughts come up for me. The image remains *my* birthday present, from *my* daughter. Now I must invite the image to speak. In order to move into the realm of the _spiritual_ with this image, I must separate a bit further and honor the reality of the image as something autonomous, something separate from and greater than my projections. I accomplish this by inviting the image to speak and recording the dialogue in my witness writing. I write down whatever comes. If

64   Elements of Studio Practice

my mind judges what comes as absurd, I write that down, too. As it so happens, when I first ask the Goddess cycle triptych to speak, I receive a firm "no." I was busy and accepted that answer, planning to resume the conversation at a later time. When I returned to the image, some weeks later, a dialogue ensued:

ME: *Will you speak to me today?*

CRONE MOON: *You spout such false wisdom. Why do you think I am so compressed and black? Do you think it's just Adina's perception or that of girls her age? I am showing you the truth. You have a long way to go to own and claim and even discover the "fullness" of age. Look for signs of fullness and life in older women and bless them.*

ME: *I feel the truth of what you have to say. It's a little embarrassing. I know it intellectually, how can I really know it?*

At that moment, I look over at my bookshelf and my gaze alights on a volume of short stories by Grace Paley. A beautiful sepia-toned photo of her adorns the cover. Her thumbs are hooked in her pockets, and her white hair flies around her face. She stands in a soft-focus landscape in which her feet and legs seem to dissolve into the earth at the bottom of the image. A black crow stands next to her on the grass. She is an old woman. I take down the book and turn it over. I read a comment on the back cover: "People love life more because of her writing."

CRONE MOON: *YES!*

I open the volume at random to a story entitled "Living." I read it and laugh and, yes, I love life more. This is what I receive from the image when I venture into the spiritual realm. Beyond the joy of receiving a gift from my daughter, beyond sharing an exchange with another artist, lies a piece of wisdom both unique and universal that comes forward through witness. The fullness of life is a time to love life more. This gift comes with the awareness of death that the Crone brings. I resolve to seek more about this lesson. I bless Grace Paley. I ask that my work may make others love life more. The Crone Moon winks at me and I say thank you and get back to work. The world is a magical place; when we practice witness, we get to know that firsthand all the time.

I witness my work when I create alone as well as when I work in a group. In groups, however, witness has the added dimension of allowing us to share with great immediacy the kind of gifts that came to me alone witnessing the Goddess cycle triptych. If you are skeptical, try witnessing among others and see if it makes the messages feel more real. Witness is also a key element in creating communal space that is safe and allows multiple truths to unfold. Some days we are unaware of what the person next to us is creating; other days we are tuned into the chorus of messages resounding through the room. At the conclusion of the artmaking time, we always sit with our work—looking, noticing, and paying attention to what the Creative Source has washed up on the shores of our consciousness for this day. Writing time lasts from fifteen to twenty-five minutes depending on the group. Younger children can speak from their hearts without writing. Most of us, however, go through a clarifying process when we put words down on paper. The purpose of writing instead of simply speaking about one's work is to reinforce that the words that come are primarily for the artist and image, and only secondarily for the group. The purpose of witness is not to explain our image to others. Sometimes artists compose their witness as if to instruct the group; this is an intrusion of ego and is unnecessary. The Creative Source will often convey something to another artist through your words, but it is not your job to consciously try to do so. In fact, conscious attempts to share wisdom often come across as pompous and inflated. Reading aloud is a good remedy, as usually the artist immediately feels the unmistakable warmth of hot air emanating from her words and resolves to notice and curb this tendency in the future. I speak from experience.

The image reveals its deepest truth in dialogue. My primary reference for dialoguing with images comes from Jung's work in active imagination. Shaun McNiff (1992) and Mary Watkins (1984, 1999) have added to my understanding of dialogue as well. The nature of dialogue with the image is best captured in writing. The intention of writing is to extend the creative act, to promote the relationship between the artist and image, and to mediate the separation of the artist from the image as the artmaking time comes to a close. When most people begin to speak extemporaneously about their image, an immediate objectification takes place. They almost always begin by sharing what they tried to do, what failed, or what they meant to "say." Art as a spiritual practice reverses this relationship from one in which the artist creates by using materials to one in which the artist receives an image as a gift from the Creative Source via direct engagement with a sacramental taking in of materials. In other forms of spiritual practice, the Divine is mediated via dreams, meditation, or prayer. For us, image making and witness writing are the vehicles. Each artist's witness notebook becomes a personal wisdom volume that is an endless resource of personal teachings from the Divine to our particular soul. Consulting my ten years of witness writings for this book has been a humbling and invaluable lesson for me. I see how I've revisited the same themes over and over, how I've learned the same lessons in ever-deepening ways.

It is true that we share our witness writings by reading them aloud when we work together in groups, but a witness is a record of an intimate moment between you and your soul. For that reason, witness reading must never be coerced or cajoled. In fact, I would rather discourage reading until an artist feels they must read because the image demands to speak through them. As a facilitator, especially with adolescents, I feel the press of their silence and am forced to notice my own vulnerability when I read in their silent presence. Yet I violate the process if I convey that they are reading for me, to please or placate me. I must honor their silence as much as I honor their words. Otherwise I am just another adult trying to get something out of them. I have learned volumes from sitting with those who choose not to read. In a class at the School of the Art Institute, one student did not read a single witness until the last day of class. Throughout the fifteen-week semester, I watched myself and my projections as they arose in my mind: "She doesn't get it," "She hates the class," "She is just coasting through." I noticed my fears and how they evoked judgments. When she read on the last day, her witness was full of gratitude for being allowed her silence; as a very shy person, she has often been encouraged to talk. She felt accepted for herself and not forced to produce. She taught me a priceless lesson in trusting the process, and I am forever in her debt.

Those of us listening are privileged to be there, supporting the exchange between artist and image and often learning from it. Those of us listening serve as reinforcement and an external manifestation of the principle of witness consciousness. We are actually the embodiment of divine acceptance in that moment. That means we hear and receive, but do not judge or comment. We may indeed feel judgmental. We may think and feel all sorts of things like jealousy, boredom, cynicism, elation, love. But the rule is to keep it to yourself. What we feel and think rises and falls like so much mist. We remain just breathing in, breathing out, so that the artist speaking can more fully experience their own words and the words and wisdom of their image. If we were to share a strong response with an artist, it would be like naming her and saying, "This is who you are." The artist can easily become caught in the expectation of the group and play a role for them. Instead, artists are encouraged to pay close attention to the feelings that arise in them when they regard the image and hear themselves read the witness. Often, it is in the speaking of the words in the witness that the emotion arrives or catches up to us. Those of us in attendance hold the space to support that meeting between artist and soul. As we feel boredom, for example, in hearing ourselves recite a stale half-truth, we also notice something that attracts and enlivens us in the work of another. Next time, we are free to reference that artist and follow the thread of what has new energy to revitalize our work. To witness is an act of divine service.

We may find that ideas, emotions, or the images themselves remain in our awareness long after the artist has finished speaking. What sticks around to haunt us deserves to be invited into our own process, not dumped on someone else. The practice of "sharing feelings" is highly overrated. The artist is free to write all sorts of judgmental statements about himself and his work in his witness and to read them with gusto. The object is simply to notice what comes up.

We in the group act the way the internal witness does during traditional meditation; we are present, unchanging, yet somehow subtly registering the effect as best we can, in a state of openness and compassion. It is a practice for the artist reading to be bold enough to speak the truth, no matter how full of "warts" or how tender. And it is a practice for the listening artists to recognize the experience of compassionate disinterest. We do not need to fix, correct, soften, or enhance the experience of another. Sometimes there are sighs, tears, and even laughter during a witness reading, but verbal comments are not made. In addition, the artist reading just reads; she does not digress into sidebar explanations or additional comments, even if she has written something like *This is really stupid, I hate what I made, I don't want to write about it.* Her truest feelings are acceptable, along with her resistance and anything else that comes along. It is not important for us to know exact details. In fact, it is not important for us to even literally understand the words that are read. I have experienced witnesses read in languages I do not speak and have been profoundly moved by the sound of the words and the emotion they convey. I have heard witness writings sung as opera and recited in gibberish. All versions are welcome. From time to time, an artist will make a comment or when reading a witness will digress into explanation. I will gently stop her and remind her of the no-comment rule. This is as much to reassure the others that the rules have meaning as it is to guide the artist back to the practice.

There is a particular moment that stands out in my learning about this practice of no-comment when I felt the power and veracity of witness. A young woman was working through her experience of being raped. Her images were brave and heartbreaking. As she read her witness aloud to the group, all of us present were deeply moved. She spoke directly to the image of the rapist in her witness; she said she was taking back her soul, her life. A woman next to her placed what I'm sure was meant to be a comforting hand on the artist's shoulder. She shrugged it off sharply and kept reading. That moment became an image for me. What flashed in my mind was how our choice of action defines the narrative in any moment. When we choose action, and even more so when we speak words, we violate the narrative of the artist speaking, even when we consider our intentions to be supportive. As I witnessed these two women, I heard this narrative within myself:

> READER: *Don't put your hand on me as if I am the "Rape Victim" and you the "Comforter." I will not let you freeze this moment in time with you in that role and me in this one. I am alive and moving, I take my soul back and go on. I am "warrior" in this moment and in the next. I and not you will define who I will be. Do not, with your "good will," rape me again.*
>
> COMFORTER: *I see your pain, I don't want to think it could ever be mine. If you are the "Victim" and I can be the "Comforter," all's well for me, that's the symmetry I'd like to have, thank you, you are the victim, after all.*
>
> READER: *You could walk out after this group and be raped. Because it happened to me doesn't mean it can't happen to you. Trust me, the act itself is only one type of violation. Being defined by your fear and that of others is just as bad.*

COMFORTER: *I see your point, I am really helping myself, not you. I release you from my selfish desire for comfort.*

Now, none of this dialogue was spoken by either party; it all occurred inside of me in a split second. I accessed it later when I wrote a witness to the feeling of agitation I experienced when I observed the images of the comforting hand and the rejecting shrug. The interaction between the two women was like an art piece that I witnessed within myself on a subtle level. Had I spoken my experience, I would have objectified both artists. In that moment for me one was "brave, honest, fierce woman," while the other was "stupid do–gooder woman." I was judging them both. Both are potential parts of me. Until I find out about my judgments, I can't compassionately see either woman as a complex, multifaceted person struggling in the moment with what it means to be human. When I began to write about this incident, a witness I received in 1997 on the subject of judgment came up in my rereading and seemed very apt. It had this to say:

IMAGE OF A HEART: *Judgment labels, it's like playing freeze tag with life. Once you call it something, its hard to let it continue in its natural cycle and turn into it's opposite.*

ME: *But if it isn't named, can't things escalate into something worse?*

HEART: *Judging is naming, a kind of naming, but not all naming is judgment.*

ME: *Heart, you sound a lot like mind.*

HEART: *I do, don't I? I've told you that when "mind" quiets down the heart's mind can speak.*

ME: *Okay, so naming isn't necessarily judgment.*

HEART: *Right, funny I should say this, but naming with compassion is mercy, remember that thought creates reality so think merciful thoughts and you will name and discern rather than judge and the cycle can continue instead of getting stuck.*

ME: *So judgment stops process?*

HEART: *Compassion names each person's highest motive instead of dividing people into good guys against bad guys. That way the kaleidoscope of life can keep turning. . . .*

ME: *What causes me to judge instead of discern? (Do I really want to know?)*

HEART: *You asked. You judge to stay out of the drama, to be safe and to try to avoid pain. See, I told you, compassion seeks out your highest motive.*

Avoiding pain is very human so you don't need to judge yourself either, that's your fear.

ME: *That if I don't judge others I'll be forced to judge myself? Right, the bottom line fear is that there must be a bad guy and to ensure it isn't you, you seek to judge someone else as the bad guy. So are you saying there's no bad guys? What about Hitler?*

HEART: *I'm saying that you all need to name behavior and experience but with compassion so it can continue to evolve. To not name is to assent to another's naming, surely you've heard my famous saying: "silence is complicity"? If you wait too long to discern you'll almost be forced to judge. So, my advice is name early and often, with compassion which evokes change for the better, coaxing behavior upward, redeeming the sparks of goodness in every situation. Got it?*

My job is to recognize that in order to really see each of those women, I have to see what they evoke that lives in me. Otherwise, I risk turning them into objects and not seeing them as real, complicated, ever-changing people. By naming my experience internally, instead of externally, I don't force them to be defined by my drama. I have a choice about how I relate to others at every moment. Whether I idealize or demonize someone else, when strong feelings come up I must first accept them as a mirror so that I avoid doing harm. Reflecting on this experience, I realize how often I imagine that I must shield others from how bad things are or have been for them, that I think it is my job to make it all right or to explain things and make them make sense. But most of all, I see that I was avoiding the idea that I could ever be a rape victim; I was separating myself from the impact of the artist's narrative by creating my own. My drama was about creating an object lesson from even the worst event, leapfrogging over the emotions aroused by the event itself. My intention, however, is to become ever more mindful of providing space for experience to be authentically witnessed. Without my judgments, I can own the lesson for myself that whatever arises in me as a narrative of the event has much to teach me.

The no-comment rule is the most controversial aspect of the practice of witness. Simply stated, we refrain from making comments to others about their work. The no-comment rule is related to nonjudgment. Before we can honestly hope to get to a place of nonjudgment, we have to begin

like michele cassou

The Practice of Witness

by embracing our judgments as teachings for ourselves. If we try to re-press them, we will simply blurt them out at an inopportune moment. We simply notice emotional reactions of like and dislike internally or in our witness notebook. We all make judgments all the time; if we are mindful, we notice them, let them drift away, and then move on to the next thought. For those judgments that have more energy or tend to linger or even to fester and grow, we must invite them into our process and get to know what they are trying to tell us. Every judgment I have about another person tells me something about myself—what I require or what I am re-sisting. If I notice that I am judging Jane for using too much paint, I sit with my stinginess and inquire about its origin. Is there something I do not feel entitled to that makes me resent Jane's seeming generosity to her-self? Witnessing my judgments is an antidote to gossip, which is often the discharge of tension that our judgments generate within us. Through the practice of witness I learn to thank Jane (silently, internally) for bringing my attention to what I am lacking, rather than talking about her or berat-ing her for her wastefulness.

Is each and every comment harmful? Isn't it unnatural to restrict commenting? The primary reason for refraining from comment is to fos-ter and reinforce each artist's relationship with their own internal wisdom and guidance. We practice no–comment in our artmaking and witness to learn how to hear, to discipline ourselves to be fully present even when our own thoughts arise to distract us. This doesn't mean we refrain from all comments in every sphere of our lives. That would be like attempting always to sit in the lotus position because we do so in meditation. The work of Marshall Rosenberg and others in the field of Nonviolent Com-munication suggests that human beings have a long way to go to under-stand how to hear one another. Mindful commentary is a great goal that often seems difficult to attain. Practicing no–comment is a wonderful way to learn discernment.

Certainly the Divine speaks to us at times through others. Few of us are discerning enough to know when the Creative Source is speaking through us and when we are, as artist Karla Riendl once put it, leaving our "mind prints," like greasy fingerprints, on the work of another. Speaking or otherwise making evident our interpretation of an artist can be a form of violation, as the example of the woman who had experienced rape attests. We must first consider the comment we feel pressed to make as one we need to *hear* rather than *speak*. The judgment we feel inside is one that we are making, and perhaps strongly resisting, of ourselves. When we invite the judgment to our table, it will reveal the true grievance, which we can then attend to through witness or further image making.

Refraining from words is a part of learning mindfulness. Words are powerful; we create reality with them. Yet most of us use them indiscriminately. So the first challenge is to suggest that each artist take any comment she is tempted to make inside, and either release it or listen to it for herself. Images speak to all of us. It is a common occurrence for the art of another to speak loudly to me, to echo something in my witness or to show me an alternative. I gratefully accept this gift. Having shared this practice with many different people over time, I still remain challenged by and thoughtful about witness writing and the no-comment rule. The goal of the practice is not to discourage communication or to suggest that there are never appropriate times to seek or share commentary about artwork. The no-comment rule is especially important for new artists and those in the tender stages of beginning creation. I am not out to protect artists from negative comments; positive comments can be equally intrusive. It is simply that when no comments are made by others, especially close to the moment of creation, we can more easily listen to our image and the inner wisdom it has come to impart. It is especially important for the facilitator to refrain from comments, which will always seem to have extra weight. As a facilitator of artmaking in the studio, my goal is to create conditions that enable artists present to connect with their inner teacher, not to be that teacher. My direct comments would erode the sense of being fellow artists and fellow travelers on the path to awareness of the Creative Source. After a few times, most people no longer notice the lack of comments and become comfortable with the intimacy and freedom that comes from knowing no one will say, "Oh, how sad" or "You should hear what happened to me" or "You're so good, I can't draw at all."

Children are the exception to the no-comment rule. Young children are still close to their uninhibited imagination and will witness quite spontaneously, engaging in dialogues with images, toys, and pets. If we join into such activity with children, our responses should be honest and not attempts to teach children a lesson from our advanced perch of knowledge. With adolescents, art as a spiritual practice is especially challenging. We all have unprocessed information and experience from our adolescent years, a time of accelerated learning that we spend much of our life unpacking. The images and witnesses of young people often bring to awareness some of our own unresolved themes. Again, our own work must remain true if we are to engage in this practice. Otherwise we are doing something else. We hold as an article of faith that the Creative Source will engage with any person who asks. To act as if we must interpret an image is a violation and deprives the young artist of claiming her truth and power.

Adolescents will often seem very self-conscious at first; we need to appreciate that the very act of deciding when to read and when to refrain is a powerful one. No one must ever be coerced into reading a witness. The nature of witness writing is that it evokes metaphorical texts, allowing us to convey great intimacy without having to spell out the details of our life—unless we choose to. What we share is our emotional reality. This enormously valuable skill—integrating emotional content with the written word—is the basis of poetry.

Participants, especially adolescents, mention the freedom they feel knowing no comments will be made. When I take this practice into the rest of my life (a big challenge for me), I find life far more peaceful. I am less likely to get caught in struggles with others, and I can avoid the depletion of churning out words when it would be better to simply listen to the comments and sit with the feelings driving them. Refraining from comments is not the same as repressing our judgments, positive or negative. Rather, it involves befriending oneself and noticing what comes up—without mindlessly letting it come out. Acting this way is utterly counter to our present culture, in which spilling one's personal material for an audience is daily fare on television. I suspect that this is simply a phase in the development of discernment and eventually will die down.

Gradually we can begin to practice mindful commentary in special times that are planned for such an event. I have engaged in this practice with my Art Institute students, who often present a body of work as a final project and request that their fellow students witness the work. It

is required that the student showing the work make
receive no harm and that the students witnessing make
intention to do no harm. Misguided action is another pit
tary. Images often arouse strong, positive feelings of
connection. It is common to mistake this invitation from
see the artist as more than an ordinary person reflecting
sparks.

When I was an art student in the 1970s, I saw and experienced often
that when a female student presented strong, authentic work, a male instructor would typically respond with positive commentary and sexual
advances. Students sometimes felt flattered at first and coerced and confused later. There seemed to be little awareness of this behavior as an act
of appropriation of the student's creative energy. In a similar vein, work
that challenges a teacher might be attacked or ignored. When strong feelings arise, our task is to sit with them. We locate the internal aspect that is
being touched and call it forward into our own work.

Artmaking will shine a light on our incompleteness. We witness con-
trasexual parts of ourselves (such as the boy who represents the artist
in my story in part two) as unrealized potential asking to be activated.
Strong sexual feelings, fascination, and attraction are common responses
on any spiritual path. Art allows us a safe arena in which to explore these
potent forces. Witness writing helps to integrate these images and their
potential into our total personality without doing harm to others in the
process. It is the ethical responsibility of all teachers, therapists, and anyone engaged in work with others to recognize the privilege and power
that accompanies witnessing the truth of others.

Within the basic method of art as a spiritual practice, there is one exception to the no-comment rule. At the end of group artmaking time,
after everyone who wants to has read his or her witness aloud, there is
usually a brief time for questions about the process and expressions of
gratitude. The continuous flow of energy that characterizes the creative
process depends upon gratitude. The act of giving thanks creates an
opening for more energy to flow into our lives. Yet this practice of expressing gratitude seems to be unfamiliar to many people. It is a common
cliché that all of us, especially in the privileged West, have much to be
thankful for; yet the daily practice of expressing gratitude is not common.

people, for example, say any form of thanksgiving before or after meals. Rabbi Zalman Schachter-Shalomi says that our present world suffers from being severely "underblessed." He reminds us that Jews have a blessing for any and every occasion, and even an all-purpose one, the Shehechiyanu, for blessing the particular moment we are in.

Studio practice has been an amazing way to become conscious of the effect of saying thanks. It arises spontaneously in the studio that someone in their witness writing will express thanks for the images and words of another artist. We slowly come to realize that we are each a mirror of the Divine and that what we need to see or hear is always before us, perhaps in the guise of the very ordinary person laboring next to us to draw a tree, or in the words of a teenager reading their witness after weeks of remaining silent. Whenever I am feeling dry and uninspired, I know that I have neglected to express gratitude to someone in my life or to the manifestation of the Divine in everyday life.

Seeing gratitude as a fundamental aspect of the creative process was a great revelation. More often I tend to be aware of what is wrong. I can be very critical. By contacting abundance and recognizing its presence in our lives, we enable more to flow. Expressing gratitude is also related to being busy. Stopping to say thanks takes us out of ourselves, out of the future and past, and locates us squarely in the present moment. A special opportunity for gratitude arises when something unpleasant or disappointing happens. We make the intention to discover what it is in the experience we are to say thank you for. This is not to deny the pain of hard times but simply to acknowledge the simultaneous reality that wonders exist within disasters and our experience of life depends to a large degree upon our interpretation of events. We can exercise choice regarding our interpretation of events even when events themselves may be beyond our control.

I was devastated in 1987 when I did not receive tenure at my university teaching job. Yet without that loss the studio work of the next fifteen years might have remained a theory rather than becoming an immensely fulfilling reality in my life. I remain deeply grateful for that turn of events even as I remember the pain I felt at the time. As frustrating as the rise to war is in America to those of us who want peace, it has revitalized the exercise of free speech and our awareness of the preciousness of democracy.

The Truth and Reconciliation Commission in South Africa brought to light the brutal history of apartheid and helped to heal a country in the process. The witness provided by the TRC instructs the world and shows that even on a global level, there is the possibility of gratitude within tragedy. This is a gift within a dark time, one that helps us live with and be in paradox. This mystery deserves our gratitude. We need not label war "good" to be grateful for and more mindful of exercising free speech.

To receive the maximum grace and blessing from our lives, we must honor both joyous and difficult occasions. Celebration of important life passages can become real through creative acts. We receive the gift of blessing hidden in the core of tragedy when we creatively engage with the events of our lives. Tremendous energy is released when we say "Thank you." Artmaking imbues life's challenges with richness and potential, allows us to relax and experience life as a flow, even in difficult moments that we share with others through making and doing. I was leading a five-day workshop at the Cape Cod Institute in Nauset, Massachusetts. I arrived there in some internal turmoil and was very focused on myself and my internal conflicts. My artwork mirrored all the murky, muddy, imprisoned energy I was wallowing in to me as well as to the participants. I would gladly have traded mine for anyone else's image. It was hard to keep breathing and just be there. And although I knew that being in a difficult place as the facilitator teaches more than if I am sailing along, I hated that stuck, murky feeling.

On the fourth morning, I received a phone call from my mother-in-law right before I left to teach. She had suffered a heart attack and survived. She was in good spirits, taking in stride a few days of pain, an emergency surgical procedure, and the fact that my husband and I were out of town during all of this. She breezily assured us she was fine and we needn't interrupt our trip. I arrived at the workshop in a completely different frame of mind. I discussed the idea of gratitude with the group, which had so far slipped my mind because I was so caught up in trying to think my way out of my own problems. I suggested to the class that another way to use intention is to dedicate the merits of one's work to someone who is suffering or in need and to call down the Creative Source in gratitude for that person instead of for oneself. Our witness then, tends, to focus on another person rather than our self.

Figure 11. *Personal Prison*, by Pat B. Allen. Aluminum foil, hot glue.

I made the intention to give thanks for Natalie's survival and for her health and well-being. Like magic, my artmaking that day provided a breakthrough for me. I constructed a garment out of aluminum foil suggested by the imprisoning grid that had appeared in my previous drawing and paintings (figure 11). As I put it on and took it off, I experienced the joy of the creative process. My prison was of my own making, and I was free to leave it at any time. As I focused on gratitude, I experienced a shift. Other participants also experienced shifts that day. Perhaps it was the cumulative effect of a week of studio work. Several people in the workshop made specific intentions or dedicated their work to family members or friends who were suffering.

I suspect that taking creative risks on behalf of someone we love is a bit easier than taking them for ourselves. I am my own obstacle far more often than someone or something else is in my way. We hold ourselves separate from suffering, thinking that will keep us feeling safe. In fact, the practice of witness teaches me that it is open recognition of pain that allows healing energy to flow into it and begin to create change. The feeling of joy was palpable in the class as we witnessed the love that poured into the images. Sharing the burden of what we carry is probably part of it as well; the love of others mixes with our own and we are less alone. When we take ourselves lightly we can see the light in someone else. Helplessness and deadlock dissolve in the paint water as we create on another's behalf.

Giving thanks need not wait for our image making. When you feel dry and constricted, uncreative and even hopeless, stop and take a minute to think of someone who deserves your gratitude. It could be a teacher from elementary school, the paperboy, a friend, a stranger who smiles at you on the bus, or an elected official who serves your community. You can give thanks for the color of fall leaves or the delight of a hot shower. Notice what begins to happen. Usually I find that as I think of more and more to be grateful for, the energy of creativity begins to flow. An image arises as praise and celebration. Gratitude makes me want to give. Artmaking is a powerful way to dwell in gratitude. Instead of a flitting unnoticed through my mind, a thankful thought can blossom into a meditation. I have made it a practice to create small healing paintings for friends and family members who are ill or are experiencing a special occasion. It allows me a way to witness the person, really notice who they are in my life, and give thanks for all I receive from them, all I appreciate about them. I believe I send healing energy to the person this way, but I know for sure that I am free from worry while creating and that the process generates positive energy. Yet I also almost always experience a moment of thinking, "This is pretty cool, maybe I'll keep this for myself." I feel a physical constriction when I think that thought, but that passes when I relax and let it go and bestow art on its rightful recipient.

We can witness life passages through artmaking in the same way we can witness suffering and special occasions. When my daughter was approaching the age at which menstruation was likely to begin, I created a box for her. It was a sort of portable altar, full of mystery as well as practical things. The outside was painted black and red and closed with a tie.

artmaking for rites of passage

When opened, it folded out and had a goddess figure, a medicine bag with homeopathic medicine for cramps, a velvet purse with sanitary products, an amulet, and a letter welcoming her to womanhood. When she left for two weeks of camp, and had not yet begun to bleed, we packed it in her trunk. As it turned out, she did not get her period until after she returned from camp, but another girl did, and Adina used her box to help her friend make that moment sacred. Our own forms of creative celebration can channel and transform the energy of the moment for the highest good.

Studio practice can begin in very small and subtle ways. Witnessing is a skill that can easily be practiced with objects other than images you yourself have created. In a setting where there is insufficient space or time for artmaking, we can still do our spiritual practice, for example, with images collected from magazines mounted on black construction paper or a small object brought from home. We make an intention and then simply choose an image, either randomly or by attraction, and go through the steps of the witness writing process: describing what's there, cataloguing feelings and thoughts, dialoguing, and seeking meaning. It is remarkably effective to work this way. One can start to use art as a spiritual practice using any combination of intention, artmaking, and witness. Don't forget to say thank you.

Teachings emerge from the witness writing about images. It is good to review your work at regular intervals. At the end of six- or seven-week sessions in the studio, participants are encouraged to take out all the artwork they have done and to reread all their writings, both intentions and witnesses. This review is an integral part of art as a spiritual practice. Often, themes will emerge or a piece of wisdom will stand out that shocks the artist, who wonders, "Who wrote that?" Although I do this practice of review each time along with everyone else, I also review many years worth of writings when I sit down to write a book like this. I am repeatedly stunned by what I have been given, the richness of the insights, how quickly and thoroughly I forget them, and also how each day I begin over again to learn. Having a great revelation doesn't mean that it stays in the forefront of the mind, guiding me ever closer to enlightenment, whatever that may be. I forget and fall off the chair and struggle again and again; but like a boulder gradually being smoothed by flowing water, I get softer

start & maintain
a simple,
ever modified,
studio practice

over time, more porous. I am humbled and reminded that *prac*
key word. If a revelation visits only for an instant then flies a
okay. I can climb back on the chair in the next moment. Retur.....
and again is a crucial part of practice.

The chapters in part two will share some teachings that have emerged
from artmaking for me and others who have engaged with these simple
tools over time.

Studio Teachings

Introduction to Part Two

When I reach through the hole at my center the gift eludes me. Whatever it may be I can possess it only as that mystery which beckons from the greatest distance and draws my heart deeper into the quest.
—Meinrad Craighead (1986, 55)

There is a great awakening going on that is coming forth in chaos. It is a time of great danger and great opportunity. Old orders are collapsing all over the world. Civil wars of externalized internal conflict rage in countries around the globe. Our country casts the conflict as American "good" against terrorist "evil." Spiritual traditions are being shaken to their foundations. Underlying weaknesses or fault lines are being exposed, such as sex scandals within the Catholic Church. Entrenched systems like apartheid in South Africa and communism in Eastern Europe and the former Soviet Union have fallen.

In this time of ever–profilerating numbers of paths to which we can commit our attention and effort, our imagination is both our greatest resource and our most formidable adversary (Allen 1995). Many people have turned to fundamentalist religion to seek clarity by creating or returning to rigid structures that define right and wrong according to stringent guidelines. Others distract themselves from their existential anxiety by clinging to the empty promises of consumer goods and celebrity culture. Spiritual traditions, and more recently the humanist and transpersonal psychology movements, offer a different answer: to create union and peace within the individual heart, which then will naturally manifest in the world.

The world is in the midst of great pangs of rebirth. But the path of renewal also beckons, inviting us to dive deeply into what has been and to find the sparks of rebirth hidden in what has become dry and remote. The path of renewal is the realm of the creative imagination. Artmaking is a

the Adaptive challenges

practice that urges renewal, exercises the creative imagination, and allows for new images to emerge through the efforts of ordinary people. Artmaking allows us to choose from among the infinite possibilities in each moment to be peace, to be truth, and to be love.

Morihei Ueshiba, the founder of Aikido, says: "The Art of Peace functions everywhere on earth, in realms ranging from the vastness of space to the tiniest plants and animals. The life force is all–pervasive and its strength is boundless. The Art of Peace allows us to perceive and tap into that tremendous reserve of universal energy" (Ueshiba 2002, 47). While there are many ways to tap into the universal energy, making art is one that is available to anyone and that helps us relearn how to say "Yes!" to life, even during dark times, through its deep and abiding pleasures of making and doing.

Part two, the "teachings" section of this book, presents the emergence of renewing images that speak eloquently to those who listen. Chapter 4 shares an extended witness to one group session in the studio, giving a flavor of the communal aspect of the studio process. Later chapters relate stories of the teachings received by other artists and myself as we worked in the studio. The Web site www.patballen.com hosts a virtual studio where readers can participate by responding to images and witness writings posted there.

Guiding images are waiting for us if we choose to receive them. They are not asking us to found new religions in their image according to the old ways of hierarchy. Rather, they appear to us clothed in whatever shape will help us understand our dilemmas. These images may at first feel unfamiliar and startle us. In fact, they come to restore balance. God has been conceived of as Father, Savior, and Warrior for so long, it is no wonder She now manifests as Mother, Nurturer, and Peacemaker in the art of so many women. When the voices and images of part of the world's people are suppressed, that balance disintegrates. Our task is to learn to dance with, to flow with, these images. No image should be clung to as being more true than another; no image gives a final and definitive picture of reality. What comes to me helps to balance me; what comes to you helps to balance you; and, taken together, all our pieces help to balance a larger whole. The images all arise from the place of infinite possibility, and that place is the core and basic home of every person.

My primary image teacher has appeared as the feminine face and body of God. In Judaism she is the Sabbath Bride and Shekhinah. She has come to me as Kali, the Hindu Goddess who cuts through illusion with her flashing sword, and as Kwan Yin, Buddhist Goddess of Compassion with her silver vase of cool water. For my friend Annette, She is the Dark Mother, the African Goddess, She of All Faces. To balance all these powerful feminine images, I have also been graced with male teaching images like the Emperor and his counterparts, the Fool and Death (see figure 26 on page 164). Many artists in the studio receive images from nature—the sun and moon, trees and animals. Images of children, babies, old crones sitting naked on a crescent moon all speak to the willing eye and ear. The image as teacher takes the form that will intrigue, instruct, inform, and delight us. The image is an angel, says Shaun McNiff (1995). He refers to the original conception of angels as being messengers. Like Abraham in the Bible, we must invite angels into our tent as honored guests and serve them refreshment if we are to hear their messages and receive their direction.

The imaginal realm waits within us; we rend the veil between worlds with our paintbrush, chalk, and crayon. This section will share teachings, stories, and images from studio artists, including myself. When working with others in the studio and hearing their witnesses, we find that others' images become as alive for us as our own. In this way, we learn tolerance for and appreciation of difference; we release fear by viewing and living with images other than our own. The images become our familiars, our guides, as they teach us to travel back and forth between our accustomed lives in the world and the realm of all possibility, the infinite beyond our finitude. The imagination is a net. As we sweep through a day, certain images stick in our minds then begin to take root and grow there. When we tend our creative life like a garden—cultivating it with attention—wisdom grows in the form of our own personal teachings. I have the greatest respect for the teachings of all the great spiritual traditions. In this age of instant access to information via the Internet, we have access to Buddhist sutras, the Torah, the Koran, countless contemporary thinkers, and the growing body of popular wisdom brought together by Oprah and her colleagues. As we seek to understand life, we no longer find ourselves limited to the tradition into which we were born. With so many choices, we must be careful not to flit among traditions, alighting on each only long enough for a superficial engagement. We must cultivate a deep intuition regarding what is true for ourselves and what is not. For many of us, the voices we long for are those that haven't yet been recorded—those of women, children, adolescents, water, rocks, earth, and trees. Many of us have had the experience of finding just the right book at a moment of crisis. The studio provides a place to find just the words and images we need to guide us; for their teachings lie within us, and art can grant us access.

Books and writing disguise the process of how we come to understand. Having one's words and thoughts recorded in clear lines of black type on white pages, bound and covered on a library shelf, is a form of privilege. It makes it seem as if my words have more authority, more importance, than someone else's. Lately, as some famous authors have been accused of copying the words of others or claiming ideas that are not their own, I have had to laugh. Maybe the whole question of who is or isn't an expert is beginning to wobble and collapse. The studio plays a part in the subversive process of learning to trust our inner authority and to question all received ideas. The priestess, rabbi, sage, and iman all live in that space of infinite possibility. We travel there via the image created with intention. The witness notebook records our history with our images. The stories they tell us are often personal but just as often contain cosmic truth. The images do not grow old or stale. I recently witnessed an image from over twenty years ago, and it was happy to speak. The images remind us that there is a timeless realm, the place of all possibility, and they will take us there any time we ask.

The process of intention and witness developed in a communal setting. It became a method that supports groups of people making art together and sharing their truth in a safe way that doesn't overwhelm others who participate side by side. A dedicated studio space is a wonderful environment, but it is not necessary to have a special space to engage in the process. Certainly, artists enjoy working in a studio when possible, just as practitioners of meditation find it inspiring to practice in a temple or retreat setting. But, once established, the disciplines of intention and witness are very portable.

Dedicated studios provide a sanctuary as well as a public home-space (Timm-Bottos, personal communication, 2004). For me an ideal

world would have several studios in every community. ⸝
would have a space where students could experience a sup⸝
out to reconnect with their higher self via freely created artwc
secret fantasy that churches and synagogues will eventually h.
in-residence to hold studio space for their congregations. It wc
kind of chapel for art as prayer, a place for the social justice comn ⸝ce to
practice discernment before taking action, a place for congregants to
renew their connection to sacred symbols through hand and heart. But
really all that is needed is a studio as *mishkan*, or portable sanctuary. This
can be as simple as a shoebox with a few supplies and a corner of the
kitchen table after the kids are in bed. The intention to commune with
the Creative Source is powerful and will provide a means to expression.

4
Call and Response
The Group as Witness Environment

Trying to convey the nature of what transpires in a studio when a group of artists are at work can be maddening. Though it helps to show the process, even a videotape edits the experience. I invite you to conjure images of the artists at work in your mind's eye. While the stories of individual artists give a glimpse into a personal experience of art as a spiritual path, the aspect of being witnessed in a group cannot be underestimated and is lost in the telling of the individual story. The nature of the witness, the quality of attention offered to one another, and the spaciousness provided by the practice of no-comment are ineffable but vital to enabling artists to forget themselves and their outer concerns, and to enter the artmaking experience completely. In order to understand this phenomenon and to learn how to write about it, I gave over the facilitation of the Friday studio process class at Studio Pardes to Kim. I did this reluctantly. After all, I had worked for years to devise and refine a method that I could both participate in and facilitate simultaneously. I feared that I would feel left out and resentful watching others create while I "merely" witnessed their process. I resisted the idea even though I had been feeling flat and disengaged for quite a while when participating and facilitating, especially with my own artmaking. I had begun to feel the pressure of piles of images created without a destination. I felt increasingly torn over the growing separation between the images that arose in the classes and the artwork I created alone, which was often more complex. The time frame of several hours had begun to feel too short.

The Friday class consisted of twelve artists, some longtime veterans of the process and several new members. I decided to begin my witnessing in the second meeting of a new session so that Kim could establish herself as facilitator with less interference from me. She briefly explained to the group my plan to visit and observe. I didn't know exactly what form that would take until I showed up for the second class. Kim initiated the drawing workshop "Energy Made Visible," the heart of the process. We begin all sessions with this workshop, in which artists are invited to choose one color of oil pastel and a small sheet of paper, often a scrap, and begin to make marks. They are asked to explore the richness within the limitations of this practice as thoroughly as they can. The idea is to notice everything: the sense of sitting in a chair, the act of choosing the scrap of paper, maybe one that already has marks on it. The instructions given in the workshop attempt to bring students into greater intimacy with their own experience, and often go something like this: "Choose a color. Feel the blunt crayon as it touches the paper, again, again, differently again. Notice how a dirty crayon brings along traces of other colors. Do you like that? The crayon warms in your hand and smears on the paper, blending colors. Do you like that? You notice that you can put one color over another, you can obliterate, you can layer, you can scrape away color and reveal what is underneath with your fingernail, which is now very dirty. Do you like that? Yes, it is like foreplay, this act of making marks. It transports and opens you and makes you want more."

Once the artist feels finished, they can take a large sheet of paper, tape it to the wall, and continue to make marks using any and all colors. We play loud drumming music in the background as we make marks. The music interrupts the thinking process and induces a light trance, allowing us to focus simply on color and marks, simply on the bodily pleasure of touch and color. These marks are the record of each artist's energy. Standing at the wall, we make marks for at least an hour or more. Some artists choose to stay with a small piece for the whole time; others move almost immediately to the wall, tearing off large sheets from rolls of paper.

As I enter the studio on my observation day, artists are talking, laughing, catching up about family and children, getting cups of hot tea. Light streams in, catching and illuminating the colors of the dragon painted on the west windows. It is a bitterly cold January morning, and these artists have set it aside to make art and write about it. Kim sits quietly and listens as conversations subside. She smoothly moves into explaining the task of the day, making marks on paper. She reminds everyone to make an intention, to focus on their bodies, to become aware of the energy that animates them, to become present to self. She mentions that, of course, any regular member who feels called to paint or work in another medium should heed that call: "Follow your pleasure."

Some linger at the tables with journals; others move directly to the large rolls of black, white, or brown paper and tear or carefully cut off sheets of varying sizes. Next, these are taped to the wall with masking tape. The drumming CD that Kim has chosen unfolds a beat that is loose and rhythmic. She chooses a spot on the wall closest to the music, a spot I usually take. I am sitting at first in my work space, set apart from the classroom by a long table and the shelves that hold the art materials. I wonder at first if I should be out of sight, but soon realize I must move around the room and take different seats—that there is so much to see. Mary stands over the oil pastels, which are set out according to the spectrum, moving her shoulders up and down to the beat, shaking off the morning chill. Rebecca stands, hands on hips, looking at her piece of black paper against the paint-stained wall. She carefully tears and manipulates one corner of the paper, twisting it gently.

The drum beat gets louder and more complex. Kim is covering an irregularly shaped piece of black paper with white lines. Mary is dancing back and forth along a six-foot stretch of brown paper, making marks with many colors. Brenda works carefully on a piece of black paper. She is creating an image, a figure running into a field of peach and blue. She leaves a wide, empty border around the figure. The music shifts again to a multilayered percussion. I can pick out rattles and a sound of metal against metal. Kim and Heather share a laugh at the oil pastel bins. Mary's paper falls down; she tapes it back up and keeps working. Kim adds red and orange over the white marks.

Tom wrote his intention with a flat carpenter's pencil. He is the only man in the studio today. He works on an image of a man with a tornado of color coming out of his side. Heather has two pieces of brown paper on the wall, one above the other. She repeats circles and more circles on the lower piece, circles and ovals on the piece above. Amy, to Heather's left, begins to fill with black around some colored lines even though her paper is black. The colors leap out from the paper with the added emphasis.

I hear a rainstick and a chime in the music, and a deep bass note creates a sense of something impending. When I am drawing, I don't notice the minute details of the music. In fact, sometimes I would swear I have never heard a CD that I have played for years as background music for the "Energy Made Visible" workshop.

I feel enormous energy as I witness and record what is unfolding in the studio. Although I came in nervous and not knowing exactly what I would do, this watching, writing, and moving around feels exactly right. I am a witness. I do not feel outside the process as I had feared, but simply in it more fully. I am overjoyed at the energy flowing around the room and at my ability to swim in it and receive this new delight. The music shifts to a track with quieter sounds and whispered voices in an African language. The movement of the artists slows down, too. Heather stops for a drink of tea; Mary walks around and looks at what others are doing. Heather returns to her piece and begins to fill in her blue circles with white. Meg has drawn what looks like a large lotus flower over her initial marks. Kim sits for a while and regards her drawing from across the room, then returns to add a tornado–like shape in black over the red center.

The music shifts again and suddenly both Meg and Mary, working side by side, are adding black lines over their colorful marks. Kim adds a second piece of paper and adjusts the placement of the first piece on the wall. Rebecca carefully draws small marks in the corner of the paper she had massaged in the beginning of the session. A figure is forming. As she walks across the room, I notice that her cheek is lightly smeared with black oil pastel. She walks across the room to get a look at her piece from a distance. With dreamy looks on their faces, several artists peel paper off oil pastel sticks. Tom stops and turns from his corner to regard the room. Meg has added a second flower. Kim has added two more tornado shapes.

The CD begins to skip. Kim looks toward the sound system on the center of the altar, but she doesn't stop drawing. The skipping stops. Kim sits down and drinks some tea from her electric–purple hot cup. All the artists are committed by now to the image that has appeared. Rebecca is adding a face to her figure. Kim has added a third piece of paper. The artists have been in the studio for about fifty–five minutes. They are engaged with something that has arrived to meet them on the paper. As an observer, I realize I can't know what that is. I cannot know if any particular artist is happy or sad, frustrated or ecstatic. I can simply notice what I see and the feelings and thoughts that rise and fall in me.

Studio Teachings

It feels surprisingly good to witness the class and not participate in artmaking. The CD continues to skip periodically and then right itself. I imagine a fingerprint on the playing side and make a note to tell Kim about cleaning the surface with a cotton swab and rubbing alcohol, a trick I learned from the teenagers who come to the studio. I imagine Kim weighing whether or not to take out the CD. I relax into the knowledge that today it is not my responsibility, and I am only curious about how Kim will respond. Meg's flowers are multiplying. Kim stops the sound system and changes the CD. A few artists turn to jokingly complain. Kim jokes back: "I was hoping you wouldn't notice, but then you're supposed to notice everything!" Now Kim plays a CD of drumming and flute music by Kodo, a Japanese traditional music ensemble. It is much crisper than the whispered African voices. The sound is like being inside the drums.

Brenda sits down and takes a breakfast bar from her bag and begins to eat while she regards her drawing. Rebecca has drawn a face in light yellow lines. Heather continues to fill in her circles with white. One oval in the upper piece is filled in with magenta. Amy cuts a second piece of paper, the knife making a crisp sound as it cuts through the paper. She tears masking tape from a roll; these sounds mix with the music. The music shifts again; it sounds like the original CD, and the artists are moving more briskly and fluidly to the African rhythms. Mary resumes dancing. Kim is adding eyes to the center of her figure, nine of them in a line. She comes over and consults me about the CD and how to skip over the damaged tracks.

Meg has added a green background to her flowers. Rebecca, again across the room, stretches her arms overhead as she looks at the changes she has made. The face is gone; a burnished–looking egg shape has taken its place. Kim has switched back to the Asian music, which doesn't feel as free or mysterious to me, but more stylized. I imagine movements I might make to it. Mary is sitting down, working on a small piece of paper. Amy squats near the floor to reach the second piece of paper she attached to her original drawing. I think about the differences between African art and Asian art; the aesthetics of each culture are so different. I chide myself for making such a gross generalization and let the topic go. I notice my strong preference for African music.

Kim sits down and begins to write her witness with a little stub of a pencil. She gives a time check to the group, reminding them that they have about ten minutes of drawing time left. As if on cue, a very up-tempo piece begins to play. Mary attaches her small drawing to her large one. A cell phone begins to ring but is nearly drowned out by the drumming. Mary cuts off a new piece of paper. The music builds to a frenzied crescendo with several false endings. I notice the time seems to move more slowly as I sit and witness. More infernal Japanese flutes! I wonder if this music would disrupt my process if I were drawing. I note again my preference for African music.

I wonder if the artists will remark on my scribbling presence in their midst. Artists begin to drift off to wash hands and get ready for the witness writing segment of class. Meg changes the orientation of her piece on the wall and then changes it back. Kim lowers the music, a sign to the group that the drawing part of class is coming to an end. The energy quiets further, and I realize there has been no conversation aside from a few brief exchanges. Artists have been silent and I look forward to hearing their witness readings. Conversations float in from the bathroom, where washing off the oil pastels from greasy fingers provides a transition. Cups of tea are refilled, seats taken. Only Heather still works at the wall, filling in circles.

The artists have been in the studio for about an hour and a half. Now they begin to step out of the numinous space of creating, to begin the process of separating from the image and regarding it more completely from a place outside it. This drawing workshop, perhaps more than any other art experience, allows the artist to merge with their image, to fall into colors, strokes, and the smeared surface. Sometimes it feels like fighting, slashing, and leaning into the paper. Other times it feels like melting. It is in the moments of merger that we touch the Creative Source, losing track of time, relaxing into a state of focused but gently suspended awareness. Music aids this suspension. Some artists may not have even noticed the skipping CD or the switch of musical styles. The most jarring musical intrusion occurs when there is a shift to English and the language becomes comprehensible. In almost all English speakers, this interrupts the sense of being transported to another realm and fully awakens the thinking mind. The witness writing is a transitional state. Awareness is focused more narrowly at first on the image that appears. Often the experience feels like surfacing after being underwater. The artist at first tries to notice what is there—what colors, what shapes—to sharpen awareness even further and to enter the image with one's thinking mind open and not in judgment mode. Just look, just see. Now that the image and artist are separate, each can regard the other. After describing the piece, the witness becomes a conversation. This may take the form of dialogue, or there may ensue a series of ideas, observations, or even metaphoric ramblings that speak of the artist's judgments, insights, intruding events of the day, and stories.

After about thirty minutes of writing time, artists walk around and look at the art that has been created. Kim invites the artists to read their witness writings, remembering to ask each person to say his or her name before beginning. This part of the process is like a courtly ritual. Heather begins by reading her intention: *I engage with the process and welcome whatever energy comes.* Then her witness: *What I mostly felt while working on this piece was pure joy—and I feel joy when I look at it up close like this. I see a jumble of circular marks different shades of blue—deep Prussian blue with white—mostly white on top of blue but then blue working back into white. The marks have lost their circularity on the top layer—have become choppy and sometimes horizontal blue bands staccato across the paper like musical punctuation, as do the lighter blue areas where I used a light blue cray pas instead of getting that color from mixing. I see a visual rhythm that pleases me. The marks are exciting, energetic, rhythmic. The composition is horizontal—I tried at first to put the piece of paper vertically on the wall but I had to change it—wanted it horizontal. I also had to cut the paper in half so that it would be thinner horizontal—I wonder why I am drawn to these horizontal bands of paper? Many of my works here have been like this—those bigger ones.*

HEATHER: *Drawing, can you tell me why horizontal?*

DRAWING: *Movement across time.*

HEATHER: *Like a time line?*

DRAWING: *Generations continue on, everything is the same and different— war, greed, love, hope, poverty, wealth, violence, kindness, fear—all the same, all different, all jumbled together in this human stew. You shouldn't judge it—that's what the Hindu sages have said—you have to embrace the whole damn messy thing.*

HEATHER: *Oh, so chaos is good news?*

DRAWING: *Extremely.*

HEATHER: *So in this drawing—oh—now I see people, faces, masses of humanity and everyone, each one is beautiful—if they are ugly they are beautiful in their horror—it's all so seductive, really.*

DRAWING: *Yes—if you're present, if you're paying attention.*

HEATHER: *Like all those people on the train—when I begin to really pay attention they are all so interesting I can't write fast enough to capture their vitality, their individuality, their quirky wonder—that's the magic.*

DRAWING: *Now you're cooking.*

HEATHER: *So do you have any advice, any practice?*

DRAWING: *Yes, keep up with your observing, keep up with this mark making—follow the circles that give you the bliss.*

HEATHER: *Yes, I started with the circles, I love to make circles.*

DRAWING: *Yes, well why don't you do that at home—your practice is to make circles this week. Take Wednesday afternoon and just make circles—like you did today and see what comes up—turn on the drumming music—treat yourself to a new CD or two and go with the circles and write an observation each day—think about the wealth of all these interesting people to observe.*

HEATHER: *Thank you drawing—you've really taught me a lot today.*

As Heather reads, the rest of the artists focus on her. I find tears rising in my eyes. Heather is working to create her identity as a writer and artist. She knows she must make space in her home if this dream is to become reality. She is receiving her own guidance. Mary goes next. I notice the small drawing Mary made toward the end of the session now affixed to her large drawing. It is labeled "unremote control." Unlike most artists, who use journals or notebooks, Mary frequently does her writings on scraps of paper; today is no exception. On a beautiful scrap of handmade paper with rose petals pressed within it, Mary writes: *Intention: I stay in touch with the process I invite strength and stamina to help me on my 50 by 50 journey.* She mutters that we do not need to know exactly what the literal meaning of her intention is and begins to read her witness off a large fragment of brown kraft paper. *Wow, the power of intention! I got the gift today.*

DRAWING: *Music—movement are your answer . . . Play . . . Ferris wheels roller coasters. Prayer beads. So many images flying in at once. Pure energy flows through you, you are energy.*

MARY: *But what about these dark black lines? I thought I would not use black today at all at the beginning.*

DRAWING: *Black is the seat and direction of your power. You need to accept that your power and energy need to be directed and controlled.*

MARY: *While working on my black lines, images of my kids at school come flooding through me.* [Mary is a preschool teacher.] *They were playing yesterday, taking hollow big blocks setting them up to the shape of a television. They made TV screens on paper and taped them up to the blocks. About seven children did this. Then they got blocks or pretend telephones, sat on chairs, and began pressing their pretend remote controls to change channels on their "TV's." It was fascinating prompting incredible imaginate stories, television stations, conversations about fears and dreams. I began to recognize some of their skills and abilities, their hopes and nightmares in each press of the remote. They went there so easily—with the push of a button.*

DRAWING: *You need an unremote control. When you are remote from your feelings and energy, you don't have control over your life. You can't follow a direction. It's too chaotic. You do have to have a plan. You have awesome powers. Just press the button.*

MARY: *Thank you. I know.*

Silence follows Mary's words as we sit and take them in, letting her wisdom become our own. Rebecca goes next. Her intention is: *Don't think anymore—just do.* She begins her witness:

> *I finished reading my book this morning—a book I've been pulled into as I do with most novels, where I become the characters and their lives become mine. This is how I've always learned, through absorption. Does "absorption" ever get included as one of the intelligences, as a learning style, as a valued technique for taking in information? I ask rhetorically. So this book [A Fine Balance by R Mistry] I identify most closely in the end to the character of least strength, who lacks ambition and the ability to overcome obstacles. He lets life beat him. Why do I react to him? The characters in the story who are truly beaten by life bounce back, joke, continue living. Is this survival guilt, the guilt of the more lucky, more fortunate, that my character feels?*
>
> *On to my picture. I enjoyed doing this. Pleasure, Kim reminded us last week. That was good to be reminded. I cut my paper with a strange corner rip and spent time adjusting the rip to be a private little scream at the top right corner— a little spirit scream. Then the color first felt overwhelming and I cursed cutting a big paper (though not really so big). But once the music carried me, my lines*

grew and I didn't care what I made or where the lines went. At one point the white jiggle reminded me of hair and I thought of Venus de Milo—she stayed with me throughout, though only as a whisper. I think the suggestion of sea from the colors I chose and the wavery seashell shaped lines made me think of her, and when I stepped back, I was shocked to see a delicately shrouded oval shape that might well be a face. A face, yikes. I liked the picture, why destroy it with an awkward face? Why not try, what difference does it make? It looks like a face belongs in there so I tried it timidly, working to the drums. But the drums pulled out from under me—just stopped cold [when Kim changed the skipping CD]. Empty and gone. As though someone turned on the light in a softly candlelit room, the face was gone, as well, so I stepped back to inspect the problem, immediately knowing what to do, or try to do anyway. The oval needed to be mother-of-pearl rather than a pearl. The irregularity of color and shape has always appealed to me far more than a pearl.

Perhaps there's a face hidden in there somewhere. She's serene and protected, wrapped in her lacy shroud. She's a survivor without guilt.

Brenda goes next. She has chosen to explore an image that she began last week; that is her intention. Her witness begins:

Last week he was stepping out onto the water. This week he's running toward it, energy radiating from his outstretched hand. No ripples in the water now only a soft glow reflecting from the sky. Who is this guy?

He is the energy I never seem to have.

He is energy—light—movement—go—

He is unafraid.

He is confident.

But who is he?

A Spirit. The Spirit of going forward. Spirit of light. Spirit of "it's okay."

"Light" has more than one meaning—is he the opposite of "heavy" or the opposite of "dark"? Well?

Go forward. He is the Spirit of Going Forward.

And that's okay.

Kim follows Brenda. Her intention reads: *I connect with the Creative Source and find pleasure.* Her witness reads:

What are you circles that are being birthed? A hurricane of fire birthing a butterfly of transformation a head for a woman—a bird woman not a butterfly. Eyes nine eyes why nine eyes? White. First I created a hurricane of fire after many layers and different energy lines going in all different directions the hurricane appeared. I loved this fast-moving hurricane. I desired to be stirred up. I desire to be on fire I really can feel the pull to get out of myself. Hurricane, do you wish to speak?

HURRICANE: *Yes, pay attention here you are out onto the fire hurricane pay attention here this is a birthing.*

KIM: *Then I realized it was so I repeated the spiraling fire hurricane many times over then I could feel the next step of something energizing. So I ripped the paper and I had the shape of what seemed a butterfly or bird someone or something with wings. I worked on the wings and desired a head—the head of who or what—like a bird head?*

WINGS: *A contented happy face.*

KIM: *I say it is, but as soon as the face appeared she said: "I'm not beautiful enough I'm not feminine enough I'm alive people have to notice me."*

KIM: *You're asking me?*

FACE: *Yes.*

KIM: *Give me hints—*

FACE: *Eyes—like Klimt.*

KIM: *I've no gold.*

FACE: *Doesn't matter. I want lots of eyes.*

KIM: *O.K., I see where. So I created nine eyes. Eyes are the all-knowing.*

FACE: *The more the better—never enough eyes.*

KIM: *I feel there is more you are not saying—*

FACE: *You will know be . . . Be what I ask BE there*

KIM: *Okay, I guess—what else did you desire?*

FACE: *Waves of spirals to pull me along to calm my soul—*

KIM: *Okay, done, anything else?*

FACE: *You can be divided in many directions but if you are challenged think of me for you need to be true to yourself.*

KIM: *I will take this advice. Thank you.*

Meg, whose final image has become a profusion of flowers, speaks next. Her intention: *To feel warmth! To rid my body of the chill that has stuck with me all week. To listen to the music and move around and greet the paper! It feels good to be back here, to create something, to be myself.* Her witness:

I have lost my chill, briefly as I sit here I feel a breeze again. I hate the cold. I hate the heat as well. Spring and Fall—why can't we just have two seasons? I look at my drawing. The black outlines please me—I don't think I've ever used black like that. The other times I've used the Cray-Pas, I've just scribbled, never making a real outline of anything. I started out that way today. I wanted to try textures so I taped artificial leaves and feathers to the back like leaf rubbings. I've always liked how Brenda makes a border around her image at first I made a yellow rectangular border, filling it in with strokes. I felt confined and stifled. I rebelled and popped my strokes out of it. At first, little loops but then I made larger ones, big strokes of color, pinks, blues, yellows, greens, I had a sample plate of colors, not wanting to limit myself. I like color. Bright colors. I grabbed the black and made some leaves. The flowers came naturally. Seems all I draw are hearts, flowers, and children. What does that mean? I ask my flowers.

FLOWERS: *You like them.*

MEG: *Duh. And they are colorful. No deep meaning here. The green background feels tropical. I wish my image were a big beach towel on the sand. I hear the crashing of the waves, the calling of the gulls rather than the sound of the traffic and the screeching of brakes. I feel the sun shine down on my face. I sip a cold, fruity drink with an umbrella, a slice of orange and a (luck?)! Paradise. My picture brings me peace! Whimsy. It takes me out of the cold, back to Catalina where Greg and I looked out at the ocean for hours at a time: laughing, talking, then saying nothing at all. Enjoying our time alone. No worries or responsibilities. Able to focus on us, the beauty of the sea and sleeping late. Walking. Sunbathing. Eating lots. Drinking more. A week long date in paradise. I think I'll save my pennies and get back there some day. Till then, I'll look at you, picture, and pretend.*

My eyes turn to Kim's picture—a genie exiting the bottle. Swirling as she comes out. Taking it all in with her many eyes. A smirk on her face like she's in charge. She's got the power, she's in control. Waking up. Meeting the day head on. Willing to take what it gives her with open arms. Strong. I am woman she shouts to me.

Studio Teachings

I am intrigued by Mary's mural! Her "remotes." I watched her move with the drums, slap on the colors, large swirls all over the page. She motivated me to get the hell out of the yellow box! Thanks Mary.

Amy's images attract me. The asymmetry in the paper fascinates me. I think "how brave to make a cut like that—I'd be worried about hanging it back up or framing it." Looks like Catholic grade school was not the best place to have one's first art experience! Maybe I'll try a fun shape another day.

Amy speaks next. Her intention: *How can I get unstuck how can I get inside find the inner movement and pay attention to the force going in the opposite direction.* She doesn't write question marks. Her witness begins:

A snake with an egg in its tail winds itself around the leg of a tree that once was human but then was trapped mid-leap. The serpent aims upward at an interrupted forest. A high-heeled boot opens its mouth with a sides way smile its spindly teeth can dangle. Who knew that the big toe grid hid a prisoner with a pink dancing partner? Two huge tears of green are more than middle-aged breasts. They have inner knowing eyes that the snake wants to eat to feed its tail egg. Is that boot mouth menacing or snidely comical. There are porous openings into spaces that perhaps are moments of evaporation. Who's more (?) the tic tac toe or her pink partner who may have slipped from the prisoner's grasp. The high heeled pointy toothed mouth may have aims in the pink dancer's direction. But then it's hard to say if hers is a smile with any bite. Dangling images speak but they are hieroglyphs that say too much and like to interrupt each other, even one dangling participle looking for the main clause.

Tom, who is married to Brenda, goes last. He states his intention: *Get in touch with lots of energy.* His witness, typically brief, reads: *I took smaller image from last week and worked it in color. Too energic nervous and hot—as in radioactive. I really appreciated the "cooler" work around me today. Thank you.*

Once everyone has read, Kim strikes a small chime to signal the end of the formal witness time. Chairs scrape, some artists leave quickly, some linger to wash their hands and tea mugs and delay going out into the January cold. Sometimes there are questions, general ones, or observations about the process. Often there are expressions of gratitude. Today those came in the witness writings themselves. The sense of mind–body entrainment produced by the music persists. It takes a while for thoughts to crowd back in. A sense of peace comes from going deeply within oneself in the presence of others.

Today, observing, I realize that this studio experience evokes a quality of early life. Mary's reference to her preschool students' imaginative play helps me to see how similar their play with pretend televisions and changing images with remote controls is to the artists' mark making. In both instances images rise and fall, teasing out emotions, stories, and insights as they go. Both are play in the most exalted sense of that word. Both artists and children play life like a beautiful instrument for which there are no lessons save the playing itself. Play is an indigenous, primary form of being in the world, even of inventing the world. I am struck also by how well each image fits its artist. Each artist, through writing their intention, sets the terms and conditions of the relationship to the Creative Source in this particular encounter.

What the artist calls out for determines what the response will be. Meg's reverie about a romantic vacation with her husband provides an antidote to the "cold that stuck to her all week." While she may not be able to take that trip right now—in fact she spoke of "saving her pennies for the next trip"—she can go home and embrace her partner with a rekindled appreciation of him and their intimacy. Amy's work conveys in both word and image a playful complexity worthy of the Surrealists. It isn't necessary to speculate on a concrete meaning. She is playing out in plain view what is only known to her; the rest of us still feel the energy generated in the tension between her images.

We don't know what Tom is so "hot" about, and it is none of our business. It is enough to be washed over by the subtle dance of different currents of energy flowing through the room. Meg chooses to name the currents when she mentions the work of individual artists in her witness. Several things distinguish her act, which is a form of referencing, from simply speaking the same observations out loud. For one, whether they feel flattered or annoyed by Meg's interpretation, the artist being referenced does not verbally respond. One of Meg's comments serves to illustrate an essential aspect of referencing. She notes that she has always enjoyed the borders that Brenda often creates in her drawings by leaving a space around the perimeter of the image. When Meg tried bordering her own work, she noticed a feeling of restriction and quickly broke the boundary she set. There is nothing like copying an artistic convention to gain empathy for one another or to get to know the crucial difference between what the mind says and how the body feels.

Without it being consciously referenced, the circular form shows up in many artists' work this day. I can't help but think of enclosure and gestation as apt winter themes. The studio, too, provides enclosure. It allows each artist to be washed and buffeted by energies that nurture, soothe, and evoke responses in their souls. This is my response and may say as much about my state of gestating this writing project as anything else. Each artist calls out with an intention for something, receives response in the forms and colors of the image, and emerges with something new, nourishing, and grounding.

I have not been so completely in the role of witness before; I always create my own work along with facilitating. Now, seeking only to observe, I experience the events within this environment in a way that is qualitatively different from how the other workshop participants are experiencing them. I am much more aware of how powerful the music is. I notice the vastly different effects exerted on me by the orderly Japanese Kodo drummers and the loose, layered, improvisational African music. I use a wide variety of music from around the world in the studio, but most often I am drawn to African music. Its call and response format seems to best support this kind of artmaking. The music's purpose is not only to interrupt thinking but to awaken an indigenous form or template within the soul that mirrors our right relationship with the Creative Source. The artist Estella Conwill Majozo says:

> This form—call, answer, and release—is a metaphor for art itself and the potential that it holds. The call is incited by the experiences we have in the world, by the human conditions and predicaments within our terrain that arouse our interest or consciousness. Next comes the response, the artist's creation—the attempt to name, recognize, and instigate change through his or her creative expression. But the artist's creation is not the end of the process, as it is often thought to be. The process continues as members of the community experience the release, the

inspiration that allows them to enflesh their message and begin activating change in their own terrains. This basic human-to-human interaction signals the symbiotic relationship among human beings. When we understand this, we can go on to better appreciate the breath dynamic between ourselves and trees. We can understand our relationship to oceans and ozones and other zones within the universe. (1995, 91)

I discover something in this act of witness that gives me a new and deeper appreciation of the process. We humans are multifaceted and live in an ever-more-complicated world. I believe that at one time humans achieved self-renewal simply in nature, that being embedded in the natural world was a means to retune us to our soul and to retune our soul to the frequency of the Soul of the World. Without needing to ponder things too deeply, the deep truth of natural law simply reentered our awareness on a deep, nonverbal level when we watched the sunset or the tide go out. We re-created ourselves in the divine image, assured of being a part of a larger whole.

When re-creating became recreation, creative activity began to be increasingly mediated by commerce. Equipment, clothing, and organized adventures take the place of a simple walk in the woods followed by some cloud gazing. Communal sports and games are replaced by professional events that reduce us to spectators. The indigenous soul starves and atrophies on a diet of spectacles.

In the studio I witness artists re-creating themselves and returning to balance by dialoguing with images. The art process seems to provide a bridge to the laws of Nature, which we can easily lose touch with in our busy efforts to achieve and produce. It certainly seems true in the following stories that the communal nature of making art together and the energy of witness consciousness combine to encourage artists to move beyond the static created by the world that blocks the call of the soul. For this reason, I am drawn out of the fixed space of an established studio and into the uncertain terrain of the world. I am called to make the process portable so that we can venture into the lost places like Geiger counters seeking the call that, while nearly drowned out, must still exist in everything.

5

Recovering the Intergendered Soul

Conscious femininity is not bound to gender. It belongs to both men and women. Although in the history of the arts, men have articulated their femininity far more than women, women now are becoming custodians of their own feminine consciousness. For centuries, men have projected their inner image of femininity, raising it to a consciousness that left women who accepted the projection separated from their own reality. They became artifacts rather than people. The consciousness attributed to them was a consciousness projected onto them. That projection was sometimes an idealized image of beauty and truth, a sphinx, or a dragon. Whatever it was, it could not be an incarnated woman.

—Marion Woodman (1993, 1–2)

The first stories in this chapter depict the excavation and return of soul parts of women. I include a story of mine that involves the return of a young boy image. I have reflected a great deal on this image of a dark boy, age somewhere between seven and eleven, not quite a child, on the verge of adolescence. Carol Gilligan and her colleagues at the Harvard Project on the Psychology of Women and the Development of Girls have conducted numerous studies that catalogue the reality of girls, their loss of an authentic voice, at about the age of my boy (1991). They document the social pressure on girls to domesticate, to submit to expectations of docility and agreeableness, and how this leads to an absence of self. Lyn Mikel Brown, a member of the Harvard Project on the Psychology of Women and the Development of Girls, describes the alternative: "A girl who chooses to authorize her own life experiences by speaking openly about them resists the security of convention and moves into uncharted territory; she sets herself adrift, disconnects from the mainland; she risks being, for a time, storyless" (in Gilligan 1991, 72). The stories in this chapter reveal women for whom art made an alternative story possible in adolescence, but whose lack of some crucial element prevented the artist's story from coming to fruition until years later.

My image provoked me to ask: What are boys doing during this transitional time that is different from girls? What images do they embody? I began to think about my two younger brothers and also to notice boys in public spaces. My youngest brother would spent time alone throwing a baseball up in the air and catching it in his mitt, all the while narrating a fantasy baseball game to himself. When I was a child, boys could wander home after school, poking sticks into things, turning over rocks, and wading in the brook that ran through town. When I began to do that, too, my parents got in the car and came searching for me, saying such antics were dangerous; "strange men" were known to lurk in out-of-the-way places, waiting for unsuspecting girls. Boys, apparently, were at no such risk.

Watching boys skateboard, I discovered a kind of single–mindedness that translates ultimately into skill. A boy will ride up and down the same stretch of pavement endlessly, practicing his moves for hours. What I observed cued me to what many women lose out on: the development of self–discipline and commitment to a physical task. Ellen Dissanayake, a scholar who has studied the meaning of artmaking behavior for the survival and evolution of our species, says: "Our bodies and minds are adapted to lead a life of physical engagement, and when born into it people find it agreeable, even richly rewarding" (2004, 116). Boys climbing trees or shooting baskets over and over, even when they do so with friends, are not being social or even necessarily competitive. The activity is sufficiently rewarding in itself to be repeated. The sense of focused attention and the resulting skills are very gratifying and bind a boy to the world. The tasks girls are usually expected to repeat, such as housework, have no associated learning or increase in skill, no particular physical challenge that makes them rewarding. For reinforcement, girls learn to rely on being told by someone else that they did a good job and that their acts of service are appreciated.

Girls of my era accepted the tag "tomboy" when they spent hours in the woods or playing a physical game. As Sallie's story illustrates, such endeavors were usually extinguished by adolescence, when being a freely embodied girl raised the danger of sexual experimentation, which suggested the possibility of acquiring skills that would lead to the choice of an appropriate mate. One could be a good girl or a bad girl; those were the choices. Artmaking requires uninterrupted, self-absorbed time. Kim stopped her artmaking when her son was born; having stained glass, her medium of choice at the time, around seemed dangerous and wasn't something that could be accomplished in fits and starts between naps and bottles.

Girls trade single-minded inquiry into the physical world for the sphere of relatedness and emotion, another important and highly nuanced realm. As women, we often feel selfish and guilty for devoting time to our art pursuits, until like Sallie's, our children are grown. As the expectation to think of others before self, to take care of the needs of others and maintain harmony, takes hold in adolescence, a kind of independence atrophies in many women. The current rage for scrapbooking speaks to a kind of ingenious truce: women create on behalf of the family. They can engage with materials and the pleasure of cutting and handling beautiful papers for the unassailable goal of creating, preserving, and in some cases editing, the family narrative. I wonder what future historians will make of these documents.

Art subverts and challenges the separation of the internal realms of male/female, good/bad, active/passive. One must be very focused to create. The studio process instructs us to trade our overdeveloped sense of helpfulness for a compassionate disinterest in what others in the studio are doing. Discipline, the sustained focus on a task to completion, undergirds this challenge for relationally competent women. Art as a spiritual path teaches us a new way to relate, while intention and witness encourage our sense of discipline to grow and develop.

Getting back the boy or tomboy parts of the soul locates women in the realm of active competence. I watched my daughter grow up with the benefit of sports to instill discipline and physical prowess in girls. But given that even female coaches remain trained in a male model, we still have a long way to go to discover and integrate a fluid range of self skills. My daughter confounded her pitching coach, whose usual method of motivation was to encourage girls to compete against one another for speed. She saw her pitching as a form of meditation. When she was pitching well in practice, she experienced the physical flow and total self-absorption that I observed in the skateboarders. Yet her involvement in sports did not inoculate her against the damaging social images of women in our culture. Like many young women, she still struggled to accept her voluptuous body.

As fashion magazines dictate younger and younger, slimmer and slimmer, literally hipless models, I can't help but notice how much they resemble the physique of the preadolescent boy. Can we engage the boyish, dark, indigenous artist soul imaginally, or must we physically become him? Can we opt for a fluid range of self skills that allow intuition on the ball field and stamina in the studio, and engaged, erotic embodiment in our everyday life? Art can show a path.

The Divine Character: Kim's Story

I heard about Kim before I met her. The director of the Oak Park Art League, where I was to offer a class in the studio process, told me that Kim, one of the teachers of children's classes, had asked to cancel her class in order to take mine. I assumed that since she was teaching art that Kim was an active artist herself. It wasn't until several years later that I learned the significance of Kim's decision to take the class and begin her soul reunion through art. More than most students, who take a ride on my faith in the process, Kim asked a lot of questions. She seemed incredulous whenever I spoke of the Divine or the Creative Source as all giving. It was as if she couldn't believe that she could make an intention to ask for what she desired. At one point, when my explanations of intention did not seem to be getting through, I suggested to Kim that it is possible to make an intention to get to know what our intention is. She liked this idea and wrote: *I'm open to asking for help in writing my intention. Please give me guidance.*

It is always important for us to notice the words we choose and to be as mindful of them as we can be. There is a great deal of instruction embedded in our choice of one word over another. It is often only when we review our writings after some time has elapsed that we can see how language shapes our experience. When Kim writes, "I am *open* to asking for help," she is still not asking and so she will not yet receive. The Creative Source, imbued with divine compassion, simply holds us until we are ready. Kim's witness following that intention struggles with words:

Intention. My intent. My purpose—the reason for which something exists or happens. To have a goal. What do I want to have looked at? Centered. What does this mean? What goal? Guidance what path—where to? I'm open to guidance to making an intention. What are my guides? God is my continuous presence. I look to him always. So, God, what should my intention be? My intention for the next six weeks (the duration of the class) To feel centered—to feel the life force yes and to connect with my life force and let out my feelings inside to let my heart talk about what it is feeling not my head. To have pleasure to feel pleasure with my heart. Get rid of the judge—love instead.

Much of what Kim wrote arose from her engagement with the unfamiliar concepts I presented in the class. She writes out definitions as her mind balks at ideas that don't seem to fit her expectation of an art class or perhaps of spirituality, either. It is not uncommon for newcomers to the process to find themselves teary eyed when I describe the Creative Source as compassionate, as eager to grant our desires. Everyone is familiar with the adage "be careful what you wish for." Especially when I suggest the idea of pleasure as a path to divine wisdom, I often notice a physical response as shoulders drop, deep sighs unfold, and again, tears rise up. The final line of Kim's witness expresses the deep question at the heart of her confusion. She writes: *What about the child in me and growing older, are they together?*

Kim had majored in art as an undergraduate and had the usual art school ideas about materials and what constitutes "real" art. She went along with the idea of just making marks on paper and painting without an image or idea for reference; but when I introduced tape and foil as a sculpture medium, that was the last straw. As is often the case, the material that she disliked most yielded her first breakthrough in the process. I had never seen anyone use tape and foil the way Kim did. She covered large flat pieces of foil with tape as if a three-dimensional form were out of the question. As other students crunched and mashed the foil into figures, animals, and structures, Kim methodically laid down strip after strip of tape, creating first a background and then a figure to be placed in low relief atop the background. The Divine Character is an accordion-pleated creature who rose only slightly off the page, like a primordial being rousing itself from sleep (figure 12). The creature asked to be

Figure 12. *Divine Creature*, by Kim Conner. Tape and foil.

embellished with patterns of gold and green glitter paint, and Kim complied. It came to resemble an Australian aboriginal painting of the Dreamtime. Kim dialogued easily with her images, and they had lots to say to her. Her intention the day the Divine Character emerged was: *To be playful with the foil. To be willing to allow whatever happens, to happen. Let my imagination be outrageous."* In part her witness reads: *"I've enjoyed laying down the tape. I feel I'm soothing the creature taking care of rips mending and healing the creature as I tape.*

KIM: *Now that I'm really looking you over, who are you?*

CREATURE: *I'm a Divine Character from the supernatural world . . . I'm god-*

Studio Teachings

like with links to the ancestral world. I've come into being so my spiritual identity can be expressed through your creativity.

KIM: *Then I wonder if you should be painted swamp green?*

CREATURE: *Gold would transform me and I could express the spiritual inner nature.*

KIM: *What about the beauty spots?*

CREATURE: *Oh! Keep them. They are the radiance of my soul.*

As Kim continues to work on her tape–and–foil sculpture, her intention continues to evolve. She writes: *I intend to continue to experience my Divine Character and the transformation happening. To continue our conversations in transforming our experience together.* In her witness, she writes: *I'm allowing the Divine love to enfold me, move through me and express who I am. From that growing feeling of love, I began to experience strength, power, and security. This is about transformation of my self. The feeling of love began to grow into a sense of love and compassion for myself.*

It was in the act of making the design on the Divine Creature that Kim began to feel her own empowerment growing. The strength and beauty of the crosshatched patterns evoked ancestral power for Kim, as well as security. It was as if she were making symbolic marks that literally linked her with past patterns of spiritual identity that had become frayed and worn through time and neglect. The creature reminds Kim that compassion for herself is a crucial element of the transformation taking place. The simple act of paying attention through making marks is experienced as soothing and healing.

As Kim completed work on the Divine Creature, she made the following intention: *I want to experience that spiritual presence within me to flow into those areas I hold limiting. For my limitations to be transformed into new patterns. For these new patterns to express themselves onto my Divine Character my figure from the outer world but of the inner world.* The word *want* creeps into the intention, which will always evoke the state of lack. Often when we make big intentional leaps as Kim does here, the process reminds us that there are steps to transformation and we are wise to invite divine energy to enter our lives with some gentleness, allowing ourselves time to integrate our new learning. Kim's love affair with her soul is next expressed in another creature that did begin to gently reveal areas where Kim limits herself.

Most of the messages were about the divine spark within her that she had lost sight of. Her images, in a blaze of glitter paint, were eagerly

Figure 13. *Bird*, by Kim Conner. Tape, foil, feathers.

reflecting that divineness back to her disbelieving eyes. Kim is not a flamboyant person. She tends to choose her clothes from the conservative side of the L. L. Bean catalogue and walks with the physical assurance of the championship skier and tomboy she was as a girl and teenager. Her tape–and–foil bird (figure 13) reminded her that underneath that sensible exterior beats the juicy heart of a wild woman. Her witness to her bird, her second Divine Creature, says: *I do like the head and face. The eyes are friendly, goofy, and lovable. The tongue long and curvy so it can catch what it needs. I made the body folded back and forth like the past creature thinking this one would walk, unlike the others. But now I don't know because I hear whispers saying I don't need legs, don't you get it? I can fly. How?*

KIM: *I really don't get it. Now is the time to have a conversation spiritual creature, you don't have to whisper, just put it forth. What would you like to say?*

CREATURE: *Okay, okay. I will talk I had to whisper before because I had no way to express myself but the long tongue will do, so listen up. I don't want legs. I'm not about walking. It takes too long. My folds will flap so I can get where I need to go, but you're not finished with me. My body is long and I need feathers, bright, colorful feathers so people will notice me and see my beauty. Do these things for me and we will have more conversations.*

As Kim continued to work on the bird she made the intention: *To be open to whatever developments come and to connect with the sacred part of me from which I receive soul wisdom.* Her witness reads: *I confess I do like you my spiritual bird. Hard for me to believe you came from my deep inner soul. How pink, cheerful, fun and charming you are! I knew you existed but I can't pinpoint where you are from. How alive you are!* The bird replies: *I'm glad you called for me. I've been waiting for you to lighten up your soul—take it easy. Makes it easier for me to fly out from beneath all that heaviness you have insisted on going through. I say just toss it aside. Move it all out so I have more room to be. Then we can be one with the spirit.*

Recently Kim celebrated her fiftieth birthday with a ritual created especially for her by Annette, another studio artist. To prepare for this event, Kim went back and reviewed her life in five segments, one for each decade. Each of five women friends stood at a point around a circle of candles set on the floor. At each spot Kim spoke of life events and honored especially important people who had loved and sustained her in that time period. In her earliest years, it was her grandmother. For a period of time it was her father, who taught her to ski and entered her in her first race, which she won. At several points there were teachers who encouraged and supported her artmaking when there was little else that interested her in school.

As Kim shared the most recent five or so years of her life, I learned that the year prior to taking the studio process class for the first time, she developed a mysterious condition in which her right side became unaccountably numb. Kim is a preschool teacher and the mother of two active boys ages ten and twelve. Her husband, Bill, is a theatre designer who travels frequently. Kim has always managed the household. Every aspect of her life demanded that she work hard to sustain others. With nothing to replenish herself, Kim's soul had slowly begun to starve. She had even taken on an additional volunteer responsibility at a hospice program, helping grieving children make art projects. The Creative Source often guides us into situations to work with others who can mirror back to us some essential aspect of our own being that has become lost.

Kim's numbness became acute during a time when her husband and sons were all away. In solitude her body mutely cried out to her. A friend accompanied her to the emergency room for tests that revealed nothing. Kim's numbness was soul deep and not visible on an X-ray. One day two friends dropped off a bag of art supplies, a stroke of divine intuition. Kim says she had forgotten she had ever even made art. Once a printmaker and stained-glass artist, she had given all that up because of safety concerns when her first son was born. Another friend, the one who recommended my class, recalls thinking it odd that when their children played together at Kim's, the activity was never art. There wasn't a crayon or a paintbrush to be found in Kim's home. The first images she created with her gift of markers and paper was a series of suns, a motif that continues in her artwork today. At some point these drawings were not enough to satisfy Kim, and she longed to be able to share her reawakening creative self with others.

Once the creative energy began again to flow and spiritually warm her, Kim's art took off. There are goddess figures, spirals, and flying beings in her work. Over the past few years, she has created a series of mandalas to deepen and celebrate her renewed wholeness. The mandalas are rich and colorful celebrations of beauty and grace. An especially poignant one is dedicated to her grandmother, who loved Kim boundlessly and mirrored her divine spark back to her in her early years. Everyone who sees these mixed-media collages senses the divine energy that is held in their designs.

When we begin to wake from an emotionally frozen state, whether induced by the restrictions of our chosen roles or from some sort of trauma, we develop new creative edges that want to grow forward. Friends and family members join in the challenge of coming to appreciate the new person unfolding before their eyes. Changes can occur in relationships with others when our creative spark is kindled. Kim's creativity had never disappeared altogether, of course. Much of it had been channeled into her work as a preschool teacher. As Kim began to nurture her own art process, a coworker complained that her teaching had become less creative—an untrue and wounding remark, especially for a conscientious person like Kim. In most cases, those closest to us benefit from our increased presence as fully alive beings. Kim's young sons have spent many happy hours making art with their mom around the dining room table. As Kim lives more fully as an engaged artist in the community, she instructs her boys in many subtle ways. She provides mandala artmaking classes in the teen program at her church, where her students see her as a wise and compassionate teacher. Through sharing artmaking Kim is open to their spiritual questions in a unique way. When the family renovated their second floor, Kim's husband lovingly redid a room expressly for studio space.

For many of us who have been loved imperfectly and inconsistently in our lives, the divine energy of the Creative Source can seem like the sun, hiding behind clouds more often than shining and helping us to shine. Kim's choice in her birthday ritual to focus on each person who has embodied the sun in her life, to remember her grandmother's love through the rose mandala series, creates her special spiritual path through art. It is no accident that the sun began her journey to wholeness and continues to be a predominant totem in many of her works. Her connection to the Divine through artmaking enables Kim to be a conduit for powerful, nurturing sun energy in the lives of all who know her.

Kate in the Artist's Garden: Sallie's Story

Sallie's involvement in the studio practice coincided with her oldest son graduating from high school and leaving home for college. That same spring she graduated from art school herself, a process that Sallie had spread out over a number of years to accommodate her responsibilities as a wife and mother of two sons. The studio both filled the void left by finishing her formal art education, providing a group of artists to relate to, and afforded a transitional space to explore the new self that was emerging as she began to claim an artist identity. Sallie describes herself as living a "dual existence." Every summer she returns to her family's rustic New Hampshire home, the touchstone of her early life. Although her family moved often when Sallie was young, the house in New Hampshire was a constant presence, remaining unchanged since she was seven years old. New Hampshire represents the "happiest parts of a happy childhood" in which Sallie spent all her time exploring nature, reading, sketching, and imagining life as a Native American as she searched for arrowheads in the woods. As an adult, she continues to return every summer and, admittedly with a bit of guilt, forgets her own family as she sheds her roles as wife and mother and rejoins her family of origin in the one-hundred-year-old wood-frame house that holds their collective history.

Sallie characterizes the two selves that she inhabits as the eternal tomboy and the dutiful good girl. She remembers puberty as being "traumatic." She couldn't continue life as a tomboy and, at that stage, life identities were clearly divided up along gender lines. "Boys had all the things I wanted," she says—like freedom to explore, play sports, and not take care of others. All the interesting female possibilities seemed to fall to "bad girls," and Sallie, daughter of a minister, was not one of those. The studio process became the liminal space where the tomboy and the good girl could meet and begin to dance together and create new possibilities. Her intention for the first day is: *I want to let go . . . I want to go deep down inside. I want to touch my feelings. I'm thinking I cover up the dark stuff . . . Look for the pleasure. Do I ever let myself look for Pleasure? I am apprehensive—afraid—of this class, but I am here. My intention for this first day is to find the pleasure in making marks. My intention is to discover what I really feel.*

I always encourage artists to notice their use of the word *want*. To want is to not have. The Creative Source will give us what we ask for, but not what we "want." Sallie writes more than a few words to explore and finally get to her true intention: to find pleasure and to discover what she really feels. Her first experience is the drawing workshop where we move from a small piece of paper and one color of oil pastel to a large piece of paper taped to the wall and whatever colors we choose. Drumming music is playing during our drawing time. Drawing this way is a means to make a path into the Creative Source quickly and to reduce our resistance by making it harder to think, harder to judge, easier to enter our body wisdom through the loud percussive beat, through standing up and simply "making marks," not "drawing." Sallie's witness reads:

This drawing tells a story. I know because I wrote it on the drawing. There's a tipi in a wood and there are tall, icy peaks—mountains in the background. The sky, what you see of it, is dark and threatening. There is snow on the ground and it is near sunset—the snow is lit with red. But the red is also blood. My menstrual blood and the blood of the massacred Indians and the blood of my shattered dreams. There are plants—strange, ghostly plants growing up out of the water in the foreground. And a reflection of the moon or sun? A black cauldron maybe. A bank of bloody sunset snow. There is a border around this drawing that takes the shape of the paper, but it is broken into and out of—it contains, but it does not confine or hold everything within. And there are mountains in the border, at the bottom and the ghost-roots of the plants. There is a little red child in (on?) the tipi. There is a half-opened door to the tipi. Come in Lone Wolf. Am I the Lone Wolf? There are paths and a huge red forked tongue. Am I lying? Are you lying to me, picture?

Sallie continues in her witness to notice what felt good to her, to thoroughly describe her use of colors, to note her judgments of herself and others. She notices that she could have continued making marks for longer than the allotted time. Then she checks back in with her intention: *Did I make any move toward my intention? Do I know what I really feel? I know I love red and black and white and brown. I like my white tipi. I like those black mountains with the red outlines at the bottom of the border. I like movement—dancing while I'm drawing. And I like stories. And I like to say I'm afraid when I'm afraid and I don't have to act on that fear. Can't I just feel it and let it come with me? I think it's inherent in who I am and I can live with it. I don't want to have to explain it or give it up.*

By describing her drawing so thoroughly, Sallie extends the time she spends looking, seeing, and feeling her experience. When we stay with our experience we come to truth. Artmaking allows us to stay with feelings—fear, for example—without turning away or getting too busy to notice. We are moving when we draw, so our feelings do not clot in our bodies but are more likely to move through us and out rather than freezing our muscles and building tension that results in constriction over time. Even though Sallie could have continued making marks, stopping is also part of the process. We stop before we are completely fatigued or overwhelmed, but not so soon that we stay entirely on the surface. Sallie has sketched out the contours of who she is in this complex, rich, and metaphorical layering of marks on paper.

I originally got to know Sallie when I joined a writer's group while working on my first book. We gathered around Sallie's dining room table in her cozy and cluttered house. She first learned about the studio process by listening to me struggle to articulate it in my writing. I was surprised when she chose to partake of the process; for on the surface she seemed to have her creative life well in hand and to be a bit reserved and skeptical of things bordering on "spiritual" or "therapeutic." The walls of her home are filled with watercolor landscapes of her New Hampshire experiences done on fine Arches paper and tastefully framed. Like Kim, Sallie had some classical views of art and art materials; but in addition to making more traditional artworks, she also collects lots of junk and makes found-object collages.

Sallie arrives at the studio in spite of the fact that graduation preparations for her son and visiting relatives are claiming most of her time and energy. She writes: *There are six hundred reasons why I should not be here today, but there are one or two reasons why I should and I am acting on them.* In her first painting, Sallie owns up to her dislike and disdain of the tempera paints. With the intention to *focus*, she chose colors she hates—bright pink and teal—and with gusto paints hearts and tears, symbols she considers "anathema." Still, she grasps a basic tenet of studio work, which is to accept yourself in the moment, negative feelings and all—in fact, to amplify them in order to really get to know them. She incorporates words into her painting that she had glimpsed on a tow truck on her way to the studio: "twenty-four hour heavy duty."

> *I painted it in two or three times, in at least three colors—and it keeps getting buried. Obscured. There are red tears falling down the side of the painting but they are apples and pears by the time they reach the bottom… a naked woman is trying to sneak in the side I'm starting to self censor this witness. I see things here I'm not willing to tell. Or am I dying to tell all? How bare can we get? There's a naked woman trying to sneak into this picture. I'm going to paint her clearly, let her in. . . . I'm a mom about to lose her first-born. . . . but I'm not everybody's mom and I don't have to be perfect and I don't have to do everything and I can be that silly, ugly, big-chinned warrior child and I can be*

that weeping Madonna who can't get her act together enough to get herself into the picture, but I don't have to be the twenty-four hour heavy duty lady. And Lou may be rising up and growing away from me, but he is crowned by my watchful eye and pierced by my watchful eye and he is eating my tears which are turning to apples and pears ... he's a snake, ancient symbol of wisdom. He's got colored scales to protect him and green daggers up and down his back. He'll be just fine ... Even I will be just fine even if I never did get centered and focused today.

Sallie reinterpreted the personal symbol of "the watchful eye" that feels responsible not only for her own son, about to slither like a snake off into his own life, but for all young people. Almost always when we sit with our strong concerns, especially those that seem a bit inflated, like Sallie's for endangered teens or Kim's for young children who have lost a parent, we find our way to a disconnected part of our self. The more we learn about the self pieces of the puzzle, the more genuine and useful our work on behalf of others can become. By giving herself permission to be contrary, Sallie opened a door to those things that don't fit with her conscious self-image. It was her first step, though not altogether a conscious one, in letting the "bad girl" out. Like many first paintings by those who are ripe for a change, Sallie's contained the code for all that had been kept hidden and needed to be unpacked. Her use of color and brush strokes bears witness to the energy that can be released once an artist moves through their barriers to tapping the Creative Source.

In the next several sessions Sallie worked on letting go of "being mother to the world." Her intention is: *To touch my insides. Find the magic places celebrate the day and the beginning of summer. To say with all openness, "Here I am Lord." To answer calls from within. My intention is to have fun. Any questions? Any issues? How do I go about becoming an artist? It's too late to become an artist. The question is, what does the artist within me want to create and want to explore ... What do you do when you are displaced, I will explore this split in my life today. My intention is to explore New Hampshire and Chicago and what I feel about this split.*

Sallie's subsequent work in tape and foil (figure 14) yielded exquisite and instructive images of two parts of herself. The first image is Luna Moth. Sallie lovingly created this creature with fine detail. Crafted out of aluminum foil and masking tape, the Luna Moth has two sets of wings.

Figure 14. *Luna Moth/Dancing Girl*, by Sallie Wolf. Tape, foil, found stuff.

One set of wings represents her New Hampshire life; the other symbolizes Oak Park and her present family. After describing the image in her witness, Sallie began a dialogue: *Talk to me, Luna Moth you are a two-sided creature.*

LUNA: *I come out of your past— kindergarten, you hatched me then.*

SALLIE: *I wanted you. The teacher let you go. I couldn't believe she let you go and yet I know it was selfish to want to kill you and keep you all to myself, spread flat in a cigar box maybe, on a bed of cotton.*

LUNA: *I came back to you.*

SALLIE: *Going to New Hampshire last week surprised me. How beautiful it was. How much I loved the smells, the sounds, the feel of the air. I didn't need anything else. And then I found you squished on the road it was a gift from my past. Was I a child again in New Hampshire? Just me and my mommy. No kids. No husband . . . Your Oak Park wings are bigger.*

LUNA: *But not as firmly attached.*

SALLIE: *I could fix that next week. I think I want to make my moth a girl with two feet to stand on and five arms to try and do everything at once.*

LUNA: *Balancing will be the trick . . .*

SALLIE: *The metaphor is always the butterfly hatching out of the cocoon. I'm waiting for a girl to hatch out of the moth!*

LUNA: *Where is the woman?*

SALLIE: *She's in there, I guess. Woman Moth Woman Moth . . . Moth—just slightly more than half the word Mother. . . .*

The next part of Sallie to emerge is what she first calls the *"Me-doll" skinny, like I was as a kid, but with boobs—I thought of them as Big Boobs but they're not, especially after I bound them with tape and foil, nearly strangling myself to make a neck to hold my head. No face yet. I'm thinking big red nipples—maybe brown. Real pubic hair. This moth and this doll are holding each other up . . . The Oak Park wings may be bigger but the New Hampshire wings are stronger. But I am outside the moth but I need the moth to help stand, to help me dance. I'm dancing with the Moon Goddess. I'm dancing with the Luna Moth . . . no faces yet. No features. We're still emerging, this moth, no this goddess and I.*

In a subsequent session, Sallie continues to work on the dancing girl. Her witness reads in part: *The most fun I've had here I think is dressing my doll. A black patch of pubic hair. Red glass bead nipples. Wild gray hair. A scarf like I'd never wear. Leggings in blue silk, what a fashion plate. She had been bent, to ride the moth, weighing it . . . Where do these images come from? That doll is me—a climber, hanging by my knees, half-naked—a free-spirited child. That's who I once was—someone I miss right now. I don't like the prudish, worry-wart person I'm becoming, always disapproving of this, that and the other thing . . . I don't know how I've become so judgmental except I'm always in reaction against something. Against cars and drivers, porn on T.V. and tooth whiteners (try gesso) and ads for vaginal lubricants and English sparrows and perfectly manicured lawns and lawn care services and mobile phones and Wisk and junk mail and Venture and sales on Thanksgiving Day. I want to be that climbing, half-naked child/woman again, dancing with the moths in the moonlight (and mosquitoes?).*

With Dancing Girl holding the reins, Luna Moth has a chance to fly in some new directions. Sallie winced at that summary of her images when she read the manuscript; and maybe it feels a little too glib or corny. Images don't promise a simple, happy ending. Dancing Girl, like my Dark

Boy in the next story, carries edited parts of the self that throw up red flags. Dancing girls, after all, abound; but they are usually dancing for an audience of paying customers in a strip club. Sallie's girl dances for the sheer joy of moving her body.

Our culture offers little room for mature women beyond the mother role. Once reunited with Dancing Girl, the artist is born or reborn. Through Dancing Girl, Sallie reclaimed her sense of humor and recovered the path to the place of nonjudgment and physical engagement with the natural world that her tomboy self knows so well. It was clear that Dancing Girl didn't need Sallie's overserious vigilance and protection. As time went on, Sallie created a series of moths and dancing girls. As she continued to let her mother role recede, she also got into exercise and weightlifting and returned to that pre–wife–and–mother place to find the vitality and spark to reinvest into her creative life. I'm not sure if she is dancing yet.

Sallie is also a writer and has published a children's picture book. She has had a story incubating inside her for years that seemed more complex, perhaps a novel or a work of young adult fiction. She decided to use the studio process and make an intention *to find the story through the art.* Artists commonly sabotage themselves by becoming mired in internal arguments about whether they are a painter or a writer, a visual artist or a word artist. Sallie's solution was to employ the art to excavate the story. It took several years for Sallie to trust the process enough to really use it. She says she wanted it to work "behind [her] back" because the possibility of getting what you ask for is "too direct, even feels selfish and unmindful of others." As Sallie discussed her fear and reticence to use intention directly, she realized how her deeply ingrained Christian upbringing affects her as an artist. Predicated on a sense of scarcity of resources, the worldview she grew up with taught her that getting what she wants might mean that someone else has to do without. Sallie decided to explore these issues through the story that she had been carrying around inside herself—the story of a young girl named Kate and her encounters with an older woman artist. Sallie's intention, to discover the story through the art, leads her to the disowned "bad girl" part of herself. The group nature of the studio was ideal for Sallie to explore the bad girl. She could eat more than her share of the cookies set out for snack breaks, not help the new artists, use lots of materials, and work entirely in red if she chose. These symbolic acts of rebellion accomplished the goal of loosening the remnants of that constricting sense of being "mother to the world." Though powerful enough to manifest the intention to know the bad girl and actually let her out, these gestures remain harmless to others.

As time went on, Sallie refined her intention to include *letting the bad girl out in the garden, receiving whatever comes and letting the story emerge through the pictures.* Sallie worked on images that had until then existed only in her imagination: the house in which the artist lived and her garden, where much of the early action in the story takes place. As the story began to arrive through Sallie's witness writings, she read them aloud and many of us in the studio began to feel we were hearing installments of a lively book. Sallie found it uncanny how things just came. Soon we knew that Kate was an eleven-year-old staying with an unmarried aunt while her parents were away doing research in another country. We peered over Kate's shoulder as she snuck into the artist's backyard to explore. We listened in as Kate and her friends at school speculated that the artist might be a witch because she lives alone with cats and has wild white hair.

Sallie began to enjoy the magic of putting down her bucket and pulling up story fragments from the well of all possibility. The process gave her the power of not having to be in control. The paradox of giving up control and receiving power in return astonished Sallie. When we step into alignment with the Creative Source, we experience an enchanted state of effortlessness. As other studio members became invested in her characters and story, Sallie met her old challenge: fear of not meeting the expectations of others. The bad girl had emerged in Kate, but Sallie's dutiful alter ego was still close by.

Recently Sallie received an artist's grant to work on another project. For over eight years she has looked at the moon. She creates charts and graphs of her observations. She notes when she looks and when she forgets to look. The Moon Project is a vehicle of awareness for Sallie. It provides a kind of discipline in that she must accommodate the moon's schedule to accomplish her aim. The paradox is that in noticing the moments not seen, she becomes more aware of the opportunities around her. The project is simple and elegant and began because one day Sallie noticed the crescent moon in the east and didn't know what to make of the moon rising in the morning. She realized then that her suburban life in

Oak Park was relatively disconnected from nature and that she was hungry for a closer relationship to the natural world. This, she felt, would help her to locate and touch her own inner wisdom. She became, in her own words, a "preliterate person," discovering the moon and its cycles first-hand. She was excited to be teaching herself. The "watchful eye" that appeared in her early studio painting became a device to chart the location of the moon in relation to the perceived horizon.

Unlike the New Hampshire countryside, the flat Midwestern landscape and densely built-up grid of houses surrounding her Oak Park home made Sallie work to see the moon. This work takes her to a place where she is aware of her smallness in the grand scheme of life, and it reminds her of a different relationship to time. Sallie noted that in the artist's residency that her grant provided, where her intention was to work on the Moon Project, it took her six days to slow down and feel her way into the work. She notes that her powers of observation have grown through looking at the moon: "no matter what one looks at intently, when you draw the world, you see the world more."

Early in making the Dancing Girl, Sallie noted in a witness that *the moon charts would make a great backdrop for dancing girl.* As the artist in Sallie comes more to the forefront of her life, and honors each element of her being, she is able to combine the discipline of the moon charts, the adventure and playfulness of the dancing girl, and the ancient wisdom and nurturing order of Luna Moth to bring forth *Kate in the Garden* as a fully realized work of fiction. Like many artists who have engaged deeply with the studio process, Sallie has incorporated intention into her life beyond the studio as well. "It gives you a starting place," she says, "regardless of what you are doing."

The Indigenous Soul: Pat's Story

The way teachings come to me is messy and circuitous. When I thought about how to write about some examples of teachings that come through artmaking, I realized that it is harder than it looks. Themes and ideas thread their way through many images over days, weeks, and years. The place of all possibility, from which images come, is not governed by linear time. I have had unfinished images complete themselves through a chance encounter, as if a stranger had handed me a puzzle piece I wasn't even consciously looking for. Whether we realize it or not, all image makers are part of a vast collective web. We collect and absorb patterns, colors, and stories on a deep level. Also, those artists who develop their sensitivity are like receptors for the images that the culture needs to have expressed.

Working in the studio, we are immersed in each other's images. We reference each other, incorporating pieces of what moves us or completes us into our work. In this way we sew ourselves together in communion. To emphasize the overlapping quality of art as a spiritual path, I have woven my own images around and through the stories of other studio artists in this book. One day, I was receiving some energy work from a woman trained in Chinese medicine and a form of bioenergetics. While reading my fields, she mentioned that the energy seemed "sticky" and something about a shy child part that needed encouragement to express herself. Under other circumstances, I might well have rolled my eyes and thought, "Give me a break, the 'inner child'?" But as she spoke, perhaps triggered by her use of the unusual word "sticky," an image that I painted over ten years ago, entitled *Tar Baby* (figure 15), flashed in my mind like a slide on an inner screen. The arrival of the image in my mind confirmed for me that Danuta's perception had merit. She did some clearing work, noting that there was sadness and grief associated with the child. After awhile she saw the child dancing. Once again an image flashed in my mind, this time one I had recently painted of a dark boy dancing on one foot, emerging from a cave or a hut, accompanied by a white bird. I described the two images to Danuta, who looked startled. "You're a prophet of your own transformation," she said. I couldn't wait to return to the studio to look at both images. I knew where the painting of Tar Baby was stored, but I didn't expect to find my witness writing easily. I opened a notebook that corresponded roughly to the time I remembered having created the image, and the witness to it was on the first page. At the time I painted Tar Baby, the full meaning of the image eluded me. The image shows a small dark boy, his hands bound, his feet shackled, his eyes closed. He stands in front of a blue–gray woman, whose sharp, red–tipped fingernails grind into her palm, drawing blood. Her severed head lies on the ground. Fire rages behind her. In the witness, I ask, *Who is this headless woman?*

Figure 15. *Tar Baby*, by Pat B. Allen. Watercolor.

HEAD: *As you can see, there was no room on the page for me so I went tumbling down.*

ME: *Who decapitated you?*

HEAD: *No one, I just fell off. There wasn't room for all those pesky thoughts . . . —Anyway, we had to shut up that stupid baby.*

ME: *Why?*

HEAD: *He wanted to say things and cry out loud about them, he's really a nuisance.*

ME: *Wait, his hands are tied, he's naked, his feet are shackled and you have your hand over his mouth!*

HEAD: *Me? Oh, I do? Are those my hands? I don't think so, I have a headache, my nails are digging into my hand so I don't feel the pain in my*

neck. That's it, I told you, he's a pain in the neck. If I could just get him to
behave! He's bad, a bad child.

ME: But he looks really sad and gentle to me.

HEAD: Looks? Looks? I can't see anything; my eyes are closed. Chicken with
my head cut off, that's me.

ME: Tar baby can you speak? No? Then can you send me your thoughts?

TAR BABY: I have to stay near to her and try to keep very still. If I'm still I
know the fire will die down. I made her head fall off because I was too loud.
I can keep quiet if she helps me. We can both be very quiet. No one will make
a peep and then it will all be okay. My hands hurt and my feet do too. I'm
very cold but I'm here and we're together that's what matters.

I ask the lock on the shackles to speak.

LOCK: I'm for safety; I'm a safety device . . .

> Ties that bind, blind
> They don't mind
> Small price to pay
> To get to stay
> Together forever
> In hell . . .
> Poor tar baby and beheaded mom! Framed by dungeon spikes, a
> family snapshot, sticky, sticky, stick together.
> Open your eyes
> Listen to cries, sighs,
> Challenge the lies
> Rise, arise
> Hell is a construction, collusion, collision
> Of needs, greeds
> Growth of emotional weeds
> Even the flames in this hell are frozen.
> Open your eyes. Feel the cold, touch the sticky, black tar baby
> Tears are his solve vent (solvent)
> Cry your tears over him, welcome him back
> His love is so great he'd die for you

ME: What can shift you two? Is there something I can offer?

HEAD AND TAR BABY: Honor us see us, hear us, don't fear us.

Figure 16. *Indigenous Soul*, by Pat B. Allen. Tempera.

Next I looked at the witness writings to the new painting of the dark boy emerging from the cave (figure 16). My intention for the painting was *Today I welcome the artist and engage with her.* I imagined painting a figure of a woman stepping out of a hut or a dark space into light. As usual, the image has ideas of its own. The character that appears is more a child in proportions. As I work on the painting another day, my intention is to understand more about creative work. I ask: *Who is the writer? Who monitors and manages the creative process internally for me? Who makes it safe and right to create?* I ask to engage again with this being, the artist, the writer. The character seems to be a boy, and in the witness dialogue he asks me, *Who were you when you were just a boy?*

ME: *I don't understand the question.*

BOY: *Yes, you do.*

Me: *I guess I don't understand.*

BOY: *Active, industrious, maker of things, when you were that . . .*

ME: *When I was maybe eight or ten I made a fence once in the backyard, it was ramshackle and I painted it. My family was horrified; they thought it looked trashy. I turned over rocks and looked for bugs. I collected rocks and burrowed under piles of leaves . . .*

BOY: *The boy who doesn't please his mother runs away from home.*

ME: *But I was a girl, I protest.*

BOY: *Don't be so literal, please. You were he-she-he-she as all children are until some circuits are cut and you forget how to play certain ways or to run or to cry.*

ME: *This is confusing.*

BOY: *No it's not. Your soul is its own best friend, a bifurcated being, Hansel and Gretel, Raggedy Ann and Andy, until it comes together.*

I am also working on a pillow at this time (figure 17). I come to the studio in the low–grade sense of wonder that I live in a lot of the time— neither freaking out about something nor ecstatic. Then studio is a refuge, a respite from headlines and news stories. It is a place to get guidance on how to act. Does it tune me to a frequency of peace so I simply don't cause as much conflict in the world? The pillow says, *Comfort can be taken in rough edges, surfaces need not be slick to be beautiful.* I have stamped some words on the pillow from another witness: *Nothing is exactly any more.* I love this aesthetic of messy edges. I love the idea of boundaries bleeding into one another. The precision of sewing real garments never thrilled me this way. The pillow says: *Comfort can come with ragged edges. You can give up thinking things must be tucked in and neat. Fall in love with the ragged, the imprecise, have you ever noticed that in nature the perfection is that abundant room is made for the imperfect? Love and honor that in the world and in people. Let everyone off the hook and put your head down on the pillow of imperfection and rest.*

I enjoy having a messy pillow arrive and reinterpret women's work. This reclaiming of all things rejected: sewing, offering comfort, making items for use in the world that don't look the way I expect. Doing all this with a different aesthetic, a new agenda that reclaims simple means and thumbs its nose at a clean sleek interpretation of beauty. The witness says:

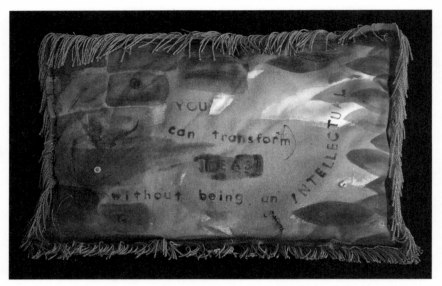

Figure 17. *Pillow*, by Pat B. Allen. Canvas, paint.

Fuck you sleek, shining wrinkleless beauty, welcome stains and edges showing. I write: *I feel a manifesto coming on, an articulated aesthetic of the poor, tired, and crumbling yearning to be set free and danced into new forms.*

I return to the painting of the dark boy / artist / writer. The idea "indigenous person" comes into my mind. How to locate the indigenous person in the soul? The definition of *indigenous* is "having originated in and being produced, growing, living, or occurring naturally in a particular region or environment." A dark boy is indigenous to the region of my soul. This word is very close to *indigent*. To be indigent is to "live in a level of poverty where real hardship and deprivation are suffered and the comforts of life are wholly absent." Indigent/indigenous. Often indigenous people end up indigent when colonizing forces move in.

BOY: *You impoverish and don't nourish what is native to your soul.*
ME: *Me?*
BOY: *All of you in the human realm. There are parts you separate and starve. You can't redeem one without the other. The mother who is unfree restricts and deforms her child.*

Roundabout, rhythmical story and play are how studio teachings emerge. Is it important to say anything more? When these words are

Studio Teachings

spoken and images witnessed in a group, without explanation or attempts to decode them, do they create change in us below the level of cognition? I think so. Part of the work seems to wander back to a place of knowing that came before books and theories in lines of type marching over a page colonized our brains. Sometimes when I sit on an airplane and every passenger's nose is buried in a book, I just look out the window and imagine myself jumping down into the sumptuous softness of the clouds. How quickly awe wears off! When we read our witness writings to each other in the studio, I often feel that we are sitting around a campfire and telling our dreams, pulling out of ourselves a deeper truth than the beginning, middle, and end that can be committed to straight lines of prose.

*

6

Renewing Tradition

At some point all of us need to engage intellectually and emotionally with either the spiritual and religious traditions we were born into or alternatives we have been drawn to as adults. This need is both personal and transpersonal. "There seems to exist a correspondence, which is not necessarily causal, between transitions in cosmic planetary cycles and changes in the religious and cultural symbols that appear on earth during various times" (George 1992, 64). The appearance of feminine symbols in spiritual discourse may be a need not only of individual women seeking a more resonant face for God, but of the planet itself. We might imagine, as scientist James Lovelock does, that the planet is a living being, whom he has called Gaia. Perhaps She wants to show Herself to us in new ways because the planet itself has reached a point in Her cycle where that is necessary.

There is a legend in Jewish tradition that the feminine aspect of God, the Shekhinah, argued with God when he banished Adam and Eve from the Garden of Eden. The Shekinah went into exile with her children (Patai, 1990, 158). Our job, some mystics teach, is to restore Shekhinah to God through acts of compassion and justice. While for generations the feminine aspect of Judaism has been somewhat dormant, now, not only in the egalitarian Jewish Renewal movement but even in Conservative and Orthodox worlds, feminine energy is seeking expression.

The way that religious symbols change is through our interactions with them. Symbols such as the cross in Christianity and the various deities in Hinduism change according to the way artists and people of faith depict them, compose prayers to them, and construct their places of worship. While there may be people who are born into a faith and culture that fit them exactly and allow them to grow and develop fully, many others seek out different paths. Important breakthroughs are often made and new definitions created when people from outside a faith tradition bring new eyes and ears to its texts and rituals. Saint Paul was a Jew named Saul of Tarsus who, although he never met Jesus, became the founder of Christianity as a religious system. "Paul's meditations on the significance of the Christ became the basis of Western understandings of Jesus' purpose, at least as much as the disciples did" (Segal 1990, xi). Martin Luther, frustrated with corruption in the Roman Catholic Church, founded Protestantism.

In contemporary times, boundaries between faiths are sometimes more permeable, admitting and incorporating customs of other groups. The insight meditation teacher Sylvia Boorstein and many others have sojourned in Buddhism and brought meditation and other practices back to enrich the Judaism of their families of origin. This is another manifestation of balancing energies, both personal and collective, of the innate drive to unfold and move toward wholeness. Image making is a valuable way to explore and integrate the received truths of any system and sift through what attracts us and has meaning without swallowing whole or being swallowed whole by another belief system. The Creative Source longs for Its stories to be told and retold, embellished and rejuvenated.

As manifestations of collective energy, archetypal symbols belong to all of us as the legacy of human creativity. Mindfully traveling through spiritual traditions via artmaking requires some sensitivity and a very clear intention. Mexican and Native American influences deeply inform the Judaism of Rabbi Lynn Gottlieb, whose congregation is in Albuquerque, New Mexico. Her respectful use of Spanish language in services and incorporation of Native American values and customs in ritual grow naturally from her engagement in her landscape (1995).

When I am drawn to an icon or image from another tradition, I familiarize myself with its original context and subsequent interpretations in order to better understand its message for me. When Kali, a familiar visitor to my artwork, was joined by Kwan Yin a few years ago, I was surprised. I knew little about Kwan Yin, the Chinese Goddess of Compassion. The two figures had a conversation. I looked up some pictures of Kwan Yin to better portray her attributes after I noticed that she looked rather masculine in a small image I painted (figure 18).

On reading further, I learned that she had originally been a male figure, the Bodhisattva of Compassion named Avalokiteshvara; over time,

Figure 18. *Kwan Yin*, by Pat B. Allen. Gouache.

the widespread devotion of women to Avalokiteshvara seems to have effected his metamorphosis into the female figure Kwan Yin (Boucher 1999). The writer Sandy Boucher says this about how aspects of spirituality enter a culture: "They come in through people—individuals who recognize a particularly compelling expression of our humanity in practice, a divine figure, a belief, a system, and make it real in their lives" (p. 5). We are all invited to become familiars with any manifestation of a divine force and to add what we learn to the rich story pool that animates human imagination. It is only through the devotional acts of humans that these deities begin to gain power in the human sphere. We dwell in the place of all possibility through our images and eventually learn what we've been called to learn. The artmaking process calls us to enter the place of no-judgment, where we are free to converse with Kali, Abraham, or the Golden Calf, for that matter.

Religious leaders may not be comfortable with the idea of retelling stories. It is interesting to learn how your faith group of origin approaches the idea of story. For example, the Catholicism of my youth didn't spend much time with the "official" story of the New Testament. We did not read the gospels as students but instead focused on the catechism, a collection of precepts we were to memorize and recite, but certainly never question. Perhaps because learning through inquiry was forbidden in the religious environment of my youth, I was delighted as an adult to find my way to Judaism, in which questioning the story and retelling it—what Rabbi Arthur Waskow (1978) calls "Godwrestling"—is the highest expectation of Jews.

I am personally energized by the Jewish belief that one story will yield an infinite store of wisdom to anyone who intentionally engages with the text. This view invites exactly the sort of approach to imagery that the studio process offers us in a very concrete and hands-on way. However, even a tradition like Hinduism, whose stories are the same and the characters very well developed, allows for different interpretations of the physical appearance of Shiva, Lakshmi, and other deities. Building Bridges, a Catholic art organization that oversees the creation of contemporary icons, has added plaques with images of Dr. Martin Luther King, Jr., Harvey Milk, Native American holy family groupings, and even an image of the Christ as a dark-skinned woman. I particularly love their image of the Catholic Mary, her Hebrew name—Miriam—emblazoned under the image of her holding a Christ figure that holds a Torah scroll. WeMoon, a women's art collective, solicits women's art every year for a calendar and note cards that celebrate the Divine Feminine as a wellspring of inexhaustible variation. Their work opens our eyes to the celebration of the Creative Source in everyday life. Images of the Divine that resemble us are deeply empowering. Otherwise, we are subtly led to equate all those who look like the picture of what our culture calls "God" with an inordinate amount of authority.

I had a powerful experience of "seeing God" one day at, of all places, a Six Flags Great America theme park. It was a steamy summer day and crowds of people were milling about the park. All of a sudden a small black boy, about two years old, realized he had become separated from his mother and began to wail. The instant I began to look around for either the mother or a staff member, an enormous black woman in a bright flower-print dress wheeled around and thundered, "What's the matter, baby?" Standing slightly behind the child, I felt myself enveloped in a force field of energy that surrounded and protected that child and made a space in the crowd around him. Within seconds the woman had scooped up the child and was talking to him about finding his mother.

I was reeling from the impact of smacking into the woman's energy field, which felt like pure, powerful love; all I could think was "She is what God looks like to me!" Sometime later I made the artwork in figure 19, which hung over the altar space in my Oak Park studio for four years. Surprisingly few people commented on it over the years. One day Fenson, a black teenage boy I worked with through our local alternative school, asked, "Who's the black chick?" I answered: "She is my image of God." He just solemnly nodded his head in assent.

The stories in this chapter demonstrate the possibility and power of new renderings of old spiritual stories and images. Annette's story is the first in this chapter, followed by my story of *Sabbath Bride*, an image in which I explore the feminine face of God in Judaism. I invite you to reflect on your own religious background and current spiritual practice as you read this section. Notice whether questions come up for you. Is a personal, private spiritual practice enough? Is our engagement with images of the Divine a dodge around dealing with the pain of the world? How does art-making lead to action or support action? These are questions that ebb and flow for me. Judaism teaches that our responsibility is twofold: *tikkun ha-olam* and *tikkun ha-nefesh*. We are called at once to heal and repair the world and to heal and repair our own soul. This is a restless edge for me that grows out of spiritual engagement. The Catholicism of my youth focused mostly on the afterlife. This emphasis, as Annette also learned, challenges one to suffer enough to become worthy of heaven. Two of my heroes are Dorothy Day, founder of the Catholic Worker Movement, and Rabbi Abraham Joshua Heschel, who wrote many important books and marched alongside Dr. Martin Luther King, Jr., in the civil rights movement. Traditions, like the images that support them, grow and change as

Figure 19. *What God Looks Like*, by Pat B. Allen. Tempera, glitter.

a result of the actions of the faithful. Art gives us a constant opportunity to examine and renew our beliefs, elaborating and expanding the faith traditions and spiritual practices that sustain us.

Resting in the Embrace of the Dark Mother: Annette's Story

When Annette first came to the studio, she never mentioned her early experiences with art or that her mother was an artist. Instead, from time to time, she would bring boxes of markers, paints, or other supplies as gifts to the studio. "They were lying around not being used," she said, as she added them to the shelves for others to share. I got to know Annette first in her role as a shamanic healer. Friends mentioned her journeying sessions, her talent for traversing the veil between worlds, her work in soul-retrieval. A clinical social worker by profession, Annette found her way to shamanic training when she discovered *Shaman's Drum* magazine and the work of Sandra Ingerman (1991). She experienced a soul-retrieval herself and found a community of others who understood travel to the spirit dimension. Annette had lived a secret shamanic life since childhood.

Annette led a "trance dance" session at the Open Studio Project, where a group of us danced blindfolded to drumming music and then drew and painted our experiences. For me, the dancing was such a profound experience of ecstatic embodiment that the painting activity seemed superfluous. I vividly remember the exhilaration of feeling completely at home in my body, with electrifying energy making me feel joyful and alive. I didn't shower for days afterward to prolong the vivid sense of being fully flesh and bones. I wondered how Annette could bear being still during the trance dance. Our wearing blindfolds, which helped to inhibit judgments and self-consciousness, meant Annette had to watch out and make sure we didn't crash into each other or the walls., In the painting I created afterward, I encountered the black dog that had been an early totem and guide of mine. He laughingly welcomed me to the realm of instinct and body. He reminded me that the ultimate aim of the creative process is to help us locate the joy and power of our physicality.

When Annette later signed up for a studio class I was surprised. Art seems a bit staid next to the power of shamanism and ecstatic dance. At a later time I experienced a soul-retrieval with Annette, and she once journeyed on my behalf to seek an answer from the spirits when it seemed my marriage was dissolving. The answer she brought gave me the faith to continue working for resolution of our problems. I mention all of this with Annette's permission; I think one of the teachings the Creative Source is trying hard to convey right now is the mutuality we need to embrace in our quest for wholeness and healing. We are meant to pass the teacher's staff from one person to another, to follow each other when we are in need, and not to become too wedded to our roles as teacher or student. Annette and I both grew up in the hierarchical Roman Catholic Church, where power flows in one direction only—from God to the Pope to the priest. The circular exchange of teaching in the studio shows us another way.

Annette became a regular presence at Studio Pardes during her work in the Creation Spirituality graduate program that was founded by Matthew Fox, a dissident Catholic priest. Fox views the creative process as sacred. In fact, Annette has incorporated collages of spiritual principles into her doctoral work, opening the wisdom of the images to others. The studio became a venue for Annette's personal struggle with spirit versus matter. Her initial works were colorful and amorphous. Her witnesses spoke of dire Cassandra-like prophecies from the spirit realm. Instead of a dialogue between Annette and her image, her witness writings seemed like spirit voices aiming to instruct the masses. I had a strong sense that Annette's intuitive gifts burdened her with an exaggerated sense of responsibility.

The beauty of the witness process is that because no comments are made, all words simply hang in the air while those of us in the room simply keep breathing. All words will speak to someone, and the speaker feels the energy or aridness of her words for herself without needing to be told. The eloquent and the learned eventually begin to realize that they are performing and let that acknowledgement enter the witness, too. It isn't bad or good; it simply is. Annette might read a Cassandra-like piece about the doom of the planet as if she alone is responsible for this awful plight. After a short pause, someone else says, "I'll read" and begins to describe a drawing of her child and how fearful she is of letting him go as he matures. The witness space shows us wholeness by giving equal time and weight to mundane observations as to brilliant metaphysical insights. We are reminded that our task is to keep breathing through both, and this balances us. As Annette spoke from the place of spiritual teacher, I found myself uncomfortable at times. As a person often given to making lofty speeches, as well as one frequently gifted with powerful information, I am especially grateful for her holding that seat and therefore that mirror for me.

After the attacks on September 11, 2001, Annette volunteered to create an art piece for our west-facing windows in the studio. Hundreds of cars drive by them daily, and we hoped to offer an image even to those who might not ever enter the studio. Through her collages, she conveyed the idea that the destruction of the World Trade Center towers was an act of transformation as well as destruction. Kali appeared in the second window with her sword of truth, presiding over the cataclysm. The final window is a golden web of images that made visible the insight that was fleeting for many, that this devastating act revealed the interconnectedness of all life.

Gradually, Annette's work began to move into life issues and her personal story—the subtext that is always beneath our spiritual searching. At the age of four or five, Annette dreamed of swinging on the stars and moon in the night sky. She was painting rainbows across the darkness and calling out in exuberant ecstasy for others to notice the beauty and to rejoice with her. She recalls being filled with an intense joy and a longing to share it with others. She called and called, but no one answered her; no one joined her. In the dream, Annette quietly closed her box of paints. She dates the loss of her deepest connection to her own soul to this time.

Annette was born into a devoutly Catholic family that was poor and had a heritage of physical and mental illness. The mystical ecstasy of her earliest childhood became overshadowed by her family's stern belief that suffering equals holiness. All the passion and wonder she had initially found in the natural world became transferred to Jesus and to Mary, his Blessed Mother. A large cottonwood tree grew in Annette's backyard, out of place in the New England landscape. As a tiny girl she would meet with Jesus in the tree, entering through the wound of a cut-off branch. She told no one of her adventures and as she grew up tried and tried to reconcile her secret mystical experiences with the harsh teachings of the Church. If the nuns taught that Jesus loved those who suffered as he did, Annette tried to embrace any suffering that came her way as a road to holiness. To please Jesus, she never complained about the abuse and deprivation she suffered, but offered it up to him instead.

As a teenager she turned her artistic gifts to painting lilies in honor of the death and resurrection of Jesus. She identified with Mary Magdalene and painted roses, the secret symbol of the one woman whom Jesus allowed in his circle. Although Annette's mother was a skilled seamstress and decorative tole painter, she never encouraged Annette's artistic efforts. She admonished her instead to focus on music, especially church choir.

Her mother's stance softened when Annette was ill, at which time art supplies and supportive attention were both forthcoming.

Annette's serious childhood bouts of meningitis and rheumatic fever allowed some time and space for her to dream, create, feel some love from her mother, and continue with her mystical explorations. When one is well, Annette learned from her mother, one had better things to do than creating visual art—such as singing, practicing piano, and helping others. Even though she had won a prize for her painting and was encouraged by the nuns, Annette could not overcome her mother's rejection of her efforts. Her creativity was eclipsed by the belief that the paramount commandment was to patiently suffer and offer one's pain up to God.

The Catholic Church did not provide an outlet for Annette's natural mysticism. When she was found eating her lunch in the cemetery, trying to combine service with her closeness to the spirit world, Annette felt sure the nuns would praise her. She was keeping the souls of the dead company, she explained. The nuns called her mother, and Annette was punished. Annette felt that being in a physical body was a sign of impurity, a spiritual defect to be overcome. After all, if she were good enough, Jesus would surely gather her back into his loving embrace in the spiritual realm. Once, Annette made a charcoal drawing of a girl full of sadness and pain. This honest expression of her own emotions through art was rejected by her mother, who pronounced the drawing "awful."

As an adult, Annette made collage her medium of choice. She hunted for images everywhere; no doctor or dentist's waiting-room magazines were safe. She even convinced the staff of a local bookstore to tell her which nights they deposited out-of-date magazines in the dumpster behind the store. From science and nature magazines, Annette culled images of the solar system, distant galaxies, and the inner workings of the body's cells. From fashion magazines she harvested all the images of women she could find; all the Mary Magdalenes would be brought home. Women of color, from countries around the globe, began to manifest the Great Mother as Annette accumulated the infinite, multifaceted face of the Divine Feminine. Finally, images of herself, her mother, aunts, cousins, and grandmothers all appeared as the archetypal turned a personal face toward Annette. For it is through working with our own story that we repair

Figure 20. *Collage #1*, by Annette Hulefeld.

the world story. One witness to a collage featuring family photographs (figure 20) reads:

As a little girl, I ran to the backyard and sat under the big cottonwood tree. I imagined that all the stars, the sun, and the moon all were hung in some kind of invisible magic "stuff" that kept them from falling out of the sky or bumping me on the head. Sometimes I wondered what it'd be like if a cloud picked me up and brought me to the stars for a tea party. I of course, would dress in glittered leaves and fancy twigs. In return for the earth dirt I'd bring as a gift, stardust would appear in my pocket. If no one was looking, I'd use my baton twirler to conduct all the different music I heard from all the beings surrounding me, seen and unseen. Back then, no one would have believed me that plants have high pitched voices, or that stones snored, or that lots of birds keep the beat! Had my mother known, she would have placed me back in the bedroom. I was clever and never said a word. I just listened. Yes, I knew that if some "big God" didn't have a plan for all the wonder, I would not stay alive for too long and neither would anything else. When my mother wasn't looking or checking up on where I was, I'd take my socks off and let my feet open their eyes to the Mother earth. During those times, I heard the ants giving pep talks to each other for they had so much work to do. I always felt sad for the worms that prayed for rain, knowing when they came up from their home, some shoe sole would "moosh" them to death . . . I learned early that you had to be careful what you pray for . . . Home was and is under my feet. The pulse of Mother's heartbeat holds me to the earth and moves every step I take.

In another piece rendered in black and white (figure 21), the Great Mother speaks to Annette in her witness:

If you look closely you'll see that I am descending into the space you call the planet. I am catching and holding the fragments of destruction and forming new circles of creation. Towers dominate. Circles contain, form, and move with the rhythms of the Universe. Don't think for a moment that I am blind to your situation. I have unseen eyes that connect to dimensions beyond your human comprehension. My heart knows all. Yes, I see a cosmic explosion and I see an expansion of the global heart. Now is the time for the planetary Soul to evolve. Divinity is breaking through the human spirit, birthing consciousness. Terrorism cannot destroy Spirit—it cannot split a soul that is wrapped in my Truth, my Compassion, and my Love. Continue to take on the wings of Life, breathe my Life. Stay awake and be my breath.

The studio process helps us see the themes that reverberate for us; these themes, which take form in our images, have their roots in our earliest experience of the world. Images shed light on abandoned parts of ourselves and let us reclaim them. Yet our images are neither personal nor collective, neither therapeutic nor spiritual. They are always and at each moment both and more. Whether we begin with the personal and work

Figure 21. *Dark Mother Ascending*, by Annette Hulefeld. Collage.

toward the collective meaning, or dance with an image from the rich trove of religious history and gradually bring it down to life–size, this work is a spiritual endeavor that helps to repair the world. Every new version of the story adds a diamondlike facet to the whole. As we share these stories with each other in our words and images, even those we might never know may find a note of resonance that helps them on their journey. Through art we infuse new life and energy into the myths that sustain us.

The Sabbath Bride and Friends: Pat's Story

My major teaching image has come in the form of a giant feminine figure, the Sabbath Bride. She appears in a painting that took seven years to complete and is over eight feet tall (figure 22). She emerged from my struggle with Judaism as my spiritual path, but much of what She in–structs me about is how the creative process operates. She brings stories of women's past and shows me new ways to understand old wisdom. She remains a powerful presence in my life, challenging and comforting me as

Figure 22. *Sabbath Bride*, by Pat B. Allen. Tempera.

I continue in learning about art as a spiritual path. She has hung in my studio and now hangs in my home. She also wants Her own book, so She doesn't tell all Her stories in this one.

I have been a convert to Judaism for over twenty years when I meet with my rabbi to try to explain my dilemma. I'm intrigued, haunted actually, by a certain image, idea—this Sabbath Bride. The songs and melodies composed by the Hasidim to honor Her will not leave my mind. What can

Studio Teachings

I read, what can I study, I ask him. Oh, and there's more. I'm afraid, afraid that if I start on this path, I'll end up, well you know . . . "Having to become Orthodox?" I am relieved when he finishes the sentence, relieved to have this thought out in the open.

I listen distractedly as he acknowledges the conflict and complains that many people seem to see Reform Judaism as the "default setting" of least possible observance rather than a valid philosophical brand of Judaism focused on social justice. Is it most in tune with the practical realities of modern life, or is it a spiritually unsatisfying "lite cuisine"? What is it that I am afraid of? Starting out as a convert, I would be an unlikely *baal teshuvah*, one who after living a secular life returns to Orthodox observance. I am long married; my child is grown. But something makes me uneasy. Even considering starting down a path that I imagine could lead to a diminished feminine role gives me a chill. I have spent my life finding my voice. I imagine the eighteenth-century Jews who composed these songs that stay in my mind as men, dressed in white, walking out together to go and pray in their *shul* on Friday night to welcome the Sabbath Queen while the women stay home and take care of the children.

It has been a long struggle for me as a convert to find a balanced path in this maddening religion—not too religious for my husband's secular family, but sufficient to feed my soul; not taking on customs that feel inauthentic, yet at least considering the wisdom of ancient ideas. I often feel like I'm walking in a labyrinth with electrified walls. I talk with my friend Dayna, who was briefly married to an Orthodox man. "It makes you feel safe," she says. "You always know what to do. All the rules are there and a whole community that follows them. And there is so much beauty in the Torah." I have other friends who are creating a sort of neo-Hasidism, taking their cue from the joyful branch of Judaism that flourished in Eastern Europe in the eighteenth century. Known for their dancing and simple wisdom, the Hasidic Jews were all but destroyed in the Holocaust. My friends follow the flowering of the Jewish Renewal movement, whose most prominent teacher, Rabbi Zalman Schachter-Shalomi, is not only a direct descendant of the European Hasidim but also the holder of the World Wisdom Chair at Naropa University, the only Buddhist university in the United States. Reb Zalman has lived the paradigm shift; he embodies the possibility of a new kind of spiritual integrity. Under his amazing inspirational leadership, members of the Jewish Renewal movement seek to reclaim all the pieces: joy, justice, study, equality, mysticism. Still, I notice the women I meet in Jewish Renewal circles are uneasy even amid the egalitarian *minyan* that has met for several years in my studio and that the men still lead much of the time.

At one service a woman notices my goddess pendant and greets me as a fellow traveler. She is a practitioner of Wicca as well as being Jewish. I mumble something and turn away. Something is churning and restless below the surface that I can't dismiss as merely New Age nonsense, but it isn't showing itself clearly. My rabbi recommends some books on Kabbalah, Jewish mysticism, but they are dry and confusing. I am circling something, but I am not yet able to see what it is.

It isn't only my Jewish friends who are struggling with a sense of displacement in their faith communities. Dorie, a close friend and member of the Methodist Church, mourns the loss of a spiritual leader in her community, removed by his bishop for performing and supporting same-sex marriage. A Catholic friend confesses in tears that she can no longer sing at church, that ashes fill her mouth when she tries to pray there, even in her progressive Family Mass community. At the same time, figures of the Black Madonna and the Great Mother are showing up in her artwork.

Suddenly it becomes obvious that I need to explore this idea through creating an image myself. There are prohibitions against making images in traditional Judaism, especially any image of the Divine, but everyone I know seems to think it's quaint that I even consider them. My intention, to explore the Sabbath Bride, seems straightforward enough. I am drawn to use humble materials—black paper and tempera paint. I am surprised at what emerges; The Sabbath Bride tells me everyone is.

SABBATH BRIDE: *My bony hand covers my fertile belly. The raven will drop*
    you there in my cavernous depths and you will sleep and be replenished by
    wonderful dreams.

ME: *Am I grandiose to try and paint you?*

SABBATH BRIDE: *No. Believe me, I am lonely for the company, I arise from*
    the candle flames . . .

I notice that I have painted a menorah, not Shabbat candlesticks.

SABBATH BRIDE: *The menorah is a symbol of wholeness, seven candles, seven days. There is more but that isn't your problem right now. It is a mystical symbol: Shabbat candles are an earthly counterpart.*

ME: *I wish the flames were lit.*

SABBATH BRIDE: *In due time.*

I let the painting be; I work on other images, including a sculpture of the raven. A month passes before I return to the Sabbath Bride. My intention is *To be filled with the light of God.* But it is Saturday, a weekend workshop on Shabbat. I write for a while before I begin painting.

ME: *I feel blocked, unready to approach you. maybe because it is the Sabbath and I am making, doing, creating, in violation of the law. Yet, I still feel too stupid to be bound by the laws. Are these my laws? Will I be able to paint today? Am I just twisting the rules to think of this work as prayer? Am I the world's biggest bullshitter and rationalizer?*

She is patient as I drift off in my self–absorbed tirade.

SABBATH BRIDE: *You don't seem to want to let me get a word in edgewise . . . it is equally false to abandon your quest because you aren't following rules. That is the coward's way out. You must look at every situation, why was the rule made? How does it serve humans?*

ME (GRUMBLING): *But that's not what the rabbis say.*

SABBATH BRIDE: *Just paint.*

The all–day workshop drags along. I am stuck—a sure sign that I am avoiding painting something that the image wants, requires. Like a storm it comes: a red horn with blood tendrils extending into the skull, a wing made of multiple sections like an insect wing, a yellow Star of David in the gaping, empty eye socket of the skull, teeth parted as if to speak. I feel afraid. Why have I painted images that are stereotypically anti-Semitic? How dare I paint this? My intention comes back to me: to be filled with the light of God. The image says: *The light of God shines making what is in the darkness visible. These images are a part of what you take on in this lineage.*

I remember years ago in a mask workshop adding horns to my mask and talking about how I thought it would be great to have horns. Later, a Jewish friend who had been in the workshop told me how embarrassed she was listening to me. I was in the process of my conversion to Judaism then and was unaware of the legends about Jews having horns. Later still I learned that this legend originated in the mistranslation of a biblical passage where the Hebrew word *keren* is rendered as "horns," instead of its actual meaning of "shining or glowing," in the description of the face of Moses upon his descent from Mount Sinai with the Ten Commandments. Did I expect that it would be simple to throw myself in with this tribe and all their historical baggage?

I gaze at the painting and see a flash of a heart–shaped space. I paint it in black over the ribs, but no, it wants to be torn open. I'm too tired; I don't want to work.

SABBATH BRIDE: *Tear the space and let your fatigue pass through you.*

I tear the heart. Energy rushes through me.

SABBATH BRIDE: *You're afraid of me aren't you?*

ME: *Yes. You seem like an exterminating angel, with your insect wings and your animal's horn, your bloody heart. Maybe I better talk to Raven, he's more my size.*

I feel so tired. Raven joins the conversation.

RAVEN: *Quit your bellyaching, you ain't seen nothing yet. You'll be burned at the stake, have a stake driven through your heart before it's all through, stake your life on it!*

ME: *What does this have to do with the Sabbath?*

SABBATH BRIDE: *You're very literal, you know. Here's a question, how can you dwell in a palace in time, a place of perfection, when evil continues in the world?*

ME: *I don't need more questions; I want answers!*

SABBATH BRIDE (SOFTLY): *Do you see the moons growing on the vine?*

It is years later that I discover the meaning of the moon, its cycles, and their connection to the work. I begin to discern that the great "She," who is the Sabbath Bride as well as all the other manifestation of Divine Feminine, has a cycle of Her own far greater than I can begin to imagine. A friend recommends a book, *Mysteries of the Dark Moon* by Demetra George (1992). George writes:

> I began to question whether the disappearance of the Goddess during the last 5,000 years of patriarchal rule might not have been due to suppression and destruction by the patriarchy, but was in fact her natural withdrawal into the dark moon phase of her own cycle. Perhaps it was simply that the inevitable time has

come in her own lunar cyclic process to let go and retreat, so she could heal and renew herself. And now she must be reemerging at the new moon phase of her cycle with the promise and hope that accompany the rebirth of the light. (p. 62)

What if all the stories we tell ourselves have flaws in them, like the mistranslation of *keren*? We make up parts to make the story work according to how developed our consciousness is at any moment. Language shapes consciousness; consciousness is expressed in our actions. I begin to chart my own cycle and learn its profound effect on my creativity, relationships, and perceptions. Whenever my work or energy is at a low ebb, I react with alarm, asking myself, "What's wrong? Why can't I get anything done? Am I just lazy?" This internal dialogue points to a prejudice in our culture wherein action is valued over contemplation or rest. According to Starhawk, "Light is idealized and dark devalued in this story that permeates our culture" (1982, 21). We have ceded contemplation to the monks and priests, but perhaps now it is time for all of us to integrate this piece as well.

In the meantime, I struggle with the painting. The Sabbath Bride's seemingly dual nature rivets me. She is creator and destroyer, merciful one and judge, all at the same time.

ME: *Does your goodness burden you then with the world's shadow?*

SABBATH BRIDE: *Yes, the Christians wanted to keep only the light, to rise out of the earthly ground and be God, to transcend their human aspects. That doesn't help at all. Those are part of me and of you and are worthy of love.*

ME: *You seem to carry the projections of vermin, the horn; this line of thought is troubling to me, is it blasphemy? Am I risking a gross distortion trying to understand this? The insect wings are disturbing.*

SABBATH BRIDE: *Would a Buddhist deny an insect its place of honor in the web of life?*

ME: *No, I don't think so.*

SABBATH BRIDE: *Read Job. All that you see is a manifestation of God's energy in partnership with human beings. Read Job and then return with your questions.*

I read the book of Job. It is an annoying story. God has too many human traits. He bargains with Satan, allowing him to deprive Job of everything—his wealth, his children, his health. Job's friends come by and find him a wretched sight. Each one exhorts him to seek out his hidden sin; surely, they assume, God doesn't punish the undeserving. Job has two choices: find his sin or blame God for being unfair. What does this have to do with me? What does it have to do with Shabbat? God is not pleased with Job's friends. He rails at them: "I am incensed at you, for you have not spoken the truth about me as did my servant Job" (Job 42:7, *Jerusalem Bible*). God restores Job's fortunes. What a crazy story. Job hangs in there, holding on to the idea that God sees a bigger picture than he does.

I get two things from the story. First, don't pretend to interpret the experience of another; there is so much more than meets the eye. This is a helpful insight in refining the studio process. We make the no-comment rule that no one can speak about his or her artwork or make comments about anyone else's. It seems harsh at first, but the idea is to foster a relationship to the Creative Source by listening to the images that show up in the painting. We listen for the inexorable unfolding of consciousness. Every person has access to a higher wisdom. It can only be gained by making space for it to be heard.

These are alternative voices to the stories we tell off the top of our heads, whether those are the threadbare narratives delivered by popular culture or the parables we swallowed whole in Sunday school. It's hard to listen with new ears, but doing so is a crucial part of this practice. Long silent and hidden, buried alive between the lines of patriarchal history, forgotten voices and stories are now beginning to emerge from the Soul of the World. Our images are the messengers. It is difficult for us to really listen to the image. Much of what comes to us when we begin this work is static from our inner judge and critic, or echoes of parents and past teachers whose own grasp of truth was incomplete. It is important to hear these messages as well, to honor them and allow them to subside so that the image, finally, will speak and be heard.

Another month goes by before I return to the painting of the Sabbath Bride. I witness: *Insect wings to pass the time, relax, face it, there's something you don't really want to see right now. It feels good to do menial work, tiny delicate strokes giving structure to something fragile. What is going on here? Something is incubating and can't be pushed. No forward movement. Sit, wait, wait, sit do nothing. Feel the space between moments, the silence between words, rules change, change of scene, changing of the guard. See your life for a moment as a slow motion film of an earthquake or the stop action film of a seed bursting. Yes, a seed bursting. We don't see that moment; it occurs underground in fertile darkness. Some things are moving and you can't see them. Don't worry, sit silently sit and deeply relax. Sit.* I do not sit easily. The best I can do is to be with the painting, making tiny adjustments. That is about as close to the necessity of just being that I can usually get, and it is enough.

A dream comes: I see myself in a costume of the Sabbath Bride. It isn't a costume in the dream; my skin is painted to resemble the Sabbath Bride painting, or I am tattooed with her image. In another dream a black man speaks to me in the gutted shell of a church. He tells me my work is to found a religious theater. Weeks pass; it is fall. The painting continues to grow organically out of the original piece that held the head and torso. I add pieces of paper to accommodate the image. This patchwork process would bother me except that others in the studio do the same. Dayna works on *Faith*, a large figure of a woman holding the world together. This process feels like using a paintbrush to rend the veil between worlds. Behind our everyday life pulses a world of primal energy that forms itself into images by way of human acts of speech, writing, thinking, and painting. Ah! Painting comes very close; it captures the timeless coexistence of multiple realities. Perhaps there is a clue to the meaning of Sabbath here. I consider that the imaginal space is the perfection and wholeness we seek to taste by observing Shabbat. I imagine that if I paint joy and spaciousness and all things, they will indeed tattoo themselves invisibly on my skin, and I will wear that knowing into the world. I paint a figure eight over the central candle in the menorah.

Sᴀʙʙᴀᴛʜ Bʀɪᴅᴇ: *Stop. You haven't looked enough.*

My eye is drawn to the infinity symbol, eight, the numerical value of the unpronounceable name of God. Endlessness, continuous flow superimposed over the central candle.

Mᴇ (ᴛᴏ ᴛʜᴇ ᴍᴇɴᴏʀᴀʜ): *You seem balanced and self-contained; I am working to bring you into focus. You are the source of the apparition of the Sabbath Bride. What do you have to say?*

Fɪɢᴜʀᴇ ᴇɪɢʜᴛ: *I am a moment of stillness. In stillness is the constant subtle flow of energy. Be aware of me, I am an image to guide you. Find my stillness daily, feel my flow, follow my dance, the dance your feet were made for. Be peace, it is different from being peaceful; full of peace is different from full of peas. You will become empty, receptive, waiting. The candle flame then ignites in the space you have made in yourself.*

ME: *I have been planning to take a meditation class. Does this mean I don't go to the class?*

FIGURE EIGHT: *Take your own advice, just do it. In the time you drive to a class, interact, say hello, goodbye and return home, you could have changed your life. Simple means, no wasted effort. I am here in you every moment, never away. I memorize your every heartbeat, quiet stillness, in-action, non-action. Do less, not more, make space. Stillness is the greatest gift you have to offer. If you can be still, what others see when they behold you is their own true face.*

ME: *But the detachment of all this scares me. Won't I evaporate or drift away?*

FIGURE EIGHT: *No, you think you need to be treading water, but you only need to float.*

The following week my intention is to watch my energy and stay with it carefully. I ask this question: *Is it sacrilegious to work on the painting of the Sabbath Bride on Shabbat?* I have to trust my energy and the fact that I mean no disrespect. I witness: *Frolicking fish swimming toward the river, running through Shekhinah's veins* (figure 23). *They look so happy. Stars dancing, moons hanging on stems. Does anyone wish to speak?*

THE FISH: *We are one with life, we are one with the water yet we have form, we sparkle, we shine and ultimately we are eaten by one another. How many times do you need to hear the same story? There isn't anything to do, to say, to get to this eternal moment. Where is your energy?*

ME: *I'm tired. I need a rest.*

THE FISH: *So let go completely of painting, this writing should be writing your way out of it. Leave it on the page so that when you return we are like total strangers you've never seen, we surprise you completely. Let this moment end and be open to the next. The secret of Sabbath is to become one with nothingness, rest, annihilation of ambition. Let yourself fall like the figure dropped by the raven. Everything continues but for the moment you cease to be involved, detached you just flow on neutral, no trial no trials and tribulations. You are a dream and your sleep deepens to where dreams can't find you. When you awaken you have new eyes. You are a new dream. You are all the mystery that is. So accept your imperfections. Stay so small that you could fit inside your own ear and listen carefully.*

Figure 23. *Sabbath Bride*, detail (fish).

If painting brings me to this place of stillness then it is indeed prayer and sacred homage to the Divine. As fish are to water, I am to painting. Yes, painting this way is indeed a valid observance of the Sabbath. It would not be the same if I were painting a sign, or making a painting for sale; but in this way of working I am finding my way back to something ancient and sacred. Rabbi Abraham Joshua Heschel, author of *The Sabbath* (1951) and one of the foremost Jewish thinkers of the century, would deeply disagree with me:

The idea of the Sabbath as a queen or bride did not represent a mental image, something that could be imagined. There was no picture in the mind that corresponded to the metaphor. Nor was it ever crystallized as a definite concept, from which logical consequences could be drawn, or raised to a dogma, an object of belief. . . . Some do not realize that to personify the spiritual really is to belittle it. (p. 60)

I would argue that the way in which I made an image of the Sabbath Bride was a deeply devotional act. I would not expect someone reading this book to adopt my image of the Sabbath Bride any more than I would try to pursue the black woman who scooped up the child at Six Flags and try to get her to found a church. The point is that in order to see the Divine, one must *see* the Divine. As I and other women engage with the feminine aspects of God, we see Her in many places—in the eyes of the woman selling us fruit in the market, in our child's nursery school teacher, in our elderly mother-in-law or our roller-skating neighbor, and in each other. Rabbi Heschel's fear of dogma is groundless if we treat the image process as a continuous *midrash* that emerges over and over in new forms. To refuse to accept this form of teaching, to denigrate the power of the imagination as a means of God's instruction, is to insult God, who created that imaginative capacity in human beings. One suspects God has been waiting for us to use the imagination to praise creation rather than to perennially destroy it and each other as we have done.

An artmaking space is a *mishkan*, a portable sanctuary. Each artist working there is alone with her image and the message it brings as well as being in subtle communion with others in the space. This is a feminine form of cultural practice. The great male artists of the past had ateliers where other artists worked for them as assistants or apprentices. The studio feels more to me like a temple where we are all engaged in different acts of service to the Divine. The witness of others and our ability to struggle alongside them deepens our engagement in the process. Safety grows as we learn to travel back and forth between speaking with our images and attending to mundane tasks like washing brushes and refilling water containers for painting. The daily ordinary work reminds us that we are not ascetics flying off into the ethers but everyday mystics choosing to

Studio Teachings

dedicate ourselves to the Soul of the World by paying conscious attention to what arrives in the image—whether it's a Goddess figure, a lesson about our family, or a practical hint about how to balance the checkbook.

The work of integration happens simultaneously with the work of revelation. Washing brushes is a key task in studio practice. It engages us with the consequences of our materiality. Artists are often surprised when I tell them that some of the paintbrushes in the studio are twenty-five years old. Every time I wash a brush, rubbing the bristles firmly again and again against a bar of soap and rinsing and rinsing again until no more color comes out, I am performing an act of service. I serve the community of artists who share the brush. I honor the hog or sable or squirrel whose bristles create the brush, the tree who gave wood for the handle, the craftsman who fashioned the metal ferrule out of Earth's ore. By my action I say these gifts are valuable. I care for them. I appreciate them. I share in a subtle way with all the artists who have handled the brush. Brushes improve with use and kind handling. I have bought inexpensive brushes at flea markets for a dollar apiece. They receive the same care as the most expensive sable brush. As I rub and form the bristles against the soap, they become more resilient and shape themselves to the creative act.

Care for one's tools is an honored craft tradition. Mindfulness transforms this simple act into a meditation on our connection to one another, our responsibility to the community of creators and to the images that arrive for all of us. We are not spiritual beings when we meditate and materialists when we clean up. We are at all times multiple realities inhabiting a particular body. The conscious bringing together of the mundane and the sacred dissolves their distinctions into humble wholeness. This is one of the primary tasks of a spiritual practice: to learn to love it all and value the simple, the everyday.

When we imagine that our connection to the Divine depends on rare and special conditions, we deprive ourselves of the continuousness of life flow. We also imagine that our small acts of violence in daily life somehow don't matter, that they are separate from our "spiritual" lives. We fail to see that rushing to get somewhere makes us late, that it forces us to drive somewhere that we could easily walk, and that this is an unnecessary act of harm both to the air, which becomes polluted, and to our bodies, which become stressed out and weak. Images bring us awareness of our mistakes, our peak moments and our quiet satisfactions. If we pay attention to all aspects of the work, our discernment of the Divine in all things grows. Without the brush, there is no painting. We can no longer value our product, the art, over the brush when we wake up to their interdependence. The Sabbath Bride makes a spacious *mishkan* where I can learn and relearn these lessons.

Another month goes by before I return to the Sabbath Bride. My intention is to learn why I've been avoiding the work.

ME: *Why am I afraid of you?*

SABBATH BRIDE: *Because knowing me will change your life. You are suspended in mid-air above my cave and you can take as long as you like to fall into it.*

ME: *This Shabbat is my birthday.*

SABBATH BRIDE: *Am I invited?*

ME: *I'm not sure. I don't know if I can make that commitment. I have no idea what I am talking about. Do I think that inviting the Divine Feminine means sitting through a dull Friday night service in the synagogue? Is that really what I imagine is required? Will my family resent me, think I'm being "holier-than-them" if I demand they attend services? Will I be separated from them if I go alone? Will I lose them?*

SABBATH BRIDE: *I don't give coming attractions, stay in suspended animation as long as you need to. I've waited centuries, a while longer won't matter.*

I am struggling with the two sides of the figure: What is the interaction between them? I feel stuck most of the time, doing little things in the painting, like brightening the figure eight. Finally I attend to two small drips of paint on the leg, "mistakes." A blue drip becomes a rabbi/angel.

I thought to paint a cave around him, a spark imprisoned; but the cave becomes a house—no, a church. A cross and a swastika appear, and then the house/church bursts into flames. Then there's a pink drip; maybe it will be a little child—life and innocence to balance persecution and destruction. No such luck. Instead it becomes "insect–man," a naked, mayfly guy looking all too gleeful. Then, holding the two of them, a pair of scales appears (figure 24). This is justice?

Figure 24. *Sabbath Bride*, detail (scales).

ME (WITH MILD SARCASM): *So what is the lesson, Sabbath Bride . . . that justice is absurd?*

SABBATH BRIDE: *As usual, you don't let me get a word in. Did you happen to notice that inside the burning building your rabbi-angel is quite unscathed?*

ME: *Yes, but how is he balanced by larvae man?*

SABBATH BRIDE: *So, you think you know balance when you see it?*

ME: *Well, yes, I do think so.*

SABBATH BRIDE: *Well, think again. You could, well, one could, go to your death a martyr. Bad, right?*

ME: *Yes, very bad.*

SABBATH BRIDE: *One could be reborn as an insect.*

ME (EXASPERATED): *So what's the lesson? Nobody gets a fair deal? Everything could always be worse?*

SABBATH BRIDE: *Quit jumping to conclusions, you've got more to learn.*

I seek to understand the dark place in the Sabbath Bride. My intention is a question: *If I am dropped into this pelvis full of flames, where do I land?* I create a small image to explore what might be in there. It turns out to be a place full of glorious lights, swirling energies, in which the figure, me, is unimaginably tiny (figure 25).

ME: *It seems very random to me.*

SABBATH BRIDE: *It's not. It's just that you can only perceive the tiniest fragment of the pattern, a fraction of a fractal, so you can't see the wholeness.*

ME: *I simply have to trust that it's there.*

SABBATH BRIDE: *You don't have to.*

ME: *I do. I do have to trust, and who am I talking to anyway?*

SABBATH BRIDE: *The Soul of the Universe, the Sabbath Bride, Shekhinah, whatever you'd like to call me.*

ME: *This is starting to scare me, annihilation comes to mind.*

SABBATH BRIDE: *Annihilation isn't a concept here, purification, clarification, if you notice the stream of green in your small piece, it is a bit narrow then it reaches a wide, endless place.*

ME: *Are you saying I can be a channel for love?*

SABBATH BRIDE: *It is the sole purpose of a human life. The first step is to let go of density and return to energy.*

ME: *Do I have to die to do this?*

SABBATH BRIDE: *Not usually. Some do, it's hard work to channel light in a human form, but necessary. Accept everything that comes to you; see into it from a place of energy. Remember that the pattern is bigger than you can see and the lifeline goes into an endless well, my womb, the void. Just picture that when you lose track of what you're doing.*

ME: *Why are there different kinds of energy?*

SABBATH BRIDE: *There are three, that which emanates from the figure, the weakest because it has to travel outward through dense human form and it's just a spark to begin with. Then there's the white, swirling energy that comes from above and is multifaceted, universally so. It can end up manifesting as anything that you imagine. Then there is the green, which is My energy and it travels upward. It is love and when combined with the other two makes wholeness.*

In the picture the different energies are represented with glitter in different colors. It is as if a close-up detail of the pelvis of the Sabbath Bride was taken in a snapshot.

ME: *Why is the container of these energies a pelvis bone?*

SABBATH BRIDE: *You are a woman. You have an extra seat of love. Men*

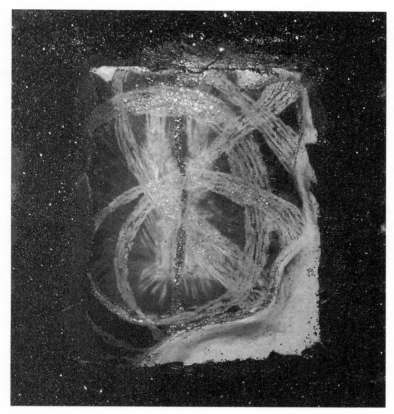

Figure 25. *Place of Glorious Lights,* by Pat B. Allen. Acrylic paint, glitter.

have just their hearts. You have a womb, which is very like a heart, a "bleeding heart," you've heard that term? It is code for feminine wisdom, the sacred heart also.

ME: *So as humans we are supposed to . . . ?*

SABBATH BRIDE: *Become conscious that you are energy, become conscious that you attract energy. Become conscious that without grounding your energy and the cosmic energy you can destroy yourself and the world.*

ME: *Okay, that's pretty simple, how do we know if we're doing it right?*

SABBATH BRIDE: *By the results, alignment of these energies never causes chaos. Not that all's a bed of roses but get used to how it feels to be lined up straight and you'll know when one is out of whack.*

ME: *But how?*

Figure 26. *Male Trilogy: Fool, Emperor, Death*, by Pat B. Allen. Gouache.

So much of my work has been to receive and express images of the feminine. I am surprised when a trilogy of male figures emerges in a series of small paintings (figure 26). They are The Fool, The Emperor, and Death, and they seem to correspond to the creator, preserver, and destroyer, a feminine divine triad that appeared years ago in my work as a series of sculptures. Intrigued, I write a witness.

ME: *How is your energy different from the female trinity?*

THE FOOL: *We're really the same—wild, electric, elemental, not departmental, sentimental, mental in green tights. I'm poised on the crown of the world, my faithful Fido in his party hat. We're both dressed for success, success of a party, that is.*

ME: *Why are you yellow?*

THE FOOL: *Yellow? Hello! Color of light, bright sight and when you block me you are full of "right." We dance against an endless sky, not bound to earth, so watch out, we can make you fly, into space without a trace, which is why you need the other guy.*

THE EMPEROR: *I reign over the earthbound and matter, I make decisions and carry them out fertile, blooming. My throne is outside on the earth, near water, sky and sun. I am kind and fair and get things done. I've told you that my energy is at your service. Use it. Enjoy it. You'll get things done you could never dream of, large and small.*

DEATH: *My energy is slayful, not playful. Without E-man [the Emperor] I'd cut down everyone who looked at you cross-eyed. I don't mind creating havoc. I'm not as well intentioned as my sister Kali. I'd kill for the taste of blood, cull the weak, who needs 'em, off with their heads!*

ME: *Okay my head is spinning. So all together, if I may summarize, your energy, each of you, is more active and action-oriented than the feminine expression of the same principles. How did the Emperor get his heart?*

THE EMPEROR: *I honor the earth, the elements, sun, sky, air, in me they all unite. I am whole; I have experienced the hieros gamos. Thank goodness or I'd never keep the other two in check!*

I feel resistance to this male energy, but I am drawn to the kind eyes of the Emperor.

THE EMPEROR: *Your quest is noble but not without suffering. For you to accept my energy means you will change. My netted armor doesn't conceal my heart, it is as open and vulnerable as you must become.*

ME: *But women are more vulnerable, our hearts are more open.*

THE EMPEROR (SHAKING HIS HEAD): *No, you are mistaken. The heart of man is more easily broken, that's why we are the warriors, to prevent the possibility.*

ME: *But you have no weapons, you have corn, a flower, an owl.*

THE EMPEROR: *My powers don't require weapons. I no longer need to fight. Believe that if you place yourself here and put me and my throne in your heart you will be able to be both brave and wise, without weapons.*

ME: *Was painting the blue clasp at your neck a mistake?*

THE EMPEROR: *No. The blue jewel is my will. Will is what you must align, align your will and be well.*

Something made me put on a lapis lazuli ring and bracelet this morning. Yesterday I purchased a lapis pendant that resembles the clasp on the Emperor's robe. I have the three paintings of the male trilogy on my writing table to aid the manifestation of my dreams. I feel their energy calling to me. A stream of images of the *hieros gamos*, the sacred marriage of male and female energy, snakes among the other work I do.

A week passes; I come to the studio fighting a cold. I write as my intention to know why I am congested. I begin my witness by addressing
the Emperor.

ME: *So there you are on your throne with all your accoutrements of feminine
power and wisdom, but where is the actual woman?*

THE EMPEROR: *You are the woman, I have learned these things so that I
can carry the signs of feminine power but I am a man, balanced by male
knowing.*

ME: *Do you know why I am congested?*

THE EMPEROR: *Con-gested, con-gestation. You are growing a new awareness. As I have studied, honored, and revered the feminine, you must study
and honor the male.*

ME: *Is that to be through Judaism?*

THE EMPEROR: *Yes. You will need to study with a series of men, you will
gain command of certain areas, and you will combine them with the wisdom of the feminine and produce a new awareness.*

ME: *Isn't that awfully grandiose?*

THE EMPEROR: *No, you said you would do this, I send you forth with this
task.*

ME: *So why congestion?*

THE EMPEROR: *There is a certain stuffiness, an inability to breathe in the
tradition—you can't hold this stuff down any more. Let go of your fears, find
my name in the Bible and let go of your fears. Study what comes before you.*

ME: *I'm afraid of the men in black coats, that they will kill me, the non-
religious Jews will kill me, my Jewish friends will be jealous of me.*

THE EMPEROR: *Welcome to the tribe! People may take issue with you but
you really have to go forward. Let go of your inhibitions, embrace study and
go forward.*

ME: *What am I still missing?*

THE EMPEROR: *It's not the Sabbath Bride you fear deep down. You don't
fear the feminine, nature, or the angel of death. It is man, men; the masculine nature that you fear will awaken your old pattern, your isolation, your
loneliness. You fear I am sending you on a lonely hero's journey, but it is
not so. You will have many loving companions, you will have teachers,
helpers, support and recognition.*

ME: *Then why am I so resistant?*

THE EMPEROR: *The male consciousness you had before was a cruel jailer. It's hard for you to imagine my vision but trust; it will be fine.*

I notice my right side is stuffy and blocked.

THE EMPEROR: *You fear domination by this consciousness. The feminine is powerful and more comfortable a haven, now that you know and respect Kali. But remember, there was a time when you deeply feared and distrusted the feminine.*

ME: *That's true, but I am also afraid of having to be a stupid kind of female to balance the male you are talking about.*

THE EMPEROR: *Quit trying to figure it out. Breathe deeply. You need not hide the compassion you've gained to accept the power I offer.*

ME: *What do I need to do?*

THE EMPEROR: *Just keep your eyes open. Who is the bridegroom of the Sabbath Bride?*

ME: *Israel.*

THE EMPEROR: *Learn all you can.*

ME: *Are you connected to my Irish ancestors?*

THE EMPEROR: *I am connected to all the ancestors of every land. This is an old road we're treading here. Right now your task is to learn from men all you can about Israel.*

As I write this section, I experience a strong sensation on my left side; my eye, neck, shoulder and rib cage all pulse. I consider the fears I expressed in that witness seven years ago in my conversations with the Emperor. I address my body.

ME: *What are my present fears of my feminine nature?*

BODY: *You worry about putting down Kali's sword of truth; you worry about the reticence you notice in men, their ability to hold their thoughts and words to themselves.*

This sounds true. I gained my voice through my work with Kali; and now I'm afraid I'm being asked to give it up. As I write this dialogue, the discomfort in my head and neck eases somewhat, but not completely. A painting of Kali done by a friend has repeatedly fallen from where it hangs in my studio window. It occurs to me to witness Annette's image of Kali. I take Her down and place Her next to me. She says: *It is time for union, do not resist, my job is to prepare the way. You've learned to speak the truth, now BE the truth.*

Speech, this has something to do with my speech. The Jewish teaching *lashon hara* instructs us not to speak of others. This is not just the obvious prohibition against speaking ill of someone, but rather of speaking about others at all. When I first read about this teaching in a book by Rabbi Joseph Telushkin, *Words That Hurt, Words That Heal* (1996), I frankly found it preposterous. So many of my interactions with women friends are spent talking about ourselves, our partners, other women, our families. It is the primary source of bonding and intimacy that we share.

Growing up, I had been deprived of this kind of sharing by the terrible stoic muteness I received as a silent teaching from my mother. She chose not to speak about her pain as she suffered with cancer or about her anger at my father, though her frustration often seemed to be expressed through injuries to herself and accidents. Years of therapy and countless images of Kali helped me to release a backlog of tears, fear, and pain. Sharing those opened me to the more mundane kind of intimate talk that women share. Am I being asked to turn my back on this kind of connection, or is it enough to make an intention to do no harm and work to stay mindful of that intention? The studio teaches us the power of words, new ways of speaking our truth. It is not the gut spilling of therapy groups. More often the stories we tell come out in metaphor, not a literal rendition.

I reread more witnesses from seven years ago. I ask the Emperor to help me discern my role.

ME: *What does it mean to make art and be of service?*

THE EMPEROR: *Your service has to do with transformation, the recognition and understanding of evil, its intricacies, its process, how it comes about, its energy. You must learn about evil, ways to respond, react, be in relation to it, this is your service.*

I can't take on this task without alignment of body, heart, and mind. I experience such separation in my life. Setting up the studio in such a way that I can facilitate and participate is my way of trying to resolve the awful separation that comes from overriding the heart with the mind. I create a thin, attenuated figure out of tape and foil that tells me he embodies the illusion of separation.

THE FIGURE: *That is my reality, alienation. Without the mirror of others I starve to death. I am the hero, alone except in very prescribed relation to others. I fight, I rescue, I honor but I also suffer because the time for heroes is over. You must awaken to separation, to know it fully in order to have the will to return to the One. Use it and find your way home, home to whole-ness, the oneness that is true. Separation is an illusion but I exist in every-one. I, the suffering, separate being, whatever is not allowed, is cut off, and sent away. You must go from oneness in order to return to oneness by choice. This life is a dance between the perceptions of oneness and separa-tion. Meditate on me, strive to see me, know I am in each person.*

ME: *Won't it overwhelm and exhaust me to see the suffering in people?*

THE FIGURE: *No and yes. I said see, not necessarily do anything. See and let what you see pass through your personal heart into the heart beyond your heart. Let your personal heart be melted, shattered. In the personal heart the suffering of others lodges like glass shards or hardens the heart like stone. The heart beyond your heart is like water, it washes, cleanses, purifies. If you saw someone actually in my state, to feed me would be to kill me, yet that would be the impulse of the personal heart. The heart behind your heart knows to bathe me, hold me, honor me, witness me, purify me and later, food for me will appear. The pelican tearing her own flesh to feed her young is not what suffering needs. Hold, see, witness, purify, redeem your own suf-fering and that of others. Then watch it turn into a dove and fly away. This is witness. This is transformation.*

How is it possible to learn this way of being with suffering? How is it possible not to be like Job's friends—judging, seeking answers and expla-nations, seeking to fix and to mend? How is it possible to know what is right action, as opposed to mere reflex action that does more to comfort the observer than the one suffering? Painting teaches this lesson. When I stay with what doesn't work, what is frustrating and unaesthetic in a piece of work, I make space for the "Aha!" of the aesthetic resolution. This is the moment of transformation, when a shift occurs, due to honest witness; something softens, opens. Is it possible to live this way? I think so, with art as a path. Painting, for example, keeps the heart that is beyond the per-sonal heart, open. I am present as a witness, a conduit for divine energy.

When you look at what is happening to our world—and it is hard to look at what's happening to our water, our air, our trees, our fellow species—it becomes clear that unless you have some roots in a spiritual practice that holds life sacred and encourages joyful communion with all your fellow beings, facing the enormous challenges ahead becomes nearly impossible. (Joanna Macy 1990, 55)

I need not judge or label another's experience but merely be present to it. In that space of acceptance things begin to soften. During witness reading in the studio sessions, I find that the artmaking I have just done, whatever it has been, opens me so that the words of others can fall into that place of spaciousness and compassion. A ground has been prepared for true listening. "When we bear witness, when we become the situation—homelessness, poverty, illness, violence, death—right action arises by itself" (Glassman 1998, 84).

So I turn to the Sabbath Bride, who began this story. There is a naked androgynous figure at the base of the painting, looking up at all that is unfolding. At the top of the painting is an ancient prayer: *Nachazir et ha-Shekhinah limkomah b'Zion uva-teivel kulah* (Let us return the Shekhinah to Her place in Zion [Jerusalem] and in all the world). Shekhinah, the feminine face of God, has always been hidden in plain sight in the Jewish liturgy. I address the prone figure.

M E : *How does all this work?*

H E / S H E : *Mandela sat in prison holding the space of peace and justice inside himself. He is that now. You are asked to hold this story.*

I remember traveling to Jerusalem in 2001, about six months before a devastating cycle of attacks and reprisals between Israel and the Palestinians began. I was privileged to say the prayer for Shekhinah's restoration on the Mount of Olives with the group I was traveling with, which included spiritual teachers and authors from many traditions.

M E : *Is the awful war and violence part of restoring Shekhinah to Zion?*

H E / S H E : *I am just a visionary. I see what has been centuries of torture and violence born of fear that the Divine had abandoned the world. Those of you alive today must decide how long war must be the way you choose to usher in Her return.*

M E : *Fear.*

H E / S H E : *Of course there is fear. What have you learned from all your work?*

M E : *Create a space, an open space for change to occur. Have an intention. Witness what is, then ask for a vision of the world you'd like to see.*

While writing this chapter, I came across an old issue of *YES! A Journal of Positive Futures*. I flipped through the magazine and found an article titled "Building a New Force" by Michael Nagler, a founder of the Nonviolent Peaceforce. Begun in 1999, NP aims to "create space for local groups to resolve their own disputes peacefully" (2002, 49). At the behest of local groups, NP deploys hundreds of peace workers to protect human rights, prevent violence, and enable peaceful resolution of conflict using such methods as protective accompaniment, international presence, interpositioning, and witnessing. NP witnessing includes monitoring events and disseminating information internationally to the media and the general public via words and images.

> What most impresses me is the ethic of non–partisanship that NP espouses. You are not there to protect one group from another even when your actions do have that effect. You are there to protect peace, for everyone, and that means getting in the way of violence against anyone as did the African–American woman from Michigan Peace Teams who covered a fallen Klansman with her own body when he was attacked by an anti–racist mob. (p. 51)

I return to my dialogue with the prone figure.

ME: *Can you help me summarize this learning?*

HE/SHE: *It is time to take what you've learned inside the studio outside into the world. Peace is the message. It is not some sort of insipid, solemn, limp thing. Celebration of life, that is what peace is. You can get peace through war, by simply bankrupting yourselves, wearing yourselves out. That is one way to create the necessary space. This is a long and painful and difficult and unnecessary path. You can have peace if you become peace. Ride the Life Force Lion, you do not need to fight and destroy him.*

When I consider the words of this witness I have a deep sense of not knowing how this wisdom will manifest, yet at the same time a feeling of hope. To celebrate life, can that really be our primary job? It feels too good to be true, not serious enough. Yet, as I write these words, I feel the smiling countenance of the Great Mother, of all the women in Annette's collages, of the Sabbath Bride welcoming me home.

Let us hope that, during the Goddess' long sleep she has effected a transformation at the deepest level of the feminine energy that will allow us to pass through the destruction of the old order, like the Phoenix, rise out of its ashes and soar. . . . Transformation can only occur in the dark. (George 1992, 105)

I accept this challenge. I know in my deepest self these words are true. HE/SHE: *Be a good and neutral mirror, let your heart break. Be a witness, not tied to a stake before a firing squad but standing with arms wide open, breathing in, breathing out, feet planted firmly on the ground. Do not try to turn the tides with your brilliant explanations. Even when you witness a fevered frenzy, a breaking all apart, breathe and breathe again. Sigh. Soon, actually not always soon, sometimes it takes a very long time that feels like eternity, but lets say soon anyway. Soon the turn to laugh and dance will come around and you will be ready: limber, warmed up, and eager to join in.*

7
Reclaiming the Indigenous Soul of the Artist

Art is a spiritual path to the true, indigenous soul of the ordinary person. The path is inclusive, democratic, common, and diverse. The aesthetic of art as a spiritual path exalts simple, readily available, everyday materials that reclaim and recycle as well as celebrate ordinary life. These choices are sometimes made out of necessity but more often out of an ethic of care for the material world. We redefine trash as raw materials for creation, and learn to return to the sense of abundance of the natural world. Those of us following art as our spiritual path encounter chimeras of contemporary consumerist society: waste, excess, commodification, and exploitation. Rather than judging these demons, we invite them into our practice in the studio to see what we can learn from them. We work with what arrives both in image and in material. We engage with ideas as well, asking to be guided by the Soul of the World to new definitions of wealth, success, productivity, work, play, sharing, gift, meaning, and community.

The studio is a space where ordinary aspects of experience become sacred through our intention to know the Divine in all things. We pay sacralizing attention to that which is neglected, cast off, and despised in the world, as well as to parts of ourselves that have been neglected, shunned, marginalized, or overlooked. In personal terms, we acknowledge and celebrate the gifts that come in unlikely packages like aging, failure, endings, and illness. Our work is also about recovering memories and retelling stories. The hallmark of this approach is the practice of exchanging judgments for curiosity.

Artists who have embraced this way of knowing may be accomplished painters or poets, but they are also teachers, clerks, lawyers, business people, engineers, therapists, factory workers, and students. The soul can never be bound by definitions, and so the studio is home to all who enter. Each story in this chapter provides some personal information about the artist's life to help contextualize their image and witness. Imagine you are overhearing an intimate conversation between the artist and her soul. You as reader are the witness. It is both a gift and a privilege to share these stories, which are ordinary accounts of art made with simple means, art that creates light and thereby enlarges what is known for all of us. Even while cultivating compassionate disinterest toward the stories that artists share, I remain aware that each story and each artist is my teacher. My intention is to hold the space in such a way that the story can spread out, grow, and change. No artist is bound by one definition, one material, one theme, or one style. Paradoxically, the studio process allows more information as well as intimacy to be shared, precisely because the hearing does not imply a condition of material responsibility. We see images and hear witness writings about the joys and sorrows of others, but we do not take action on their behalf. But what this also implies, and this is important, is that while art as a spiritual path may manifest as a group practice and engender a sense of communion—that is, deep sharing—it does not automatically create a community in the truest sense of the word. Our responsibilities toward one another are clearly circumscribed. We are definitely committed to doing the work of engagement with our soul through the images that manifest and to appreciating that we are all part of something larger. This is the communion part. Through this discipline of listening deeply and suspending judgment as well as letting go of the urge to fix or help, we may indeed begin to learn skills that will benefit the communities through which we act in the world: our families, places of work and worship, teams, social groups, and volunteer commitments.

Those who make art together over an extended period face the same major challenge that any community must confront: remaining true to the group intention—in this case, making a safe place for art—over any particular individual desire. Operating within a culture that has individuality as its supreme value, an ongoing intentional art community has much to teach us. Imagine how public discourse would change if people aligned themselves with the intention to do no harm and dedicated their participation to the highest good for everyone before attending meetings and community events. Witness trains us to relinquish our desire to try to craft an immediate solution, and instead guides us to create space where new possibilities can arise. Listening to the stories in the numinous, fragmentary poetry of the image and witness, we collect seeds to plant in our-

Studio Teachings

selves. When I read the stories, I imagine a patient gardener, loosening the soil around the base of a plant so that it can grow and flourish. On this path, we cultivate our soul by creating images that allow new possibilities to sprout.

Sorting through received truths about our lineage and who we are in the world is one of the primary acts of evolving human consciousness. This is not a wholly independent act, of course, but one influenced by the stories reported in the culture. The term *transgender*, for example, was not in wide use when I was an adolescent but is invoked increasingly in contemporary discussions of identity among young adults today. Such a word may expand and soften our notions of self and generate new images of what it means to be male and female along a continuum, rather than at two opposite poles. For me, the very concept of gender has been called into question by the images I and other women artists have created of the little boy living within us. I activate new potentials in myself as I get to know this boy. Recently I collaborated with a fellow student in a video class I was taking. I was intimidated by the computer program we were using to edit our footage. While watching him simply try different tactics over and over to accomplish our aim, I was reminded of the dark boy in my painting. I noticed that this young man was free of the self-judgments of incompetence and simply kept at the task at hand. I felt tutored in the strategy of persistence, which was part of the dark boy's message to me.

Mary Watkins says: "'What is' and 'who one is' become radically widened as one decenters from the ego's perspective and the given" (1999, 9). Internet relationships allow for experimentation with virtual identities that may be idealized or more daring than a person's accustomed self-image. Similarly, mail art is an art practice in which objects are exchanged and sent through the postal system to other artists. There are many iterations of mail art and many intentions among mail artists. Special names and identities are often chosen by mail artists that give the safe metaphor of alter identities. When I send out a response project (such as an invitation to reflect on money and commerce) under the pseudonym "Econoclast," I experiment with being an "iconoclast of the economy." In my subsequent artmaking and witness writing, I am more aware of the multiplicity of my inner dialogue. When we engage through artmaking and witness writing with ourselves as beings with many other aspects besides the most conscious egoic one, we become aware of what story we are living and whose unfinished dreams we are weaving into form. What new possibilities are we drawing into the culture of how to be and how to act?

In the memoir *Reading Lolita in Tehran* (2004), Azar Nafisi describes how the Islamic revolution severely constrained women's choice of self-image. Wearing a chador became mandatory for Iranian women in the 1990s, Women who had dressed in contemporary Western style for their entire lives suddenly found themselves legally required to be covered from head to toe when in public. Nafisi, formerly an English literature professor at the University of Tehran, began a private class in her home for young women. She taught books she loved by authors such as Jane Austen and F. Scott Fitzgerald, to help keep the imagination alive and to provide an alternative to the inflexible dogma promulgated by the regime. Her students had grown up with these severe restrictions; and while some took off their head scarves once in the safety of Nafisi's apartment, others remained cloaked. Nafisi describes how a woman who had been one of the most conservative dressers showed up one morning wearing jeans and a shirt under her robe.

> Now, without the veil, she slumped, as if she were trying to cover something. It was in the middle of our discussion of Austen's women that I noticed what it was she was trying to hide. Under the chador, one could not see how curvy and sexy her figure really was. I had to control myself and not command her to drop her hands, to stop covering her breasts. Now that she was unrobed, I noticed how the chador was an excuse to cover what she had tried to disown—mainly because she really and genuinely did not know what to do with it. (Nafisi 2004, 296)

For something to come into being, we must be able to imagine it; we must have an image for it. What kind of self-image can a person who is forbidden to show even a wisp of hair—never mind an arm or a leg—be expected to have? They would not have a self-image at all, but would be compelled to inhabit a cultural projection that relates in no way to their individuality or volition. Nafisi also discusses how this policy has affected women who, before the revolution, had chosen to wear the veil as an ex-

Figure 27. *Woman in Purdah*, by Pat B. Allen. Pastel.

pression of their devotion to Islam. Now that every woman is forced to dress this way, the act of wearing the veil has lost the symbolic power it had when it was voluntary.

Earlier in my career, I engaged in a long process of sorting through and dismantling many of the standardized ideas I had been taught about art therapy. At that time I created a scribble drawing of a veiled woman, entitled *Woman in Purdah* (figure 27). I drew her in 1981, before the image of veiled Muslim women had become such a powerful symbol in the West. I recently revisited her to see what she had to say. When she first arrived I had an established practice of writing about images, describing them, and recording my associations. However, I had not yet learned to dialogue with the images. Although she had been stored in a file for years, I felt a strong connection as soon as I sat down with her this time. To reacquaint myself with her original meaning, I looked up the word *purdah*. It means to separate, veil, or screen. I ask her what her message is:

WOMAN: *Every woman is entitled to a time of separation; you must see the value of renewing your commitment to yourself. You give yourself to your husband, your family, your community and the world and you then must return to yourself, separate yourself . . . The veiled women in the world are simply trying to balance you women who are too much in the world, merging with everything. Your times of separation are both to renew yourself and to instruct others in the true nature of life force energy. It ebbs and flows, it must be renewed. You are meant to embody this teaching to represent mystery and the unattainable. As a veiled woman I am a powerful aspect of the Divine—I see but I do not judge—you cannot read my judgment. I am a reminder of witness.*

ME: *But women's wisdom must be brought into the world, no?*

WOMAN: *Of course.*

ME: *If women become more active, can't men separate, isn't that needed?*

WOMAN: *Men don't understand ebb and flow, they become confused. When they gather together they intensify and fight and jockey for position.*

ME: *I don't know if these ideas belong here, am I listening or making this up?*

WOMAN: *Cultivate beauty, peace, and stillness. To do this you must separate yourself. Do not always remain active, cultivate the eyes and heart of witness. What is going on must go on and mostly needs to be witnessed more than anything.*

ME: *What about fighting for women's rights?*

WOMAN: *Less is more. Less action; more witness. Practice doing no harm and seeing clearly. Beauty, which is alignment, practice this. Learn how it feels to prepare and allow things to unfold rather than to struggle and fight.*

ME: *This seems passive.*

WOMAN: *Receptive, it involves the discipline of readiness. Do trees "try" to have their leaves fall? Do they "fight" for the right to blossom?*

ME: *But humans thwart each other.*

WOMAN: *And tree roots grow through and crack concrete.*

ME: *Thank you.*

Reading Nafisi's memoir, I had a shocking realization: for all the free-dom we theoretically enjoy in this society, our lives are spent just as im-mured in cultural projections as those of women living in purdah. Our cultural trance contrives relentlessly to convince us that attaining the ideal packaging for ourselves—whether it's a luxury car, a career that suits us perfectly, a designer dress, a sexual partner who is unstintingly ardent and attentive, children who attend the "right" schools, or a per-fectly toned abdomen—will define our identity and ensure our future happiness. Nafisi says:

> I have a recurring fantasy that one more article has been added to the Bill of Rights: the right to free access to the imagination. I have come to believe that genuine democracy cannot exist with-out the freedom to use imaginative works without restrictions. To have a whole life, one must have the possibility of publicly shap-ing and expressing private worlds, dreams, thoughts and desires, of constantly having access to a dialogue between public and pri-vate worlds. How else do we know that we have existed, felt, de-sired, hated, feared? (2004, 339)

We in a Western democracy suffer not from paucity but rather from a glut of images whose net effect is to crowd out original thought. The re-lentlessness of the messages and their subtext of control in the guise of freedom bears an uncanny mirror-like relationship to Nafisi's totalitarian environment. The difference is that we ingest, partake of, and incorporate the images around us not at gunpoint, but by our own choosing. Making our own images can break the spell. We see who we are and why we grav-itate toward some cultural myths and not others. The veiled woman in my image suggests that learning to do less, curbing our ambitions and ac-tions, and aligning ourselves with nature will help us blunder less and be more effective. Perhaps the separation she suggests is from the media, the ubiquitous and unnoticed arbiter of our collective desires and fears.

One's cultural background often determines how one views art, art-making, owning art, and engaging with art in groups and through rituals. In the course of doing studio work, many artists who engage in the stu-dio process become aware that they are carrying around attitudes toward art—for example, that it is unimportant and perhaps even wrong—that hark back to childhood. I always ask my students at the School of the Art Institute of Chicago to write a personal art history at the start of each semester. One term I had nearly all–second generation artists. The tenor of the class was unlike any I've had before or since. There was an unspoken ownership of artmaking in this group that freed them to explore images and to feel entitled to show their work in public forums. They taught me how much of my work as a teacher is colored by helping others gain, as I had to, a sense of entitlement to self-expression, of respect for the value of what they create, and of courage to show their work. Over the years I have met many adults whose first entry into art is as a parent seeking an art class for their child. Classes that accommodate a wide range of ages can be very rewarding in such cases; often parents are trying to give their children an opportunity they themselves missed when growing up. My daughter and her contemporaries have grown up in a society where self-expression is taken for granted as a basic human right. Some of my richest studio experiences have been with teenagers and adults working alongside each other. Like Nafisi offering an imaginal alternative universe to her college students, we each have different areas of freedom and can create space for each other through our images.

Images and stories that are thrust upon us by others, rather than growing naturally from the soil of our own experience, have little potential to expand our consciousness. Rather, they cause a kind of imaginative constriction that maintains its hold over time; images and stories introduced by parents, religious institutions, the media, and other "authorities" continue to shape our experience long after the sources are gone. By challenging our fixed ideas, art practice provides images that both confront and advise us about our self-administered oppression. In addition to our religious or faith tradition, work is perhaps the most important story line in our lives. In my working–class family, college education was a paramount value, and all of my siblings are teachers. Art was considered risky, impractical, and not real work. Although I managed to go to art school, my father didn't speak to me for a year after I transferred there from a "real" college. Historical work identity may even give us our name. Carpenter, Brewer, Smith, and Baker are all patronymics—names that derive originally from the profession of the father. Toponymics—names derived from towns, villages, and regions—are common in many parts of the world. In our exceedingly mobile culture, we may carry a name that has long since lost either of these meanings. While a democratic society allows for transit between classes via the accumulation of wealth through education and work, many of us are invisibly bound by the unconscious restrictions or expectations of the lineage into which we were born.

For a brief period beginning in 1933, in the midst of the Great Depression, the Public Works of Art Project of the Civil Works Administration was established under the aegis of the U.S. Treasury Department as part of President Franklin D. Roosevelt's New Deal (Dijkstra 2003, 16). It was a valiant and unprecedented government effort, providing art experiences for the average person by setting up small local and regional art centers. These centers hired artists who were out of work due to the Depression to teach as well as to make art themselves. "New Deal arts projects were guided by two novel assumptions: artists were workers and art was cultural labor worthy of government support" (http://historymatters.gmu.edu/d/5100). During this brief period, working for subsistence wages from the government, many artists began to identify themselves as "workers."

> Poor, but—thanks to the art projects—relatively secure in their position in society, they did not find it difficult to recognize their economic kinship to American labor. At the same time they understood that, compared to the hardships suffered by the working classes, their own position was still one of privilege. Intent upon making a difference in what they saw as a crucial class struggle, these artists wanted to speak for the dispossessed. . . . They consciously tried to undermine the separation between "high" and "popular" culture by creating a cultural bridge between the social classes in the form of art that combined modernist techniques with subject matter that would be meaningful to those who have suffered the most from the excesses of early twentieth–century capitalism. (Dijkstra 2003, 11)

Many of these artists of the 1930s were the children of European immigrants who had fled repressive cultures. They "stood between worlds."

Finding new freedoms in America—including public education and free public libraries—they embraced opportunities to become "steeped in the ideals of democracy." At the same time, "art and life, self and society, were part of a single continuum for these children of immigrants: acts of creation were not separate from, but integral to, their experience of community" (Dijkstra 2003, 12). In addition to children of immigrants, descendants of African–American slaves gained access to art education, which was unavailable in the public schools in the South and missing even in the black colleges that were being founded. Lawrence A. Jones, an African–American man who grew up in Lynchburg, Virginia, came to Chicago to take advantage of programs at Hull House, Jane Addams's famous experiment in preserving culture. Lawrence later got a scholarship to the Art Institute of Chicago. His work in a WPA art center in New Orleans convinced him that as an artist he had a responsibility to the less fortunate: "Believing as I do that the appreciation of art cultivates in man a sincere regard for the contributions of his fellow men, regardless of race or creed, I am trying through my painting and art teaching to create a more democratic America" (2004, 6).

The political activism and concerns for social justice inherent in the work of artists of this unique period in America threatened both an arts establishment bent on elitism and a government seeking to suppress criticism. As immigrants and children of immigrants, many of the artists who benefited from the programs were at strong risk for being seen as leftists and Marxists. Both the content of their artwork and the proximity of revolutionary ideas in their cultures of origin made these artists too threatening to the status quo for the government to continue its support. With the arrival of World War II, the government–supported arts programs lost their funding to the Graphic Section of the War Services Project, which was dedicated to producing propaganda and patriotic exhortations. In 1944, hundreds of canvases produced in the WPA era were junked as rags. Following the war and the rise of an affluent and conservative America obsessed with progress, a new class of art patron emerged, one uninterested in the social realism that had marked the art of the 1930s: the corporate CEO. There was a pervasive disdain in this new cultural milieu for what one critic called "Ellis Island art" (Dijkstra 2004, 18).

The contemporary community studio movement and the opportunity for the common person to make art today echo the regional art centers that briefly graced the country in the 1930s. At that time over five thousand artists throughout the nation were involved, with more than a hundred community art centers providing classes and sponsoring exhibitions. Countless thousands of children and adults experienced art programs offered by professional artists with government support. These individuals "faced the technical problems involved in painting and sculpture, [and studied] original works of art with a new and healthy interest, [deriving] relaxation and pleasure from participating in art studies" (http://historymatters.gmu.edu/d/5100, p. 3). However, it quickly became clear that with a war on, America couldn't afford the largesse either financially or in the realm of the true exercise of democracy that the WPA art programs represented. Art history is not a common concern of people who find their way to studio experiences today. Rather, they seek relief from life stress, a chance to explore themselves in a safe environment, and support for choosing to make images. Still, if a country like Afar Nafisi's Iran can transform from a free society to a totalitarian regime almost overnight, my sense is that the preservation of democracy depends upon the imagination of the people to continually vision and re-vision the kind of world we wish to live in.

Art as a spiritual path leads both into the individual soul and outward into the community—from the Soul of the World to the actions of the artist. We enlarge and provide alternatives to each other if we see ourselves as part of a strand of meaning that has surfaced and disappeared in our history of trying to work out what it means to live in a free society. The artists in this chapter represent the working-class and immigrant sectors of American society, which only briefly claimed artmaking as a valuable pursuit. Both Dave and Lisa have found ways to intertwine their lives as workers—Lisa as a social worker and Dave as the owner of a heating and air-conditioning business and now also a gallery—with their growing identities as artists. They point the way to a kind of integration of life, work, and spirit that inspires those around them while at the same time expanding the possibilities for friends and family as well as people they encounter in the workplace.

"Bee" Yourself: Dave's Story

Dave's parents migrated from small towns in the Midwest to Chicago, where they met and married. Dave succeeded his father as head of a successful family business, a small heating and air-conditioning firm. Dave grew up in the family business and remembers at the age of seven holding a flashlight for his dad as he did a repair. As an adolescent, Dave went to college in Hawaii to get as far away as possible from the life he had known growing up. After college he returned to the Midwest but went to work for another heating company, partly to rebel against family expectations. In the long run, this job gave him valuable experience that he ended up bringing back to the family firm later on. Dave took over after his dad died and eventually built the company to five times its original size. He took pride in creating a logo and a façade for the building, and getting a fleet of trucks that bore the company name. After a while he found himself managing a staff of fifteen employees. I had always been rather charmed by the bright glass façade of the building, which is unusually colorful and original for a business in our rather staid little town.

Like many young men in our town who are following in their family's footsteps, Dave began his adult years in this town with a social life centered on drinking at a local bar. Eventually he married a woman who tended bar there. But over time Dave began to feel frustrated and unfulfilled. His father had worked day and night to serve his customers, mostly single-handedly, while Dave's mom took care of the books. Unwilling to live that way, Dave worked hard to transform the business into a smooth-running and successful enterprise that even left him time to take up golf.

When I first met Dave, his interest in golf was beginning to wane. His divorce had recently become final, and he had begun working with fused glass, an art form he had learned about on the Internet. House of Heat, Dave's company, is located in the town's budding arts district and Dave has been an active member of the local artist/business association. We attended several meetings together to negotiate some local ordinances that artists felt were restricting business. Dave's credentials as a "real" businessman and his longtime presence in town lent credibility to the artists' concerns. Dave says his life at that time was lonely and somewhat empty. No longer content to sit around bars, he participated in a few glassmaking workshops in New York and Portland, Oregon, that opened his eyes to new possibilities and made him hunger for a creative community.

After one meeting with town officials, Dave asked about my studio, which was located a few doors down from House of Heat. "What goes on in there?" were his exact words. Knowing nothing of Dave's personal struggles or his forays into glassmaking, I described the studio process and told him that the goals of participants often had to do with making a deeper connection to self, mourning a loss, and tapping into and expand-ing their latent creativity. To my surprise, Dave asked when the next workshop was starting. I told him that it began the following day, and without hesitating he said "Sign me up."

My background makes me a sucker for a man in work clothes, and I found myself grinning when Dave arrived with a journal under his arm, wearing a blue work shirt with his name embroidered over the pocket. I expected that he would not last the whole workshop and would proba-bly arrange for his beeper to go off after sitting around with the group of mostly women who rarely held emotion back in either their images or witness writings. In fact, he told me later, his reaction to the witness readings was "What the hell are these people talking about?" In his world, if he was feeling bad, well, "A beer would fix that." Dave doesn't recall ever seeing his father take time for himself; certainly he couldn't imagine his father asking himself the question "How do I feel today?" The release and freedom he witnessed at the studio was not something he had encountered before. Golf was probably the first release he had found; and art has proven even more satisfying, giving Dave a sense of accomplishment. Growing up, Dave thought of art as something to maybe look at but certainly not to do. He has used his work at the studio in several different ways. Sometimes Dave just plays, experimenting with how much water or paint he can get onto one piece of paper. Sometimes he works out designs for glass projects. Sometimes he uses the workshop for self-care.

One day his intention was: *I take some time off from the heating season and enjoy the group and the peace of making art. Slow down, breathe deep and recharge for the coming week.*

Dave worked intently for the entire session, gathering and arranging found objects on a towerlike shape. Dave witnesses the sculpture (figure 28):

> As I started to stack things together my piece became a challenge of balance. I put more and more pieces of pottery together stacking them higher and higher. Challenging the limits of gravity and strength. At one point although I knew that I was pushing the limits I just kept stacking knowing of the eventual collapse and sure enough many sections toppled over. I feel like this is a reminder to hold back on taking on too many things, too many jobs. In the heating business it's always feast or famine and it's hard to tell people that you can't help them or that you can't do any work for them for a month but that's the way it is. After the collapse of my balancing act piece I scaled back and straightened things out. I still stacked things up high but this time I took more time and considered how to make them stay up. I still strived to push the limits and set high expectations but also to stay within the limits. This past week has been so hectic and the last two weeks I have not come to art class. It would have been easy to stay at work and not come again. I'm glad I came; it gave me a chance to put life into perspective. Three hours for myself to sort things out and escape from the pace outside is very important.

The following week Dave continues to work on his balancing–act piece. His intention: *I will continue working on the balancing act piece. I liked the way I felt last week after stacking things up and sensing the limitations. During the week, work has been much better with the realization that some work will have to be passed on and the rest will be scheduled 4–8 weeks in the future. I feel balanced and relaxed.* His witness takes him deeper into a meditation on the issues on his mind.

> Today I thought about balance and teamwork how one person's support of another can make great things happen. At first the piece was short and wide . . . Then I decided to add a team of Indians, army men, and a space creature to support the piece and the piece really soared. It's amazing how when you put individuals together that you don't think fit well they somehow jell together to form the team. This past week this is how I have felt at work. Certain

Figure 28. Sculpture by Dave King. Found objects.

people had to go (and now they are gone) others have stepped up and we are moving forward. Everything seems to be in balance and I feel at ease.

In the last session of the weekly workshop Dave made an intention to *absorb what I have done and see if things have changed for me.* I was struck by this use of language: "to absorb what I have done." Many times it is easy to forget that time for absorbing new ideas and insights is a vital part of the creative process. My yoga teacher describes the final relaxation at the end of our asanas as time for our body to take in and reprogram our patterns. Dave's witness reads: *Well, some things have changed and some haven't. I feel too busy at work even though we have passed on some work and pushed other work back. Today I considered not coming to class and doing some work but I came and I'm glad. I* reviewed what I did several weeks ago and found there were some pieces I hadn't even taken out of the drawer. I found a bright watercolor from early in September and put it up behind the sculpture. I really like it. As I move closer to the piece I notice lots of things that are speaking to me but I feel a resistance to opening up and listening. Too many outside pressures and responsibilities to just stop and listen. I decide to just put the piece aside for today and wait for that conversation for another day. I think a couple of weeks to put things to rest will help me prepare for the message that is waiting to be discovered.

The next session Dave attended met on Halloween, also Día de los Muertos, the Day of the Dead. I mentioned this to the group because I feel a strong affinity for this festival and for the Mexican belief that the veil between the worlds is thinner on this day. Dave's intention referenced my remarks (It is always fascinating to learn how one's words are received!):

To slow down and try to look at my impatience. Also Pat suggested that today is a good day for contacting the dead. My father passed away a couple of years ago and my brother committed suicide almost twenty years ago. Maybe today is a good day to think about them. During the last session I made a stacked sculpture that I thought has a lot to say but that I wasn't quite ready for. So I will look at the piece and see what I can.

Dave then witnessed the piece:

I look at the piece and I see brightness. I feel a need to focus on the positives, the brightness of the pink, the warmth of the pink the softness of the fur at the bottom. I like the vertical uplifting. It calls me to look to the future and start climbing upward again. I feel like I have been letting small things drag me down. I have been getting caught up like the spiderweb in the piece shows. So I removed the spider and web and opened up the piece. It feels fresh and open and uplifting. I built up the background and resecured more taller vertical stuff. The being at the top had been pulled over by the web. Once the web was removed the being was free to stand tall. I think about throwing the spider in the garbage but I decide to put it in the stuff on the shelves (the found object box) hopefully it will help someone else. I clear my space to start working on something else. I start to think about my father. He always went to work. He worked night and day. People tell me all the time that he was great and funny. We (my brothers and sister) always tried to impress him when he was around

Figure 29. Dave King between House of Heat and Glass Gallery.

us but he always told us what we did wrong and had little to say that was good. I had a poster that said "May you always have the freedom to be yourself." One time he made a snide comment about this poster. Today I looked through the found items and I saw a bee looking out at me. I taped it to the table and wrote under it "yourself." I made a box out of foil. (My father made everything out of sheet metal) The box is open at both ends. I look through the box at the "Bee yourself" and I think the box is like the heating business. It has felt cold and hollow lately. But as I look through the box I see the "Bee yourself" and I think about it. The fact that I have been lucky enough to work at the company has given me the opportunity to start a cool glass gallery and to be myself. I wish my father had been there more when he was alive. I wish he could see me now. I think he would say that I should work harder at the company and not spend so much time on myself. So we were and are different. I'm glad I'm who I am and I wish my dad had spent more time with us and more time for himself. If you're out there listening I hope that you heard me and things are going well for you. My brother, on the other hand took and gave, wanted and needed but didn't get what he needed so he took drugs and alcohol. My father (who grew up without a father) didn't know what to do so he hid behind his work. He helped the people he could (his customers) and spent time in a place where he was comfortable and felt like he could be in control AT WORK. I am looking for the place where I am comfortable in my life.

Dave turned his former office at House of Heat into Roaring Belly Glasswerks, a gallery where he displays his handblown glass fish as well as the work of other glass artists who now make up his creative community (figure 29). He continues to run the heating and air-conditioning business and to be a force for good in the art district and business community. By following what gives him pleasure, Dave not only has enlarged his own life but also has created new possibilities for all who know him—his friends, employees, customers, and family. He recently bought a new house and is considering turning part of it into a studio space where he can host workshops and continue to make art with others.

Re-Membering: Pat's Story

Around the time my daughter Adina is thirteen and entering high school, an image comes to me (figure 30). I paint a small figure, still unformed at the edge of a grove of snaky cypress trees under a full moon over a blue sea, a letter left on the ground. Darker, this image needs to become darker. The light will come from the moon and from within the figure, maybe from the letter, a piece of ancient parchment, ancient wisdom? I address the work in my witness:

Unfinished piece I feel comfort in you in this state, like an enjoyable novel by the bedside that I haven't finished. You make me think of Adina; she is on the edge of the dark wood of adolescence where I can't follow her. Is she coming out of a dark wood into moonlight to find an ancient text to guide her? I forget she has me sometimes and in a detached way see her as alone, the way I was alone at her age. I was alone on the edge of a dark wood. I didn't know the moonlight was there, I couldn't see its shimmering rays, its cold, clear light etching particularity into the trees and rocks. You in the painting are alone and so far, naked and vulnerable in a landscape that seems to block you with its mystery. Is there enough courage to venture into the dark wood? I wandered into the wood blindly (there must be angels). Can Adina find her way? Part of me imagines it must be time for me to die now that she is this

Figure 30. *Teshuvah*, by Pat B. Allen. Gouache. The Hebrew word at the bottom is meant to be *teshuvah*, "return"; however, I inadvertently misspelled it, using the letter *heh* where the *vav* should be.

age, the way my mother died. Part of me imagines my own tombstone over me as I think impotent thoughts. But I can send her real energy; give her real love and warm hands and the message that we all enter the dark woods again and again over and over if we stay really alive.

I imagine a tiny boat on the water but it isn't there in the painting yet. The witness writes:

Tree moon water/sea the sea shimmers preventing me from seeing through its wavelets of mercy. Tree limbs wave in the sighing mist keeping me from Her inner depths. The moon watches all of us. Tree sea moon. Moon sea tree and me, a little boy, my aura surrounding me at the edge of the wood at the place where water meets the sand. We all dissolve and recombine. [Once Adina said to me, "You just happen to be my mom this time around." How does she know that? I wonder.] I'm the moon now I feel cold brightness. I'm the sea now, cold wetness. I'm the tree now I feel my roots plunge deep into Her earth. It is midnight under a full moon. I've come to wait for Shekhinah. She has dreamed me into being, her child, her little boy. I dream of Her, Mother, Creator, Destroyer, Preserver. She's in all of it, in coolness, night moon tree shore sky sea. My little aura shimmers in answer to Her moonlight. Your face is dark; Your face is light. My face is hidden. Your face is in every leaf, wave, grain of sand. Too bad I'm blind. You become Braille. Too bad I have no hands; you reach my nose as the scent of cedar and cypress. Too bad I have lost my face. I feel You under my feet. Finally I dissolve in You, we are complete. The boat materializes on the shining waves. The moon scatters her jewels over the scene. The scroll becomes a Torah glowing with fiery light. All dancing light energy. Everything is a source of light.

Robert, the man who washes the windows of the studio, leaves, his work finished. He waves as he goes off, and light streams in and falls on the floor, nearly blinding me. Why can't I penetrate the picture? It is leaving me outside. I want the boy to turn around, pick up the Torah, dance, and be consumed in the fire. I want to know what the story is now.

ME: *Do you want that, little boy?*

BOY: *What? What did you say? You're worried about catching the bus, carrying packages, what you have to do later, watching dogs walk by with platinum-haired humans in tow; you are in no shape for my message. Turning is a slow process, when I turn, I may burst into flames myself, nothing to rush. Think of what you are not facing and slowly turn to face it.*

ME: *This feels so sluggish, trickling out, not flowing, where did it go, my energy?*

BOY: *Don't worry; don't hurry. The ship is coming this way. You are straining to get away from this quiet moment. When you are in the middle of frenzy, you'll wish you were here. Ebb and flow, this is ebb, don't be alarmed. Quit wishing everything was its opposite. Remember, fully see and hold what is and notice it gradually turn into its opposite.*

Artmaking brings to our attention the multiple, richly interwoven realities coexisting in our lives, which we so often edit down to one bare strand of the story. The image evokes Adina, evokes me at her age, and then I am a little boy, the indigenous soul. Perhaps this image is an echo of the ancient dyadic representation of the Divine as mother and son. The teaching that he brings has to do with return; in this it echoes the *Sabbath Bride* (figure 22, page 148). He reminds me that everything allowed its natural course and fully witnessed, turns gracefully into its opposite. Night turns into day whether we are fearful or not. In artmaking our fear can lead us to get stuck. Witnessing lets the image instruct us before we jump to conclusions about the dire meaning of an image, like when I interpreted the rabbi and mayfly man on the scales in the *Sabbath Bride* painting. The process of natural unfolding occurs in the medium of loving attention. When we fear change or resist the turning and fight against it, do we poison the natural solution? Fear is the loss of awareness of the loving presence that is always holding all of us.

I created a series of pieces in which I witness a photograph of my mother as a young woman. I noticed this particular photo at my sister's home and asked for a copy. Before her marriage to my father, before my birth, she is of course not "my mother," but rather a woman on the cusp of adulthood, about to advance into the next phase of her life. I transferred a photo via the computer by scanning the image onto transfer paper and ironing it onto the cloth. I distressed the image by ironing over it and obliterating some of the detail. In this work I first experimented with the practice of witnessing directly on the image as part of the artmaking process. I applied rubber stamps, stencils, and handwriting directly onto the fabric.

The first witness reads:

I don't usually make art about my mother. She is really very mysterious to me. Is she just all the memories that we have? Does her essence live in a different body? Once I thought I saw her on a train. The person I saw was a black man yet somehow it seemed to be her. The space in me that she once held will always remain open. Many things have come to me through that open space. For this I am very grateful. In this photo she is young and happy. That reminds me that she felt joy I never thought of her without thinking of her suffering. If she felt joy maybe I can too?

I hear a reply: *Welcome to the house of peace.*

In another piece in the same series, I engage with her more directly. The witness on the cloth reads:

Memory fades when we unclasp our hands. It sinks into the body there it waits in our cells, hidden from view. FLOOD, sometimes memory floods me with longing: the strong desire for something unattainable If I sit in that space long enough the flood subsides. Oh the terrors of that . . . open space. No offense I say to her, but it isn't you it's more the idea of mother that makes me ache (I know she says, me too, that's everybody) ASK! ASK! She gives everything. I don't dare ask ASK! I say "Make me yours" Always and forever we are one.oneoneoneoneoneoneoneoneoneoneoneoneoneone. "Then what is there to ask for?" I say
REMEMBRANCE.

Part of the witness to the final hanging in this series says that *to learn if something is true listen to your body it never lies. You nod your head, you know that, you say. But do you know? Do you know that your body is TORAH?*

In this work I believe I am accessing the essence of the person who for a time was my mother. But then that isn't so strange when you consider that I'd happily converse with a bird made of tape and foil, a painting, a rock, or a tree. It is thirty-seven years since my mother died. I have lived more than twice as long without her as I did with her. Yet her reality is stronger now than it was when she was alive. I decide on her *yahrtzeit*, the anniversary of her passing, to honor her and our journey together and how it continues to unfold.

I create a collage using a copy of a photo of her holding me as an infant. I add a photocopy of a burned one hundred dollar bill. I have recently read about a Chinese custom of burning money to honor the dead. I think it would be fitting to add the word *kadosh* (holy), but my spelling in Hebrew is atrocious. I open a book by Lawrence Kushner to see if I can find the word but open to the page for the word *teshuvah* (return). Kushner shares this from the Talmud: "Returning home is the hardest thing in the world, for truly to return home would mean to bring the Messiah. Returning home is also the easiest thing to do, for it has only to occur to you to return home and you have already begun"

(1993, 32–33). My witness to the piece begins: *Going to Source is a great longing that flows through and animates all creation. When we create our images, we return to Source.* I ask the image to speak.

MOTHER: *Kadosh, kadosh.*

ME: *Burning money is an interesting way to mark death, a way of saying you are free of earthly constraints.*

MOTHER: *Yes, but dwell on the joy that comes from having tended the hole, the space, the entry to the void you've been given. It has allowed me to pass back and forth between realms. You have given me safe passage to be of service in the world.*

ME: *Really?*

MOTHER: *Yes. You have created a ladder and angels go up and down all day and all night.*

Managing the "holes" in the self and learning to appreciate them has been a great teaching for me. But though I have after thirty-seven years learned something about the void left by losing my mother, I am not immune from struggling with other losses. I am usually grateful to be around folks who make no bones about who they are and what their limitations are. The space in the self that comes from loss and suffering can be a point of entry—a place for grace to pass through—or it can be a tightly locked door. I recently received an opportunity to learn about having my heart shut in resistance and how hard it can be to get to the place that is the "heart beyond my heart." As usual, I learned through my failures.

In this case, I failed to make an intention before some house guests arrived for a weeklong stay. Without an intention to ground me, I agreed to go out for dinner, ate and drank too much, talked too much. And after a few days, even after noticing what was happening, I was sick—feeling cornered, sad, overwhelmed, and slightly murderous toward my guests. I tried to manage with old and inadequate tools like dodging the resentment that welled up in me as I struggled with how much of a hostess I should be. I neglected to notice how I was resisting any feeling of grief as I prepared to close my studio. Many of the longtime studio artists have a lot of feelings about the closing. I was not ready to feel my own loss, tied as it was to complicated feelings about my studio fellows. One of the guests was used to, in our previous infrequent visits, having deeply emotional conversations where every aspect of life could be dissected with some detachment. I tried to dodge these exchanges, feeling too shaky to explain my view that this isn't really a great thing. I was not really aware of how much I was grieving the important transition from the public studio I had maintained for four years. The artists loyal to the studio process wanted it to stay the same; they were happy with what had been created and deeply valued the sanctuary the studio provided. I was feeling stifled and in need of moving on. My guest expected me to respond to his suffering with therapeutic insight, something else I no longer felt much like doing.

When our guests departed, I felt angry and depleted. I hadn't been able to enjoy our visit much at all. I was reminded of an experience at the beach some years ago; a strong undertow knocked me off my feet, sweeping me along the shore until a lifeguard pulled me out of the water. The undertow of the studio closing and my attempts to navigate not only my own feelings but those of longtime studio participants threw me off balance. I had a clear intention to be mindful of others in the studio and how the closing would affect them, but had left myself out of the equation.

My guest's expectation that I act as a therapist evoked a discomfort in me I couldn't quite name at first. I just felt tired and angry, but couldn't find a way to that heart beyond my heart. The door to my personal heart was slammed shut even to me. I was forced to recall the way in which I had related to this friend in the past. We had a kind of wordless agreement that it was my role to confront him about his problems, pointing out connections between his behavior and its unhappy consequences. I played the insightful counselor, he the grateful truth seeker.

There was an element of dishonesty in this pairing that eluded me until I learned the studio process of no–judgment and witness. Our visits had always been brief–I had no ongoing responsibility. I could have an intense conversation or two, and that was that. This time, after hearing the stories and complaints over and over, I realized I no longer desired to give my previous therapeutic retorts. I hated how critical I felt. In relation to the studio, I knew I couldn't maintain the sanctuary for everyone else if it had ceased to function for me. I felt support from most people, but I am especially grateful to those, like Dave, who expressed their anger and disappointment as well as their understanding.

Figure 31. *Box of Pain*, by Pat B. Allen. Nails, beads, paint.

I went to the studio and asked these questions as my intention: *How can I balance the critic and call forth compassion? How do I deal with feeling so judgmental of another person and not harm them? How do I not drown in my own uncomfortable biliousness?* I knew I needed a box. I found a file card–size box made of wood and began to hammer nails into its lid; then turned it over and hammered nails through the bottom into the box. I created a box of pain. It felt so good to hammer in the nails. The box splintered somewhat but stayed in one piece. I painted the whole thing red, inside and out. I complained in my witness about how hateful I felt, how I saw my guest as a "box of pain" (figure 31). Here at the studio I could see the other artists through the eyes of the Divine Source. At home, I had failed. I witnessed the box, which began with a reply to my questions.

Box: *But you hammered in the nails, now you stand in his shoes, realize that to remove one nail is to risk destroying the box. It is an act of love of the world to keep one's self in one piece, one peace, piece of cake, right? After all, you didn't attack him, fall apart, or hammer in more nails . . . believe me, that is all that is asked of any human being. Your downfall was simply that you got confused about whether you should get out the pliers and yank out a few nails (my old brand of aid!) as you've done in the past and of course your small urge to smash the box. But, in the end, you did neither. You were a witness, if a shaky one.*

M E: *So, then, why did I get sick?*

B ox: *Because you had been numbing yourself for awhile before this challenge, instead of preparing for it. You were not willing to witness your own suffering until the studio closed, being busy witnessing everyone else. You resented your guest for being a big shiny mirror. It is very hard to feel compassion when your heart is closed to yourself.*

How to be of service as an artist? How to stay true to the process as a source of spiritual guidance? How not to harden my heart or fall back on reeling off brilliant formulations that explain it all? The process tells me: Make the image of what you know, as best you can, right now. Listen to the image, follow its voice, ask what it needs, and freely give it. Serve the cause of the aesthetic resolution, the point when the image feels right and it is ready to speak the truth; and when you hear and feel the "Aha!"—that is the sound of the heart opening. Step back and firmly, carefully listen; but do not give advice or come to conclusions. Be willing to stay in the discomfort of not knowing. We cannot do anyone else's shadow work, point out the places where they are in the dark and blind to themselves; we can only do our own. Feeling convinced that someone else needs to do shadow work is a clear signal that it's time to step into our own closet and turn on the light. When we do our own shadow work, we increase the circle of light so that others will come into it with their muddy shards and be willing to see what's what.

Mother, Real and Imagined: Lisa's Story

Lisa swept into the studio, rushing a bit as usual, her black hair flowing past her shoulders. She plopped down at a table and began to unpack her stuff. She had an assignment from her women's medicine circle, she told us breathlessly, that terrified and overwhelmed her. Each woman was to write her mother's story to share with the group at their next few meetings. Lisa quickly realized that she did not know her mother's story. Other women in the medicine circle cheerfully went about meeting with their mothers, interviewing them over tea or simply writing out what had always been shared. When Lisa, with great trepidation, tentatively approached her own mother about the task she faced, her mother said, "I don't have a story." "Of course you do," Lisa replied, "I want to honor you." "Make something up," her mother shot back. In that instant, in a moment of pure compassion, Lisa vowed "to honor her [mother's] wall, not penetrate it." "I am no longer making this about me," Lisa said, "This is about her." Lisa also knew that the story would come to her through images: "There was no other way."

I first met Lisa when she came to interview me for a class she was taking in social work school. She was doing research for a class presentation on alternative therapeutic healing modalities being used in Chicago. I explained the intention and witness process, watching to see how Lisa would regard this information, which was likely to contradict the principles articulated in her art therapy reading. I suggested that she do a hands–on experience for her class and explained dialoguing with images. I could tell from the serious look in her eyes that Lisa intuitively understood everything I was explaining and would have no trouble conveying it to her classmates. After she gave the presentation, she called me to say that the experience had been profound for her, her class, and her professor. She felt the professor "saw" her for the first time. I wasn't surprised. I was sure that her authenticity and deeply grounded spiritual presence came through when she presented the work. She had felt permission to bring her soul into the classroom. Lisa began to spend time at the studio, another way station for her on a path that she had been traveling for some time.

Growing up in a close–knit Italian family, Lisa attended an all–girls Catholic high school and was among the first generation in her extended family even to contemplate college. Unlike many of her classmates, whose parents were accountants or lawyers, Lisa didn't have a clue about which box to check on the career–counseling worksheet given out by the guidance department. She was overwhelmed by how big the world seemed and was confused and oblivious to all the possibilities. Lisa did not discover her talent for artistic expression until many years later in her late thirties when she returned to school to finish her B.A. and took an elective art class. Her experience in that first "real" art class planted a seed. She was astonished by what she was able to create. The class brought her closer to a sense of God than she had ever felt. "If I can make something this beautiful," she remembers thinking, "God must be in me, like they said." Colors, imagery, and form all connected Lisa to a joy she had tried but failed to find in Jesus, Mary, and the Catholic faith she had grown up in. She was far more influenced by the teachings she received from the catechism: "This is what you do, and if you don't do it, here's how you'll end up." Although Lisa attended church as many as three times a week while attending Catholic grammar school, nothing about it felt authentic to her. The most vivid memories she has of her religious milestones—baptism, first communion, and confirmation—revolve around getting the right dress. The beautiful white eyelet dress she wore for First Communion has been passed down in her family for generations. This is where her mother, aunts, and cousins poured much of their creative energy. In hindsight, Lisa recalls her mother's life philosophy as: "If it looks good, it is good." Adorning self and home provided a practical engagement with creativity, as well as communal opportunities to celebrate life and make it beautiful.

While taking her art class, Lisa also turned to gardening as a creative outlet, following her family tradition of beautifying hearth and home. Plunging her hands into the soil was as satisfying as drawing with charcoal. "Getting dirty" connected Lisa to her own life force, which had been constricted by her Catholic upbringing and the limited perception of herself that resulted from it. Lisa's mother had created the life she dreamed of, overcoming obstacles by sheer will when necessary. Lisa recalls a mosaic-style wall in their kitchen that her mother created stone by stone. Lisa's first job applying her computer skills was at Goodwill Industries, a social service agency providing work experiences to prostitutes, ex-convicts, and others in need of rehabilitation. Gradually, Lisa's interest in people's lives and stories, rather than their computer skills, led Lisa to a career in social work. Lisa considered art therapy as a profession, but was persuaded that social work was the more practical choice. Yet she constantly sought out art therapy workshops to gain the knowledge she craved.

When it came time to decide how to receive her mother's story through images, Lisa decided on the form of an altered book. She pur-

Figure 32. *Mother Book*, by Lisa Sorce Schmitz. Altered book, collage.

chased a book from a secondhand store for her purpose that happened to
be titled *How to Rethink Your Family and Remake Your Life*. First, Lisa removed
many of the pages and glued others together to create a few thick pages
to work on. The process was slow, arduous, and messy. Then she began to
witness photos of her mother to receive the story locked within the silent
images. Working with paint, found images and objects, glitter, and glue,
she constructed a deeply moving tribute to her mother (figure 32). The
photos of her mother as a child, teenager, bride, and young mother
yielded up the story to Lisa's patient attention. She excavated a narrative
that emerged not chronologically, but with soul logic. The finished book

has few words. Mostly it is a riot of color and energy balanced by poignant photos and powerful archetypal images from magazines and calendars. In places, fragments of text from the original book remain, offering prescient commentary on the images that have come to live beside them: "there are several truths"; "there is no truth"; "virtually no memories of childhood, only flash floods"; "emotions without the scenes that generated them."

At one point Lisa placed a weight on the book overnight to try to flatten the pages, which were rippling and curling from the moisture of the paint. The polymer medium she had used was dry but not completely cured. Lisa writes in her witness: *So as I sit down to work on the next section I am heartbroken to realize that my idea to flatten the book overnight was not a good one. The pages are stuck together—I must tear them apart to open the book again—it makes a grotesque ripping sound. There is damage to the blue and pink sections. How perfect! Battle scars! As I begin again the book mirrors my own ripping open as I work through this process.* The trust Lisa maintained in the process, despite this frustrating mishap, inspired other artists in the studio to make art about their mothers.

In another witness, Lisa writes: *Another day has come and gone . . . I sink deeper into the story. Once again, after each session working on this my mother looks different . . . the world looks different . . . my love grows deeper. Today is a bright sunny day. The imperfections in the pages stare back at me. But I choose not to engage them. Instead, I look at the whole picture. Searching for what I love most in each piece. How much more vivid the colors and images are when I do this. This does not mean the blemishes aren't there—they are too obvious, too much a part of the picture to ignore. Now, however, I can allow them to fade into the background—taking their rightful place in the collage . . . in the story.*

So much of the image work we do is about forgiveness, which comes from seeing each other clearly, not from denying or whitewashing the truth. To forgive is to see the divine spark amid all the (too strong and judgmental) messiness of someone's life, and to mirror back that spark. Lisa writes a beautiful prayer for her mother toward the end of her work.

My wish for you is that you soon surrender into the arms of a new God. The real Spirit of the Universe. She will hold you and love you regardless of your actions. It is simply enough that you be. May you reframe your God into one

that is not separate from you. Turn a treacherous sea into calm liquid. Where
hues of cobalt, turquoise, and lime dance in the sunlight water that gives way
to the fire and life in a young girl's heart.

Lisa's work is a strong example of the "call and response" that can occur in the studio. I was immediately moved to share my mother work with her. I was just beginning the series of cloth hangings where I had written my witness to a photo of my mother right on the fabric of the hanging. I told Lisa I had been speaking directly to photographs of my mother and felt her soul essence answer me.

Suddenly it seemed nearly every artist was receiving images about their own mother or the Divine Mother. All of us were inspired by Lisa's initial intention: *I am telling my mother's story. I am seeing her with new eyes, understanding her in new ways. I am rewriting the story I have lived with up until this moment. I am writing the true version, the hindsight version, the healing, forgiving, loving, opening-my-heart version. I am grateful for this opportunity. I am honoring my fear and resistance to this process. I am moving at a comfortable pace. I am open and receptive to the Creative Force. It is moving through me as I explore, interpret, and create this new story.*

So many artists responded to Lisa's work that we created a show, *Mother: Real and Imagined.* For the show, Lisa constructed an altar draped in vibrant cloths—purple, green, and animal-print. She placed the altered book on a stand in the center. Surrounding the book were candles, rocks, crystals, feathers, and amulets. In the installation, Lisa brought together all the sacred elements of her quest: family, spirit, art, and—most of all—deep compassion. Lisa's mother was working the night of the opening. Cousins, friends, and colleagues crowded around Lisa's work as she explained it to them. The next day, when Lisa was at work and the studio was quiet and nearly empty, Lisa's mother and aunt came to see the work. To my surprise, they lingered over each piece in the show. They stood a long time talking quietly in front of Lisa's work. Their faces shone with pride and love. As I watched them take in the power of the work I knew, I was experiencing a deep *tikkun,* a repair of the world on behalf of the Divine Feminine. The wall that Lisa had perceived in her mother when she began her project had melted of its own accord in this instant and the studio was flooded with grace.

It was spring, around Mother's Day, when we hosted *Mother: Real and Imagined*. In addition to displaying the artworks, we planned an artists' tea party. We set the party up in the middle of the gallery. It seemed important to stage the party in a public space where people could come in and view the work while we drank tea and sherry and enjoyed a sumptuous meal.

We ran a clothesline across one wall near the ceiling of the space. We invited the artists to bring laundry and hang it with clothespins on the line. To honor her mother, Mary created an installation about cleaning and housework, which inspired us to incorporate evidence of our daily tasks, the household arts, into the show. Dorie performed songs about mothers, mothering, and the Divine Mother. Kim brought in her precious collection of china teacups and saucers—each one different like the artists and each one uniquely beautiful—that she inherited from her beloved grandmother. Some of us brought teapots. While we ate, women told the stories of their artwork and their experiences. Amy began to speak about how hard it is to balance all the tasks involved in being a mother. We honored our mothers; we honored ourselves.

This show affected me deeply. It seemed important to use the space of the studio to be present in our multiplicity: as artists, mothers, daughters, grandmothers. It is important to state that these identities are intertwined, not separate. We elevated the arts of home, of friendship, and anchored them in our created expression by sharing food, story, and song. I felt the images of our mothers witnessing us as we enlarged the space that women can inhabit. One artist's completely honest call evoked a response from so many. The significance of that show continues to ripple through our group of artists and through the community at large.

8

Art and
the Big Picture

In truth, neither art nor artists will save the world. Only a new way of being can do that—one that knits people together and inspires a different vision, an ethos of generosity and caring. Only when we dissolve our historical ties to the modern paradigm of materialism and overcome our habits of passivity and consumerism, is there any hope of moving toward a more spiritually informed way of looking at the world.

—Suzi Gablik (2002, 30)

Throughout my career I have grappled with the question, "How can I make art and be of service?" The answer I have received is that the methodology described in this book—intention and witness—can lead us to right action on behalf of the Soul of the World. These simple tools are the technique of noticing; they provide us with the means to listen past what our minds already know, to find a solution that originates in dialogue with the heart of whatever or whomever we are called to serve. Intention and witness are reliable means of raising the marginal ideas to the forefront, of seeing what we are missing. If art is a spiritual path, it must lead outward from the individual listening with the body, mind, heart, and soul into the commons, that place where we are called to serve. To be authentic, this path must be well trod both inward and outward.

What might art in service to the Creative Source look like? Thirty years ago art therapy was one answer to that question. Twenty years ago I thought the right answer was to set up a storefront, fill it with art materials, and invite ordinary people to make art out of their lives. At that time, I willingly subordinated my individual artist self to the ideal of creating a sustainable image-making community. I had a lot of ideas. Mainly, I just wanted to save the world. I believed that once the world was finally saved—and not before—I could make art freely and happily.

I got a different message from the Soul of the World.

SOUL OF THE WORLD: *Become spiritually fit for what comes your way. When you are suffering, suffer. When you are rejoicing, rejoice. Don't avoid the pain you see but also don't seek it avariciously. Activism can be as materialistic as anything else. Perhaps when you fully and freely make your art the world, or at least you, will be saved.*

ME: *That's a pretty self-indulgent view, don't you think?*

SOUL OF THE WORLD: *Thinking you can save something besides yourself, that something needs saving, is pretty arrogant. Are you sure you understand what you've been writing about?*

ME: *Well, maybe not entirely. I really get it on the small scale, when it gets into the big picture I fall back on other ideas. I get intimidated by "social responsibility," "activism," "community organizing."*

SOUL OF THE WORLD: *Your job is to listen, to witness, to attend, not to fit into some fashionable rubric. When its time to act, you'll know. Don't forget Dan Berrigan.*

When I was in college, still half in the fog I grew up in, just waking up to the fact that there was more going on in the world than my mother dying, I happened to be at Colgate University during an antiwar rally where Daniel Berrigan was one of the speakers. He said a lot of things, but what I remember was a suggestion he made: "Don't just do something, stand there." This phrase has stuck with me ever since. I felt I had been standing there watching my mother slowly and painfully die of cancer for years, and it hadn't helped at all. I didn't know then how to engage with suffering, my own or hers. I simply absorbed and held all the sadness and rage inside me. Yet here was Berrigan, this man who poured blood on draft records and spent years in jail protesting the war in Vietnam, suggesting that we just stand there.

I believe he was saying, "Bear witness," and asking us not to be mere bystanders angrily blaming or spouting platitudes. He was advocating an active attending–to, a feeling into, a deep listening, until right action presents itself. I believe he was suggesting we refrain from mindless action and that we consider the effect our actions might have. To stand in witness to what we believe is no small task. To have the patience to wait and the courage to see the correct action and then take it is a discipline. To care for those entrusted to us is no small task. To begin to envision the ways to "knit people together and inspire a different vision" is a task that art is made for, as the stories in this chapter attest.

> Attentively noticing the world, we find ourselves particularly attuned to certain issues, problems, situations. As though singled out by our temperament, history, wounds and passions, particular aspects of the world soul call us to them. The path of individuation is in part a fine-tuning to the ways in which we are called and obligated. Both its meandering and its insistent directions reflect the ways in which the world has entered us, insinuating themselves in our histories and stories. (Watkins 2004, 15)

Ten years spent in the public sphere, attempting to involve others in the enterprise of artmaking, led me to contemplate the larger issues of cultural forms, of how we participate in creating culture. For now, I answer the question of how to be of service by following my restless mind into the *mishkan* that is the studio and engaging with the ideas that I feel called to question: What is community, and how does art build, affect, or sustain it? How does commerce affect art and artmaking? What is the right relationship of personal art practice to work in the world? What are the next ways that intention and witness can engage the world?

We are gradually awakening to the ramifications of envisioning the entire world from the standpoint of commerce and profitability. We inhabit a larger story from which there is no escape and in which we all have a role to play in the rebalancing that must occur. With the marketing of products as our culture's highest value, even the self comes to be seen as a commodity to be "branded" and sold. What is art in such a world? What is the meaning of a Japanese businessman purchasing a Van Gogh painting for a sum greater than the gross national product of some countries? Is the value enhanced because the painting was not valued in its own time? By privatizing prisons and allowing them to bid for service contracts with corporations, have we covertly reestablished the institution of slavery? If art is to be a spiritual path, a commerce-free zone of creativity must be established in which such ideas can take up residence and be contemplated over time, generating images that instruct us. The studio can provide a *temenos*, or sacred space, where we can sit with our images and attend to them in dialogue together.

Rather than aspiring to success in the mercenary and mostly inaccessible high-end art world, arts professionals of all kinds are increasingly seeking to serve their respective communities as cultural workers. But what is a community? According to *Webster's*, the word *community* encompasses several meanings: "a unified body of individuals"; "people with a common interest living in a particular area"; "an interacting population of various kinds of individuals"; "a group linked by a common policy." I always look at the words in the dictionary surrounding the one I am considering. I find that words with a similar root often amplify my reflections. There is *communion*: "mutual participation"; "an act of sharing"; "intimate fellowship." Implicit in community is *communication*: "a process by which information is exchanged between individuals through a common system of symbols, signs, or behavior." And on the same page we find *communism*, our onetime national bugaboo, a system of enforced state-regulated sharing. Communism represents the antithesis of our enshrined national value of rugged individualism. As I reflect on the nuances of these words I begin to see what my concerns and issues about community and art might be. How do I learn to share, participate with others, communicate in a way that is satisfying and authentic? How do I accomplish the involvement with others required of community without losing myself, abandoning my desires?

If I expand my field of vision one aperture stop larger, I also ask: How does my work as an artist influence or even serve others? If I have an idea for a project in my community, how do I responsibly include the feelings and ideas of others without giving up my artistic vision? Artists sometimes have about as much sensitivity to the ecology of a community as a Wal-Mart Superstore opening in a small town. Richard Serra's now-infamous public art sculpture *Tilted Arc*, which bisected Federal Plaza in downtown Manhattan, destroyed the common space shared by workers and pedestrians. It was eventually taken down after citizens petitioned to have it removed. Paradoxically, the irritating presence of the imposing steel sculpture may have surfaced a community that was previously unidentified. Serra never professed to have service or even consideration of the community as part of his plan. This is astonishing, considering that his enormous steel sculpture significantly altered not only the urban landscape but also the sightlines and paths taken by ordinary people. In response to the petition to remove his work, he brought a lawsuit against the government. The Federal District Court ruled against him and the work was removed (Gablik 1995, 79–80). While Serra represents an extreme example of some of the values of modernist art, it seems fair to question whether it is time to revisit the prevailing values that guide art experiences for the larger community. Suzanne Lacy asks whether or not art can build community:

> Are there viable alternatives to viewing the self in an individualistic manner? And, if so, how does this affect our notion of "success"? Can artists and art institutions redefine themselves in less spectatorially oriented ways in order to regain the experience of interconnectedness—of subject and object intertwining—that was lost in dualistic Enlightenment philosophies, which construed the world as a spectacle to be observed from afar by a disembodied eye? (ibid., 81)

Lately I've been trying to let go of my grand schemes for saving the world; instead of making big plans, I want to deepen my trust that the Creative Source will show me how to be of service. It feels wrong to me that today's service organizations operate so much like businesses. Even friends of mine in the clergy have commented that employing "strategic-planning" approaches to recruitment of members and other aspects of congregational life have attained a disquieting ascendancy within their congregations. Rather than becoming resigned to the hegemony of the business model, I feel compelled to look again, to consider that there is value in approaching problems from more than one angle. I seek the marginal ideas that perhaps hold energy ripe for reinvestment in the commons. Nature tells us that monoculture can't survive, but how do new forms that challenge established models—or at least provide alternatives—come into being? The archetypal psychologist Mary Watkins tells us:

> When perceived through the heart, the imaged presentation of "what is" leads to longings and imaginings of what might be. It is

for this reason that cultural work on every continent listens attentively to the images—the poetry, the music, the art—that convey with passion and intensity what is being lived. We know that such listening may with grace bring into being images of the most deeply desired, utopic images toward which a community orients itself in striving. Such intense listening is like the fire that bursts the resistant pod of seeds, yielding a potential otherwise imprisoned. (2004, 17–18)

I wonder what would have happened if the unhappy workers had witnessed the Serra sculpture and appended their witness writings to their petition. Would a wildly expensive court proceeding at public expense have been necessary if Richard Serra could perceive the experience of his work through the eyes of those for whom he, if blindly and inadvertently, created it? Possibly so, considering that he is quoted as having said: "I don't think it is the function of art to be pleasing. Art is not democratic. It is not for the people." But my experience says that hearing open-hearted witness opens the hearts of those who hear as well. Perhaps the continued call and response of Serra's work might have influenced his view.

To be sustainable, I believe new cultural forms as well as new forms of serving one another must allow for inquiry, engagement, and celebration. I believe that such forms can grow out of a concerted engagement with the Creative Source and a willingness to take direction from the unfolding that the Creative Source continually tells us is our natural birthright. (Do the trees "try really hard" to get their leaves to unfold? an image recently asked me.) There are an infinite number of ways to serve the Creative Source or, as Rumi says, "to kneel and kiss the ground." I look at the different possibilities as cultural forms whose underlying assumptions must be brought to the surface through continual intentional critique.

We must also realize that each of us is called to different areas to lend our heartfelt engagement. Robert Hinkley employs his twenty years of experience as a corporate lawyer toward the elimination of corporate abuse of the environment, human rights, public health and safety, local communities, and employees (Cooper, 2004, 5). Because Hinkley has witnessed the corporation closely, he has a perspective those of us outside its immediate culture lack. He has worked to surface the underlying assumptions of corporations. The responsibility for the critique of culture falls to all of us; it is the birthright and the responsibility of everyone living in a democratic society. The goal is not consensus but multiplicity—not bland, unchallenging art, but various opportunities for engagement, for call and response, for culture that reflects the awesome differences we share.

In this chapter I examine three cultural forms of art practice that have inspired me. Each embodies art as a uniquely flexible spiritual path—having a clear intention, a different level of complexity, a different relation to commerce and community, and a different scale of meaning and influence. The stories begin to show the way in which the Creative Source works by activating through circumstance the potentials and tendencies in individual artists to come forward and step into the "big picture" with their work.

Art for Peace: Barbara's Story

Following the events of September 11, 2001, classes were cancelled at the School of the Art institute of Chicago, as I am sure they were at many universities, especially those in large cities like Chicago where the fear of additional attacks was palpable. My friend and colleague Barbara Fish invited her students to her home to make art. With the intention simply to bring comfort, connection, and clarity to one another, this small group gathered around Barbara's dining room table to share their fears and ground themselves in the creative process. Ever since, each week on Friday night, they have repeated the ritual. Lighting a candle and sharing food, they create images together. Their overarching intention has remained the same: to make art in community and increase their awareness of their responsibility to the world. If Barbara is out of town, someone else provides the space, and Barbara observes her practice wherever and with whomever she finds herself on a given Friday night.

Anything can be brought into the image space—personal concerns, world events, work-related problems. Barbara says: "By working to regain and maintain a present and clear attitude of peace, we contribute to peaceful solutions . . . we hold the space for each other to respond to challenges creatively instead of reacting out of fear" (Fish 2003, 1). There is no charge for the group, which is called Art for Peace. People find out about Art for Peace by word of mouth. Following the first meeting, Barbara sent a note inviting everyone in her apartment building to join Art for Peace. Group members who have moved went on to establish "peace cells" in their new environments. One of the original members joined the Peace Corps. She stayed in touch with the group and let them know she had established a peace cell in the community in Micronesia where she was assigned. Participants agree it is an act of service to witness one another in this way, as well as a form of self-care. Each week they renew their commitment to living in the paradox of maintaining personal peacefulness while also remaining awake to suffering: their own, each other's, and the world's.

The members of Art for Peace have considered and rejected ideas of becoming larger, becoming a nonprofit organization, or moving to a public space. They maintain a simplicity and humble elegance rarely found in present-day cultural forms. At the 2001 American Art Therapy Association annual meeting, they publicly presented their work and encouraged others to create their own Art for Peace groups. Their presentation was not motivated by ambition or designed to earn them accolades, but purely to share something they have found rewarding. Barbara likens the work to the yogic practice of *seva*, meaning selfless service, performed without attachment to results.

Art for Peace fills a need both for spiritual practice and for public ritual, and does so without imposing any religious doctrines or political ideologies. It allows for inquiry, engagement, and celebration with those present. While new people and random guests are welcome, a few core members are nearly always present. Their commitment to each other extends beyond Art for Peace and includes helping each other out in their lives as well. Both the individual soul and the sense of community among members are nourished. What is unique and defining is that unlike the forms of established religions, which serve to hold in place centuries-old ideas and identities, artmaking—the central act of Art for Peace—allows new ideas and images to enter the culture. For example, Barbara and the other peace artists have found that while it is not always possible to take action in the face of difficult events, artmaking is calming and dissipates anxiety, allowing clarity to arise. In spite of their clear and present consciousness about painful truths, these artists do not become paralyzed or retreat from reality, but accept whatever guidance comes to them in the service of peacefulness.

Barbara's work with Art for Peace has deepened her understanding of how art can serve as a valid, even life–saving, response to individual experiences, group concerns, and world events. Her research inquiry into "response art," art made to clarify her work as a therapist and educator of art therapists, led her to formulate the concept of "harm's touch," the psychological impact upon therapists and other helpers of moving through difficult work with others. Therapists often find their emotional lives blunted by the stories of trauma, abuse, and neglect they hear day after day. And they witness not only the personal pain of their clients, but also the social injustices and pathological cultural structures that give rise to and exacerbate many of their clients' problems. Barbara has found that making art about a client's stories helps to contain them outside her body, allowing her to maintain a heart connection to the experience and to remain an empowered witness to her client.

Working as an art therapist on a high–security inpatient unit for adolescents left Barbara with an accumulation of painful experiences. Not only did she take in the stories of trauma told by her patients, but she also witnessed the deterioration and demise of a once highly regarded milieu treatment setting. When a new conservative political climate swept through the healthcare establishment in Illinois, the children were reclassified as delinquent and the dignity and care that had characterized their treatment was exchanged for an ethic of punishment. This resulted in the unit's having a volatile atmosphere; on several occasions the Chicago police were called in to quell patient attacks on employees. A hospital policy directive mandated that at least one staff member of a few that the children trusted was to be assigned to the unit at all times to ensure some semblance of order and to subdue uprisings of panicked adolescents who felt unsafe in the turmoil. Barbara was among this group of trusted staff.

Despite her reports of patient abuse as the standard of care was violated, Barbara was ultimately helpless in the face of a changing system. Barbara experienced a soul–deadening malaise as drastic policy changes began to compromise her efficacy as a therapist and child advocate. Nevertheless, she was able to keep her heart open to the children during the demise of the hospital. She continued to meet with the children, create a momentarily safe space for them, and provide art to hold their stories. Sadly, as soon as the bureaucracy could arrange it, the hospital was closed and the children were removed to detention settings. Many of the patients, wards of the state, had lived on the unit for years. Barbara watched in dismay as these children—the most difficult and damaged in the state—lost what once had been a loving home space. Sweeping these children out as if into the gutter was surely an ugly act. James Hillman writes that "the question of evil, like the question of ugliness, refers primarily to the anaesthetized heart, the heart that has no reaction to what it faces, thereby turning the variegated sensuous face of the world into monotony, sameness, oneness" (1992, 64). For years Barbara carried the stories of these children inside her and in the images she made to respond to them. When she began her doctoral work, she found that these images were calling insistently to her, demanding that she tell their stories, that she finish the work she had begun in the hospital with the children. She started to recognize what loss and harm she herself had sustained from the closing of the hospital, and from being the recipient of the children's stories, images, and grief. In response to this recognition, and knowing that she needed to heal from this pain before moving on, Barbara began to intentionally excavate her soul through painting.

Mary Watkins writes: "When perceived through the heart, the imaged presentation of 'what is' leads to longings and imaginings of what might be" (2005). One of the images Barbara received was a hunchback figure whose face resembles hers (figure 33). She began to recognize the deforming effect that carrying around all the stories was having on her soul. Her image tells her: *You hold on to too much. The lesson here is to move through your exploration. You have to let go as you move on. You can't take everything with you.* She held on to her experiences at the hospital in many ways: through her art, through images of the children's art that she uses to teach art therapy graduate students, and in unresolved feelings in her body.

Barbara has begun to create the images and write the stories of those to whom she had lovingly attended and to see that although she couldn't save them or the hospital, she offered them clear attention during their work together and provided the gift of a loving mirror of their worth as people. The hunchback image reminds her that her work in supervising students takes her into many dark places, including shelters and prisons.

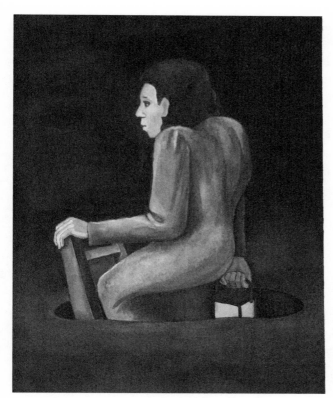

Figure 33. *Hunchback*, by Barbara Fish. Watercolor.

You move repeatedly into places that are concrete containers for pain. Human suffering, How can you not be affected? Everyone is affected by the world's pain. Most will not see it. They will wrap themselves in a paradigm that does not let them see. If you want to know what's true, you have to see. Then you can decide what to do. You can hold it like I do and let your body twist to contain it, or you can be a conduit. Let it move through you. Become a channel to let these things move toward expression. Let your images become portals. Others can choose to learn what you know by experiencing your images. The only way not to be harmed is to become useful as a way to help these images find expression.

The image then further explains that those whom Barbara sees can't make themselves visible; they are locked up, out of public view. If she chooses to be of service to them, she must decide what kind of witness to be: *Don't become a witness that is merely a container. You will calcify. The only way to be healthy is to be a vehicle. Witness, reflect, express. These are the three arms of response art. It happens in the process and it happens over time. Let yourself know the in-the-world part. Show your art at every opportunity.*

Art for Peace continues as a support of the unfolding discipline of response art for Barbara and her fellow peace artists. As she reclaims her soul, she will perhaps follow in the footsteps of Morihei Ueshiba, one of history's greatest martial artists and the founder of Aikido, which can be translated as "the art of peace." Ueshiba says:

> The Art of Peace begins with you. Work on yourself and your appointed task in the Art of Peace. Everyone has a spirit that can be refined, a body that can be trained in some manner, a suitable path to follow. You are here for no other purpose than to realize your inner divinity and manifest your innate enlightenment. Foster peace in your own life and then apply the Art to all that you encounter. (2002, 41)

Making Art, Being of Service:
Dayna's Story at the Open Studio Project

Dayna came into the world with a strong sense of justice and a high sensitivity to the pain of others. The central question she grapples with is how to manage being in the world without despair. As a child she managed by creating a world in her own imagination and not attending to the ordinary dissonance that occupies many young girls. She didn't care about cliques and their mandates about clothes or activities that were in or out of fashion. Dayna related mostly to her sister, who was close to her in age, and to her own art. When other children were bullied or picked on, however, she would fiercely intervene on their behalf. Now, as executive director of the Open Studio Project in Evanston, Illinois, Dayna has found a way to integrate her imagination with her commitment to social justice.

I first met Dayna in 1989, when she was a graduate student in art therapy at the School of the Art Institute. She organized a show, *Women against Violence*, and invited me to be one of the speakers at the opening. Dayna was moved to create the show in response to a number of shocking events that year. A young developmentally disabled woman was raped by a group of four boys on the football team while nine others watched in Glen Ridge, New Jersey. These events and the culture that supported the boys and complained that they would be "scarred for life" if they were forced to stand trial were the subject of a 1997 book by Bernard Lefkowitz called *Our Guys: The Glen Ridge Rape and the Secret Life of the Perfect Suburb*. The assault of the woman known then only as the "Central Park Jogger" took place in New York City. The then twenty–nine–year–old investment banker, Trisha Meili, revealed her identity in 2003 with the publication of a book about her experience. At the time of the attack, the public was given a story of five teenagers, boys of color, on a supposed rampage with thirty or so other teenagers that evening in Central Park, an event that led to the coining of the term *wilding* to describe the acts of April 19, 1989. The boys were convicted of inflicting rape, sodomy, and a beating that left Ms. Meili with permanent brain damage. Subsequently, another man, Matias Reyes, a convicted serial rapist, came forward and confessed to the crime, asserting that he acted alone. Ms. Meili, who has no memory of the attack, has stated that she will never know exactly what happened. The convictions of the five boys were vacated in 2002. Finally, closer to home, a young woman was abducted at a cash station in Chicago and later murdered. She was to have interned at the same hospital as Dayna that summer; her name was Dana.

Dayna's focus in the art show was to raise awareness about the prevalence of violence against women in our culture and to point out that it occurs across racial and economic lines, against women in all walks of life. The show was a powerful antidote to the stereotypes that were strengthened in the media following the attacks. The lawyers for the football players tried to portray the disabled girl as a Lolita who had seduced the boys. The media portrayed the young African–American and Hispanic boys in the Central Park incident as a dark force threatening the city. Dayna's idealism in conceiving the show was impressive. But I was perhaps most struck by her organization and determination in gathering the artists and her success in drawing a large and interested crowd—made even larger by her arrangement for television coverage—to participate in a sophisticated dialogue about the issues. She found donors to cover the printing and framing costs and, at the event itself, raised two thousand dollars for a local women's shelter. In sum, she created a forum for the idea that art can raise consciousness and change the world.

A few years later, Dayna, Deborah Gadiel, and I founded the Open Studio Project. Our intention was to make art and be of service in the world. None of us was satisfied with the art therapy approach that seeks to treat problems in individuals without addressing the social and cultural contexts in which those problems arise. The six years of the original Open Studio Project served as the laboratory in which the process described in this book was received and refined through our work together and with others. During that time, Dayna developed a style of painting highly detailed miniatures that combine meticulous realistic details with poetic narrative elements.

I and many others learned from Dayna that artmaking can be a means of staying awake to the messiness of life without going mad, and that it can help us to take compassionate right action. An important example of this comes from the experiences Dayna had with Helen, her elderly unmarried aunt. Dayna was a primary support person of Helen's—accompanying her to medical appointments, taking her shopping for clothes, and running other errands with her. Helen, like many elderly women, was slow moving and set in her ways. Dayna, who also had a young child to care for, would at times become impatient with Helen and found it stressful to remain compassionate. When Helen eventually had to move into a nursing home, Dayna helped to choose one that was well regarded and faithfully visited her there. Witnessing the smells, depressing surroundings, and lonely residents of even this high-quality nursing home proved exhausting for Dayna. She turned to her art to hold the sadness, fatigue, and frustration that make so many people distance themselves from elderly relatives. Dayna came to the studio and poured her energy into detailed renderings of the nursing home and of Helen and the other old ladies (figure 34).

In witness writings, these women spoke both as individuals and as manifestations of the Crone, a powerful archetype:

Do not cover me up! Dag nam it! I've been swept into the dark corners of despair and death for centuries. I am not to be feared. I have a lot of power. I am not feeble and useless. The world needs my energy. Every time you turn your

Figure 34. *Crone*, by Dayna Block. Watercolor.

face from Helen's fingers jabbing her dentures to get the tuna fish out, every time you try not to leave your lips on her wrinkled cheek too long, every time you avoid the rotting smell in her breath you avoid me and you can't avoid me, no one can. Release me from this black charred heart of ash. I have something to contribute. I am in all your hearts. I lurk in your basements. I rummage in your attics. I creep into your dreams and sleep beneath your beds. I watch while you fuck and sleep and eat and live. I watch and rot and wait for you to catch up to me. You in your endless tasks, busyness, movement, avoiding me, avoiding what you can't avoid. You better fucking embrace me and my stench and my brittle bones and my sagging skin and my reckless whiskers! Because I am your destiny. You better figure out my worth while yours seeps away with each passing breath.

The power of these women is evident in their words. They were thus dignified by being fully seen and held, neither sentimentalized nor transmogrified, but simply witnessed in their truth.

Dayna's witnesses challenged all of us to consider how we treat the old and to reflect on the inevitability of our own aging. These tiny images had a great impact on me as a teaching of both truth and compassion. In a witness writing I was given this practice: *Whenever you see an old woman, look at her and silently bless her for her contribution to the world. You don't know what or where it was. Notice your judgments, release them.* I found this practice liberating. I began to see beauty in old faces and could imagine the spark within the soul of each old woman as a mirror of the Divine.

During our time together at Open Studio Project, we learned how important it is to the survival of a community studio program to have a connection to a local community. In Chicago, Open Studio Project was a storefront curiosity passed daily by busy young professionals who flocked into Chicago's Near West Side to occupy new lofts and condominiums renovated during the gentrification boom of the mid 1990s. Our dream was to create a "public home space" (Timm–Bottos, personal communication, 2004) where these young professionals would work together with less financially advantaged local residents to create a vision of a community that could accommodate a diverse population. Regrettably, this never came to pass. None of us were rooted in that community, and at the end of the day we were eager to get home to our own families. We didn't grocery–shop there, or use the library, or worry if the schools were good enough for our children.

Dayna transplanted Open Studio Project from its original location to Evanston, the community where she and her family live. Along with Sarah Laing, Ted Harris, and a host of other dedicated artists, Dayna has created a vibrant nonprofit arts and social service agency that is embraced and supported by the Evanston community. Open Studio Project now has a life of its own, providing art with intention and witness to all interested individuals. They have free and scholarship–supported programs in place for people of all ages and serve youth after school in affiliation with violence prevention agencies from around Evanston; programs are also available for women who have experienced violence. OSP is a public home space that brings people from many backgrounds together in a safe environment where they can speak and hear each other's truth. The process of intention and witness supports individuals doing work to understand their own lives through art and writing. In addition, it supports OSP the agency. OSP's board of directors uses the process to define the organization's goals for growth and development as a nonprofit in tumultuous economic times. Ideas such as a universal ethic of care are implemented in planning and fund-raising as well as in the classes and workshops.

Dayna believes strongly in the power of intentional group process as a guide to creating community. A nonprofit agency is a democracy, and an art studio is a unique environment in which to practice and enlarge our understanding of democratic principles. Sharing power is a challenge in any enterprise; but, as Dayna says, when difficult decisions present themselves, OSP board members and staff can return to the studio process to reconnect to the guidance of the Creative Source and clarify their feelings and thoughts before taking action. The studio is a place where one can "just stand there" and make art until clarity arises. Making art is a process of discernment that keeps egos in check and participants grounded in their ideals. By noticing discomfort and creating an image to understand it in the safety of nonjudgment, a culture of transparency develops in which the struggle toward authentic and compassionate action is supported by all as an intrinsic value. The parameters of the culture throughout OSP are that respect for people and relationships come first. The studio process fosters an inherent belief that the Creative Source never guides us to harm one another. People involved with OSP are expected to use the process first and foremost for themselves, with the faith that doing so will allow them to participate in the community at their highest level and lead them to raise funds and manage programs in the right way.

OSP is a subtle force for good in the Evanston community. Its workers do not seek to actively change anything, but rather to lead by embodying the intrinsic values of the commonweal. Their teen participants often struggle with verbal skills, making writing and reading a witness a challenge. Dayna says: "On a person-by-person basis, we develop ways to encourage them to use language . . . access their own voices and to learn from their own artmaking process . . . there is an inherent respect for every person who participates at OSP, respect as a co-creator/artist and as a human being with something of great value to offer the world; respect as a source of genuine wisdom." The writing and reading aloud of witnesses allows each person to tap into a place of eloquence that might eventually become accessible in school or everyday discourse or when the opportunity arises to advocate for justice. People who appear quite ordinary and even at times unappealing reveal their divine spark in their artwork and witness writing.

When I left OSP for my own community, I knew that the intensity of the day-to-day rigors of a nonprofit setting, even with the support of the process, was not my path. I am deeply grateful to Dayna for nurturing OSP into its full potential. She has, with the help of many others, taken the process into the practical realm of raising money, working with other agencies, and cultivating a viable community home space unique to Evanston. Because she is not only an "arts professional" but also a mother, wife, and active citizen, fully engaged in the life of community, Dayna is constantly able to be a witness for her deeply held values and ideals. The balanced growth depicted in the OSP annual report supports this experiment in intentional democracy. Tapping into the Creative Source for guidance makes the difficult work of living our ideals bearable, even joyous. Ever mindful that they are serving a higher value than mere self-interest, the artists of Open Studio Project, under Dayna's leadership, thrive personally and shine a beacon of hope to all who enter their simple art space.

Amazwi Abesifazane: "Voices of Women"

I enter the Betty Rymer Gallery at the School of the Art Institute of Chicago to view an exhibit of "memory cloths" created by women in post-apartheid South Africa. One hundred and fifty pieces are being showed, and all share the same elegant format of presentation. Each colorful ten-by twelve-inch cloth cloth is matted within a simple frame and contains three major elements: a visual depiction of the artist's story, a color photo of the artist, and two paragraphs of the text of her story—one in English and one in her native language. The cloths are rendered in a combination of embroidery, appliqué, and beading. As I view the first piece and read the text of its story, my eyes fill with tears. I try to move to the second cloth but find I can't take in any more information—my heart is brimming. The combination of the simple stitched form, the photo of the woman's face, and the stark facts of the violence of her story simply stop me in my tracks. I wasn't expecting to be so completely overwhelmed or to find that the project was guided by an application of intention and witness on a scale greater than any I had seen before. The gallery director, noticing my response, invites me to join a class session that is about to begin. The creator of the project and two of the women involved with it were addressing a class on African popular culture.

That was how I came to hear Lindiwe Baloyi, a longtime social activist who serves as chairperson of the Amazwi Abesifazane Committee and head of South Africa's Women's National Coalition in KwaZulu–Natal, and Promise Tholakele Zuma, an artist/stitcher in the project who works as an area coordinator and stitching–group facilitator for the project. When Promise speaks in her native Zulu, Lindiwe translates for us into English. A slightly built and animated woman, Promise tells us how intimidated she was when she first began to participate in the program; she did not have sewing skills and certainly did not consider herself an artist. She leans into Lindiwe, putting her hand on the larger woman's shoulder as she expresses how amazed she is to now be helping other women and to be traveling to the United States to talk about the project. When it becomes clear that the art students attending the class are at a loss for questions to ask, Andries Botha, founder of Create Africa South and originator of the memory cloth project, explains to us his passionate commitment to the recovery of the soul of South Africa.

A well–known contemporary South African sculptor and an Afrikaner, Botha "moved away from mainstream sculptural production" in 1984, when he began to work with thatching, wattle, and wax—materials drawn from "the South African landscape" (MacKenny 2000). Tires and telephone wire found their way into his work as explicit references to the barbarity and squalor of the apartheid era. That same year, he founded a community arts workshop for disadvantaged South Africans and personally sponsored several artists. In the early 1990s, Botha served as visual arts chairperson for the newly elected democratic government, to which he submitted a proposal for the creation of a national cultural policy for the arts. In 1994 Botha founded a women's textile collective. *Home*, an installation created in 1997, appears at first glance to be a generic house surrounded by a white picket fence. Inside, inscribed on the walls, are quotations from statements given to the Truth and Reconciliation Commission by perpetrators of violence.

Botha says: "I would like to see myself as operating in many domains as a creative person: One domain is the manufacture of objects, the other is responding as creatively as I possibly can to the emotional and societal context in which I live" (MacKenny 2000). In his quest to understand "cultural citizenship," he has consistently examined his own identity as a white Afrikaans male. In 1998 he created *South African Skin*, a series of photographs that features—among other things—images of white South African men's tattoos. The men "are defeated, but their skin carries the map of optimism or arrogant history" (ibid.).

Apartheid was instituted in 1948 and maintained until 1994, when Nelson Mandela was elected the first president of the South African democracy. According to Botha, those decades of brutal oppression completely devastated the traditional lifestyle and psychic infrastructure of South Africa's indigenous people. In the ten years since the end of apartheid, South Africa has made many strides forward, and in spite of a growing black middle class, much of the black population remains poor.. The decision to forgo Nuremberg–type trials in favor of the Truth and Reconciliation model had many complex reasons. Desmond Tutu, chair of the Truth and Reconciliation Commission, says: "We had to balance the requirements of justice, accountability, stability, peace and reconciliation. We could very well have had justice, retributive justice, and had a South Africa lying in ashes—a truly Pyrrhic victory if ever there was one. Our country had to decide very carefully where it would spend its limited resources to the best possible advantage" (Tutu 1999, 23).

The TRC amnesty process had as its foundation the policy that if a perpetrator of political violence came forward to tell their part in crimes against their fellow citizens, whether at the behest of the government or in some other context, the crime was then completely expunged. The victims gave up their rights to pursue criminal charges or civil damages—a tremendous sacrifice. It would have been very difficult to make charges stick in many cases in criminal proceedings because most of the violence was carried out by the state, which also had the means to cover it up. In addition, unlike in Nuremberg, where Nazi criminals were tried by an international court made up of the victorious Allies, the TRC, the victims, and the perpetrators were all South African citizens who somehow had to learn to move beyond the past and live together in a new way.

This enterprise required a profound exercise of the human imagination, and South Africa met the challenge. Many models for retributive justice exist, but South Africa gave the world its first secular model of restorative justice. Such an imaginative leap was made possible by the African philosophy of *ubuntu*, which underlay all the TRC's activities.

> In the spirit of *ubuntu*, the central concern is the healing of breaches, the redressing of imbalances, the restoration of broken relationships, a seeking to rehabilitate both the victim and the perpetrator, who should be given the opportunity to be reintegrated into the community he has injured by his offense. (Tutu 1999, 54–55)

When I read about *ubuntu*, I felt I was being given a puzzle piece I had searched for all my life. Adversarial justice never made sense to me; simply placing a wronged party in opposition to an innocent party ignores the complexity of human relationships. One party is expected to shoulder blame while the other assumes the disempowering role of victim. Neither emerges from the process whole.

A powerful underlying factor in *ubuntu* is the sense of how the "religious other" is regarded. Dirk Louw calls for an ideal that is a "decolonized assessment of the religious other," and by implication of those who are racially or culturally "other" as well. Ubuntu requires that while acknowledging differences, one should fall into neither absolutism nor relativism when regarding those differences. Instead, we are called to privilege the concept that we are all, whatever our beliefs, part of a larger spiritual whole (1998). Through our relationships within this rich intersubjective matrix, we become who we are and what we can be. A related traditional African idea is *seriti*, an energy, power, or source that makes us ourselves and unites us in personal interactions with others (ibid.). I compare this to my use of the concept of the Creative Source, of which each of us is a part and from which we all partake of the same source energy.

> *Ubuntu* directly contradicts the Cartesian conception of individu-
> ality in terms of which the individual self can be conceived
> without thereby necessarily conceiving of the other. . . . Thus un-
> derstood, the word "individual" signifies a plurality of personali-
> ties corresponding to the multiplicity of relationships in which
> the individual in question stands." (ibid., 3)

In my experience of reading and hearing witness writings read aloud in the studio, I have no doubt that a larger force is speaking to us and through us to each other. Additionally, through the infinite variety of im-ages, we come to know intimately the multiple elements that make up our personalities. It is far more difficult to cast the world in reductive di-chotomies—black and white, good and evil, sacred and profane—when one has witnessed apparently irreconcilable potentials, for example a commitment to peace and the ability to perpetrate violence, coexisting in oneself. It is astonishing and thrilling to discover language and concepts that have existed for centuries in Africa that support the studio discover-ies. Through apartheid, the South African government tried to negate the existence of multiple realities and enforce a culture of black–and–white thinking. I feel deep gratitude for the South African struggle for liberation from this system. South Africans, black and white, have fought with their bodies and hearts to resolve conflicts with which most of us in the West-ern world have grappled only symbolically. We have an enormous amount to learn from the literalized version of the archetypal forces of dark and light that has played out in South Africa.

Deeply moved by witnessing the Truth and Reconciliation Commis-sion's work, Andries Botha in 2000 founded a nongovernmental organiza-tion called Create Africa South. The organization's first project was the crafting of the memory cloths of Amazwi Abesifazane (Voices of Women). Botha's realization that "the body is the primary site of all creativity" and that a "woman's body is the fundamental site for the recovery of a society" led him to consult with SEWU, the Self-Employed Women's Union (Botha 2004a), about how to realize his vision. Botha believes that all people are endowed with the energy of the Creative Source. Creativity transcends the "power-drenched" assumption that people with specialized training cre-ate art that is more valid than that of people without it. Botha asks:

Why do cultural practitioners accept that the museum, gallery, curatorial triumvirate exclusively negotiates their complex thoughts and emotions as creative commodification? Why do these particularly Western definitions for cultural practice become our desired role model, purpose and value within an increasingly complex and diverse cultural world defined by unique and contested cultural realities? (2004b, 16)

Indeed, why do we unquestioningly accept the version of reality fed to us by professionals and so-called experts? Is the world not less interesting, less free, and more homogenized when all of us do not exercise our right to add our imaginative contribution to the whole? Botha recognized that the TRC retrieved accounts from a relatively narrow stratum of society and that those accounts would become South Africa's history. This was especially true since presentations were limited to accounts in which a political motive is present or the "gross violation of human rights"—defined as killing, kidnapping, or torture—occurred (Tutu 1999, 45). This limitation was ostensibly necessary to make the TRC's task a practicable one. But its effect was to exclude from the process of national healing those people, primarily women, who had been the most silenced and marginalized during the years of apartheid. "Images of the past commonly legitimate the present social order through shared memory" (McEwan 2003, 743).

What is striking about the memory cloths is that in response to the originating prompt—"Tell about a day you will never forget"—women relate stories not only of political violence, but also of everyday tragedies that beset the lives of people trying to survive under adverse conditions—natural disasters, family members killed by AIDS, animal attacks, local disputes, and drunk driving. Also portrayed on the memory cloths are accounts of violence inflicted by security police and, perhaps most disturbingly, at the hands of comrades in the struggle for liberation. Creating an archive that isn't only spoken and transcribed, but also recorded through imagery and women's craft, allows these women's accounts to be both heard and dignified.

The memory cloth represents a melding of two traditions: the Zulu love letter (http://minotaur.marques.co.za/clients/zulu/bead.htm) and the European sampler. The former is a kind of beaded broach, usually given as a gift by a young girl to a young man, that carries an encoded message; the latter is a needlework picture traditionally made by women, embroidered with a homily or Bible verse, and hung in the home. Botha insisted that the women sign their work and that their photos be included in the presentation. In this way they become neither faceless victims to be shielded from view nor anonymous crafters from the Third World, but individual artists bearing witness to the complexity of their life circumstances.

Voices of Women has multiple intentions: to provide a forum for women to come together and tell their stories in peer groups and be witnessed by others; to alleviate the stress of life in post–apartheid South Africa, which materially has changed little for the citizens of the rural areas; and to remotivate people to move on from the past. In addition, the women learn or re–learn traditional skills of cloth work and bead work, form artists' collectives and begin to sell their artistic products to the world market. The most significant intention of Voice of Women, however, is to create an archive to augment and complement the work of the Truth and Reconciliation Commission. Despite having suffered acts of violence that were often extreme, indigenous women from rural South Africa were not widely included in the TRC process.

> These personal testimonies of how apartheid directly affected the lives of individual women, when amassed, become a collective indictment of the malfeasance of the system. And because they are visual and handmade, they are able to move viewers' emotions, juxtaposing the almost childlike images created by these women against the devastating seriousness of what they depict. (Becker 2004, 3)

The history of apartheid compounded by the present HIV/AIDS epidemic has devastated the black male population of South Africa: "Women are left alone to secure the future." But women, although physically intact, have experienced, along with the entire population, a "devastation of the soul" (Botha 2004a).

Botha hoped to respond to questions from the students and engage in a dialogue, but it seemed that they were as stunned as I was by the work that filled the gallery. He told us that in addition to sheltering Voices of Women, which he calls "a solution of the imagination," Create Africa South is collating the poetry of Mazisi Kunene, a major contemporary black South African poet. A women's health education class has also grown out of the work. As women sat together and sewed, it became clear through discussions that many did not have information about their bodies, their rights to self-determination, or facts about the AIDS crisis. At present the death rate in KwaZulu-Natal, the province where Voices of Women originated, is greater than the birth rate (Botha 2004b, 13). Create Africa South is committed to exploring and expressing the relationship between society and creativity by responding imaginatively to the needs of the people as they emerge.

A profound theme that comes through in reading accounts of the work of the Truth and Reconciliation Commission is the spiritual nature of the work. In addition to TRC Chair Desmond Tutu, three other members of the clergy were appointed to the TRC, which consisted mostly of lawyers but also included physicians and psychologists. Archbishop Tutu recalls that they began the process with a spiritual retreat: "We sought to enhance our spiritual resources and sharpen our sensitivities. We sat at the feet of a spiritual guru, who happened to be my own spiritual counselor, while we kept silence for most of the day, seeking to open ourselves to the movement and guidance of the transcendent Spirit" (Tutu 1999, 81).

The Commission's work ended with a retreat at Robben Island, where Nelson Mandela had been imprisoned for twenty-seven years. Each day of the TRC began with a prayer, and the atmosphere created for the victims to testify included prayer, hymns, and ritual candlelighting in honor of those who had died. Archbishop Tutu wore his purple cassock and so stood as the archetype of spiritual leader. Called upon by journalists to justify the spiritual nature of the hearings, Desmond Tutu explained that it was crucial to the TRC process to recognize the inherent spiritual context of the task of reconciliation and healing.

The point is that, if perpetrators were to be despaired of as monsters and demons, then we were thereby letting accountability go out the window because we were declaring that they were not moral agents to be held responsible for the deeds that they had committed. More importantly, it meant that we abandoned all hope of their being able to change for the better. (ibid., 85)

The work of Amazwi Abesifazane convinces me that in the studio process we are recovering the wisdom of ordinary life, of the indigenous soul. It has been alive and flourishing in Africa, where we are privileged to see the enactment of the Soul of the World in the clash of two peoples. We are given extraordinary models of art in service to the world, not only to the individuals who have become liberated in South Africa, but to all of us. We are offered new models of justice, of politics, of creating culture and writing history. All is not gilt-edged; much is still guilt-edged. Desmond Tutu describes the disappointment of many South Africans that more white citizens do not grasp that they have much to gain spiritually from owning up to their role in apartheid. That gain cannot be claimed, however, as long as the material conditions of blacks and whites remain so stunningly disparate. Confession, forgiveness, and reparation are all necessary for true reconciliation.

Each of us must realize that whatever form our privilege takes, it is not our own; it was created through the efforts of those who came before us. In many cases, it was created at the expense of others as well. We will never grasp the gift and promise of the wonderful concept of the inter-connectedness of all beings until we also accept the interconnectedness of our responsibility to one another and the world. It is my fervent belief that with the intention to open to these truths, we will be given images to instruct us in how to proceed. "If we are going to move on and build a new kind of world community there must be a way in which we can deal with a sordid past" (Tutu 1999, 278). Andries Botha gives us a re-markable model of an artist willing to engage with what is, and the women of Amazwi Abesifazane give us a model of how that that en-gagement can create a vibrant community that discovers its own needs and how to meet them.

9
Building Image Communities

"I think it's time for us to face the soul of the world," writes mathematician Ralph Abraham (in Sheldrake, McKenna, Abraham 2001, 65). "Traveling up the great chain of being toward the world soul, we may get in touch with things that precede any capability of verbalization, that seem to reach out for contact, that are learning to communicate in a language we can understand" (p. 92).

I "think" so, too. Experience, however, shows me over and over that the Soul of the World does not yield Itself to thought.

SOUL OF THE WORLD: *That knife is too sharp, cuts too clean, you've thought too much. Drop your gaze down to the eyes in the soles of your feet, stand on my green body and speak what you feel.*

ME: *I feel such sorrow that I fall to my knees.*

SOUL OF THE WORLD (SMILING): *Now lie down, body to body, and let us finally speak, heart to heart, soul to soul, open and let me flow into you and then you will see, thought will not suffice. You must see and hear and smell and touch.*

Whenever I am really stumped, I lie down on the earth. Even in my postage–stamp–size backyard, with power lines crisscrossing the sky above my head, I hear the truth when I am body to body with the earth. Sometimes, when I am walking the dog, I stop to stand under a tree. I look up and feel the loving energy streaming down on me. Standing under the tree, my feet on the earth, I open to its voice, I understand its speech, which is rarely in words. I ask a question and my eye may light on something in the landscape that gives me the answer I seek. For the longest time I have known in my bones about the transformative power of images and image making in groups. I have tried through the practice of art therapy, through founding two community studios and doing consulting for a number of others, through initiating community–wide art projects, to think my way into how best to manifest the transformative power of artmaking with others.

Over and over I have also learned that thinking gets in the way. I have learned about the limitations of our present cultural forms, our fixed ideas of how to do things, the illusions we have chosen over the simple example of nature, which we are a part of and apart from. The Soul of the World is saying, *Stop, slow down, listen, watch, remember to give and receive. The creative process is a form of respiration, give out, receive back and stop long enough to learn how to give and receive.* In creating image communities, I have tried out the form of nonprofit organization in the Open Studio Project and a business model at Studio Pardes. While the idea of Studio Pardes as a "for-profit" business felt incorrect, there are no more nuanced ways for designating what a public space where my name was on the lease and I signed the checks might be called. Both raised enormous questions for me, both philosophical as well as practical. How does the model we choose affect the presence or absence of the Creative Source? What is the best use of my energy, as an artist or as an entrepreneur? What is a fair amount to charge for workshops that honors the value of my time and the cost of rent, materials, and maintenance? As a nonprofit at OSP, we planned fundraising events, which, while they raised cash to supplement fees for workshops, took an enormous toll in time and energy. As a for-profit enterprise at Studio Pardes, we planned shows and sold artwork, taking a percentage for the studio. As I record these strategies, they seem perfectly reasonable, and, evaluated objectively, they were even successful. All I can do is witness the discomfort that grew in me as I saw Studio Pardes in danger of becoming partly a store with items for sale. The half-mile area that my town has designated as an "arts district," in which Studio Pardes was situated, originally had a number of working artists' studios. Now it is almost entirely a retail district, with charming shops, many selling handmade items by individual artists. The expectations of shops are different from the expectations of an artist's workspace. Most artists, like myself, found the two expectations at cross purposes. The main way that most people have of interacting with art is to buy some. Buying art is a perfectly fine thing to do; I do not begrudge artists who sell work, as I have certainly done. But the selling of art in some way conflicts with the engagement with art as a spiritual path. As I sit with the lasting unease that rises in me about the relationship of commerce to art as a spiritual path, I feel like the proverbial blind man trying to describe the elephant. I don't yet have enough information.

I am deeply grateful for those who can, like Dayna, stay with a form, in her case a nonprofit community studio, and work patiently to transform it, I found I could not. She continually tempers the enthusiasm of those within OSP's board and members who imagine bigger would be better by guiding them as a community to return to their intention and receive guidance from the Creative Source about how to manifest that intention most authentically. After despairing of my own failures, I realized that the answer is not in doing away with the forms and existing models, which have value in spite of their imperfections. They must be helped to evolve. The answer that interests me is instead to create simple, small experimental forms that can allow us to invite some of the thoughts that bind us into the creative process, where we can surface our thoughts and feelings and examine how deep our allegiance is and should be to certain ideas—for instance, that profit is the ultimate good. This idea is so embedded in our culture as to be almost unquestioned. We don't realize we are following the model of the corporation without asking if it fits our circumstances or needs to be modified. As Robert Hinkley's work shows, when we trace the origin of profit as the ultimate aim, we begin to see how such an idea can be shifted. He says: "Corporations act the way they do for one simple reason: they are bound by corporate law to try to make a profit for shareholders . . . in 1886 the Supreme Court determined that corporations were entitled to the rights of citizenship under our Constitution. Since then, the corporation has developed into the worst kind of citizen: one that claims all the rights but shirks the responsibilities of citizenship" (in Cooper 2004, 5). Hinkley is working to change the mandate of the corporation so that the corporate code reads: "The duty of the directors henceforth shall be to make money for shareholders *but not at the expense of the environment, human rights, public health and safety, dignity of employees, and the welfare of the communities in which the company operates*" (ibid). This simple addition of twenty–eight words to a standing law is a revolutionary change in intention.

In small, sustainable image communities, like Barbara's Art for Peace group, we can allow ourselves to be instructed by the Soul of the World.

When the members of that group had been meeting for a while, ideas began to arise such as "maybe we should take this into a public space, invite a larger group, have a show." Being together and remembering their basic intention—to remain peaceful—helped them discuss and decide what to do about issues of ownership and taking credit for the group. We need transitional spaces and we need a lot of them; they need to be accessible, abundant, and free.

I have noticed that in most situations, once a person has paid money for something, his or her feeling of obligation stops. The transactional model of exchange actually inhibits creativity to some degree. As the Creative Source reminded me in the witness cited at the beginning of this chapter, *"the creative process is a form of respiration"*—or, as Estella Conwill Majozo says, a form of call and response. Lewis Hyde writes: "As the artist works, some portion of his creation is bestowed upon him. An idea pops into his head, a tune begins to play, a phrase comes to mind, a color falls into place on the canvas. . . . with any true creation comes the uncanny sense that 'I,' the artist, did not make the work" (1983, xii). When we open to the Creative Source, we receive a gift. Most of our dealings in life are transactional; we buy almost anything we want. While money is an impersonal currency that offers universality and convenience, it blunts the development of relationship. Hyde says: "It is the cardinal difference between gift and commodity exchange that a gift establishes a feeling-bond between two people, while the sale of a commodity leaves no necessary connection" (1983, 56). Unlike my husband, who searches for the cheapest gas when filling his car, I go consistently to the station where I also receive the gift of added service. The owner has been willing to drive out in his truck when I've been stuck to jump-start my car and has performed other acts of generosity that bind me to him in loyalty. I was sad when he installed pay-at-the-pump credit-card service, even though it saves time. Now I just exchange a wave with whoever is operating the cash register inside the station, if they aren't staring off into space in boredom. When ideas are surfaced, we can weigh whether convenience and profit are more valuable than personal contact, than saying hello to a live person and hearing about their recent vacation or their grandchildren. Do we want connection? The Creative Source surely does.

Paradoxical as it may seem, it is precisely such simple and crucial ideas that arise when one sits in the studio, makes an intention to see what is, and follows the image to the message it holds. It occurs to me that we need to nurture and support a commerce-free zone of creativity for ourselves, our neighbors, and people we don't yet know. Wherever we are guided by intention and witness—whether in neighborhood image making, creativity circles, or situations like Amazi Abesifazane—we can witness and record the history of ordinary people, which makes us more mindful of our own lives. We can surface the ideas that underlie our actions and expectations, and decide intentionally, and with guidance from the Creative Source, whether they serve us.

Such artmaking opportunities can begin a tiny movement to recover what Hyde calls a gift economy (1983). "We might picture differences between gifts and commodities . . . by imagining two territories separated by a boundary. A gift, when it moves across the boundary, either stops being a gift or else it abolishes the boundary" (p. 61). We need to relearn gift exchange precisely because there are so many boundaries that need to be transgressed. Hyde continues: "Because of the bonding power of gifts and the detached nature of commodity exchange, gifts have become associated with community and with being obliged to others, while commodities are associated with alienation and freedom" (p. 67). Having a choice of commodities is one kind of freedom, one on which our culture and our corporations concentrate a great deal of effort. One could spend a lifetime, several even, sorting through the available types and brands of face creams, cars, telephone long-distance plans, breakfast cereals, cable television services, stereo systems, and exercise equipment. But this freedom only has value if our basic needs are authentically met outside the sphere of commerce. Although television commercials would have us believe otherwise, we cannot purchase meaning or a sense of belonging.

I first began to think about these ideas when spontaneous gift giving emerged in the studio. Mary, one of the artists who exhibited their work in *Mother: Real and Imagined*, was engaged with ideas about her mother, who had valued cooking, cleaning, and taking care of her family. Like many of us, Mary rebelled against a circumscribed role as housewife and mother. In her art, she witnessed the act of cleaning as a divine act of service. She brought nontoxic cleaning supplies and cleaned a section of the wall on which many artists had left drips and marks while painting. She framed the section of clean wall with masking tape and witnessed it. She recovered the dignity of sacred service and recognized the gift in her mother's life of service to her family. She created handmade invitations to invite artists to come for a cleaning day at the studio and brought lunch for everyone. She made it clear that everyone was welcome to eat, whether or not they could stay to help clean. Some artists, not wanting to or unable to clean, could not accept the gift of lunch and made various excuses to leave right after the class. Some stayed for lunch and left; a few stayed with Mary and I and cleaned. I felt uplifted and energized as I scrubbed the floor alongside Mary. I had witnessed a true gift exchange—not to me directly, but to the Creative Source and to the space of the studio.

During a retreat I took in Arizona to work on this book, I received an image of a woman dressed in saffron robes, her head shaved like a nun or monk. She sits on the ground in a desert surrounded by mountains, a serene expression on her face. She holds a begging bowl. She speaks about an essential element of the creative process: *We open ourselves, and something like grace, some deep and mysterious force, flows into and transforms us. It is a relational experience.* Martin Buber (1970) says: "This is the eternal origin of art that a human being confronts a form that wants to become a work through him. Not a figment of his soul but something that appears to the soul and demands the soul's creative power. What is required is a deed that a man does with his whole being: if he commits it and speaks with his being the basic word to the form that appears, then the creative power is released and the work comes into being" (p. 60).

Like Mary, many of the artists described in this book are responding to the Soul of the World as they relearn and reinvent ideas about service, work, value, and gift. We are called to work together in a way that mirrors the generosity of the Creative Source back to Itself and to each of us. We must see the Divine in everything if we are to survive. We can't simply think "Oh, we are all connected" and point to cell phones and computers as our primary evidence for this. We are being called to define self and other in new terms, but with old means—images and the support of others.

Images initiate the shift, and the presence of others allows us to amplify it through the process of witness in a group, which yields changes that transcend mere thinking, changes that reverberate on every level of our intersubjective being. Joanna Macy (1990) says: "The self is a metaphor. We can decide to limit it to our skin, our person, our family, our organization or our species. We can select its boundaries in objective reality. As system theorists see it, our consciousness illuminates a small arc in the wider currents and loops of knowing that interconnect us" (p. 59). Macy characterizes our growing awareness as a "greening of the self" and observes that "we are beginning to realize that the world is our body" (ibid., 60). She says that letting the energy of the earth flow through us gives us buoyancy and resilience. These are the very qualities that we access and cultivate in the studio process. Art *is* a way of knowing.

To form an image community, take two or more people, sit down together at a table or tape paper to the wall. State an intention collectively as well as individually: What do you really wish to call into your life? Write down these intentions. Make marks on the paper in a way that gives you pleasure, with whatever materials are at hand. After a while, sit down and look at what has been created. Notice what captures your attention, and write what comes. Then read to each other the new stories you've received. Next week, do it again. Light a candle. Bring food. Bless one another. We can recover all we need to know.

> We can reinhabit time and our own story as a species. We were present back there in the fireball and the rains that streamed down on this still molten planet, and in the primordial seas. We remember that in our mother's womb, where we wear vestigial gills and tail and fins for hands. We remember that. That information is in us and there is a deep, deep kinship in us, beneath the outer layers of our neocortex or what we learned in school. There is a deep wisdom, a bondedness with our creation and an ingenuity far beyond what we think we have. And when we expand our notions of what we are to include in this story, we will have a wonderful time and we will survive. (ibid., 63)

Art is a path to this place and these stories. If we engage our images, they will sketch a map to our survival.

References

Allen, Pat B. *Art Is a Way of Knowing*. Boston: Shambhala Publications, 1995.

Ayto, John. *Dictionary of Word Origins*. New York: Little, Brown, 1990.

Badiner, Allen Hunt (ed.). *Mindfulness in the Marketplace*. Berkeley: Parallax Press, 2002.

Barron, Stephanie. *Degenerate Art*. Los Angeles: Museum Associates, 1991.

Becker, Carol. "*Amazwi Abesifazane* (Voices of Women)," Betty Rymer Gallery, School of the Art Institute of Chicago, 2004. Exhibition pamphlet.

Botha, Andries. Informal lecture. Betty Rymer Gallery, School of the Art Institute of Chicago, April 30, 2004a.

———. "Reclaiming the Emotional and Public Self." Amazwi Abesifazane. Betty Rymer Gallery, School of the Art Institute of Chicago, 2004b. Exhibition pamphlet.

Boucher, Sandy. *Discovering Kwan Yin, Buddhist Goddess of Compassion*. Boston: Beacon Press, 1999.

Broner, E. M. *Bringing Home the Light*. San Francisco: Council Oak Books, 1999.

Brown, Lyn Mikel. "Telling a Girl's Life: Self-Authorization as a Form of Resistance." In *Women, Girls, and Psychotherapy: Reframing Resistance*, edited by Carol Gilligan, Annie G. Rogers, and Deborah L. Tolman. New York: Harrington Park Press, 1991.

Buber, Martin. *I and Thou*. New York: Charles Scribner's Sons, 1970.

Clapp, Thaddeus. "Art Within Reach," *History Matters*, May 17, 2004. http://historymatters.gmu.edu/d/5100.

Conwill Majozo, Estella. "To Search for the Good and Make It Matter." In *Mapping the Terrain: New Genre Public Art*, edited by Suzanne Lacy. Seattle: Bay Press, 1995.

Cooper, Arnie. "Twenty-eight Words That Could Change the World." *The Sun*, no. 345. (September 2004): 4–11.

Craighead, Meinrad. *The Mother's Songs: Images of God the Mother*. New York: Paulist Press, 1986.

Dijkstra, Bram. *American Expressionism*. New York: Harry Abrams, 2003.

Dissanayake, Ellen. *Art and Intimacy*. Seattle: University of Washington Press, 2004.

Donaldson, O. Fred. *Playing by Heart*. Deerfield Beach, Fla.: HCI, 1993.

Fish, Barbara. "Art for Peace: Practicing What We Preach." 34th Annual Conference of the American Art Therapy Association, Mundelein, Ill., 2003.

Gablik, Suzi. "Connective Aesthetics: Art after Individualism." In *Mapping the Terrain: New Genre Public Art*, edited by Suzanne Lacy. Seattle: Bay Press, 1995.

——. "Art as Activism." *IONS Noetic Sciences Review*. December 2002, pp. 29–30.

George, Demetra. *Mysteries of the Dark Moon: The Healing Power of the Dark Goddess*. New York: HarperCollins Publishers, 1992.

Gilligan, Carol, Annie G. Rogers, and Deborah L. Tolman (eds.). *Women, Girls, and Psychotherapy: Reframing Resistance*. New York: Harrington Park Press, 1991.

Glassman, Bernie. *Bearing Witness*. New York: Bell Tower, 1998.

Gottlieb, Lynn. *She Who Dwells Within*. San Francisco: HarperSanFranciso, 1995.

Heschel, Abraham Joshua. *The Sabbath*. New York: Farrar, Straus & Giroux, 1951.

Hillman, James, and Michael Ventura. *We've Had A Hundred Years of Psychotherapy and the World's Getting Worse*. San Francisco: HarperCollins Publishers, 1992.

Hyde, Lewis. *The Gift*. New York: Random House, 1983.

Ingerman, Sandra. *Soul Retrieval*. New York: HarperCollins Publishers, 1991.

Jacoby, Mario A. *Longing for Paradise*. Boston: Sigo Press, 1985.

Jones, Lawrence A. "The New Orleans WPA/FAP." *History Matters*. May 17, 2004. http://historymatters.gmu.edu/d/5100.

Kushner, Lawrence. *The Book of Words*. Woodstock, Vt.: Jewish Lights, 1993.

Lefkowitz, Bernard. *Our Guys: The Glen Ridge Rape and the Secret Life of the Perfect Suburb*. Berkeley: University of California Press, 1997.

Lerner, Michael. *Jewish Renewal*. New York: Grosset/Putnam, 1994.

Low, Adam. *The Definitive Dalí*. London: BBC Television, 1988.

Louw, Dirk. "Ubuntu: An African Assessment of the Religious Other." *Paideia*. 1998. www.bu.edu/wcp/Papers/Afri/AfriLouw.htm.

Lovelock, James. *Gaia*. Oxford: Oxford University Press, 1979.

MacKenny, Virginia. "Andries Botha." *Contemporary Art in South Africa*. 2000. www.artthrob.co.za/00apr/artbio.html.

Macy, Joanna. "The Greening of the Self." In *Dharma Gaia: A Harvest of Essays in Buddhism and Ecology*, edited by Allan Hunt Badiner. Berkeley: Parallax Press, 1990.

Majozo, Estella Conwill. "To Search for the Good and Make It Matter." In *Mapping the Terrain: New Genre Public Art*, edited by Suzanne Lacy. Seattle, Wash.: Bay Press, 1995.

Martin, Tim. *Essential Surrealists*. Bath, U.K.: Parragon Publishing, 1999.

McEwan, Cheryl. "Building a Post–colonial Archive: Gender, Collective Memory, and Citizenship in Post-apartheid South Africa." *Journal of Southern African Studies* 29, no. 3 (September 2003): 739–757.

McNiff, Shaun. *Art as Medicine*. Boston: Shambhala Publications, 1992.

———. *Earth Angels*. Boston: Shambhala Publications, 1995.

Meili, Terry. *I Am the Central Park Jogger*. New York: Scribner, 2003.

Morrow, Lance. *Evil: An Investigation*. New York: Basic Books, 2003.

Nafisi, Azar. *Reading Lolita in Tehran*. New York: Random House, 2004.

Nagler, Michael. "Building a New Force." *Yes! Journal of Positive Futures* 23 (Fall 2002): 49–51.

Patai, Raphael. *The Hebrew Goddess*, 3rd enlarged ed. Detroit: Wayne State University Press, 1990.

Pennebaker, James. "Putting Stress into Words: Health, Linguistic and Therapeutic Implications." *Behaviour Research and Therapy* 31, no. 2 (July 1993): 539–548.

Schoeman, Stan. "Beadwork in the Zulu Cultural Tradition." *TheZulu Beadwork Language*. June 30, 1996. http://minotaur.marques.co.za/clients/zulu/bead.htm.

Segal, Alan F. *Paul the Convert*. New Haven: Yale University Press, 1990.

Sheldrake, Rupert, Terence McKenna, and Ralph Abraham. *Chaos, Creativity and Cosmic Consciousness*. Rochester, Vt.: Park Street Press, 2001.

Starhawk. *Dreaming the Dark*. Boston: Beacon Press, 1982.

Telushkin, Joseph. *Words That Hurt, Words That Heal: How to Choose Words Wisely and Well*. New York: William Morrow, 1996.

TRC (Truth and Reconciliation Commission, South Africa). *National Unity and Reconciliation Act of 1995*. www.doj.gov.za/trc.

Tutu, Desmond. *No Future without Forgiveness*. New York: Doubleday, 1999.

Ueshiba, Morihei. *The Art of Peace*. Translated by John Stevens. Boston: Shambhala Publications, 2002.

Waskow, Arthur. *Godwrestling*. New York: Schocken, 1978.

Watkins, Mary. *Waking Dreams*. Dallas: Spring Publications, 1984.

———. "Pathways between the Multiplicities of Psyche and Culture: The Development of Dialogic Capacities." In *The Plural Self: Multiplicity in Everyday Life*, edited by John Rowan and Mick Cooper. New York: Sage, 1999.

——. *On Returning to the Soul of the World.* Woodstock, Conn.: Spring Publications, 2004.

——. "On Returning to the Soul of the World: Archetypal Psychology and Cultural/Ecological Work." In *Festschrift in Honor of James Hillman.* Woodstock, Conn.: Spring Publications, forthcoming (2005). http://uploads.pacifica.edu/gems/watkins/OnReturning.pdf, p. 17.

Webster's New World Dictionary of the American Language, edited by David B. Guralnik. New York: New World Publishing, 1993.

Woodman, Marion. *Leaving My Father's House.* Boston: Shambhala Publications, 1993.

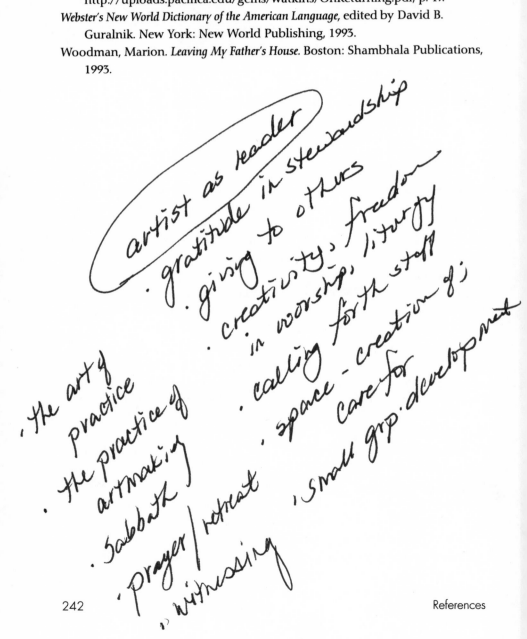